T0337977

Startup Accelerators

Startup Accelerators

A FIELD GUIDE

Richard Busulwa
Naomi Birdthistle
Steve Dunn

WILEY

Library of Congress Cataloging-in-Publication Data:

Names: Busulwa, Richard, 1980- author. | Birdthistle, Naomi, author. | Dunn, Steve, author.
Title: Startup accelerators : a field guide / Richard Busulwa, Naomi Birdthistle, and Steve Dunn.
Description: Hoboken, New Jersey : John Wiley & Sons, Inc., [2020] | Includes index.
Identifiers: LCCN 2019047697 (print) | LCCN 2019047698 (ebook) | ISBN 9781119638599 (hardback) | ISBN 9781119638650 (adobe pdf) | ISBN 9781119638605 (epub)
Subjects: LCSH: New business enterprises. | Entrepreneurship.
Classification: LCC HD62.5 .B878 2020 (print) | LCC HD62.5 (ebook) | DDC 658.1/1—dc23
LC record available at https://lccn.loc.gov/2019047697
LC ebook record available at https://lccn.loc.gov/2019047698

Cover Design: Wiley
Cover Image: © Rusty86/Getty Images

Printed in the United States of America
V10016322_121319

Contents

About the Authors

Richard Busulwa (PhD, MBA, MInnov) is a researcher in the Business School at Swinburne University of Technology, home to the Australian Graduate School of Entrepreneurship. His entrepreneurship research focuses on startup evolution, entrepreneurial learning, entrepreneurial well-being, and strategy for startups. He is co-author of *Strategy Execution and Complexity: Thriving in the Era of Disruption.* Richard is a startup co-founder and seed investor in cloud, IoT, AI, blockchain, property, and niche professional service firms.

Naomi Birdthistle (PhD, MSc, BA) is an associate professor of entrepreneurship at Griffith University and visiting professor at Alto University. Naomi has published research on entrepreneurship education, entrepreneurial ecosystems, and high-growth firms. Her research has received numerous awards including Emerald Literati, Ernst & Young Entrepreneur of the Year, and the Institute of Small Business and Entrepreneurship (ISBE) and Ireland's Network of Teachers and Researchers of Entrepreneurship (INTRE) awards.

Steve Dunn (MBA, BA) is CEO and co-founder of LEAPIN Digital Keys, a startup that delivers NB IoT smart access control solutions. Since its founding, Steve has led the startup through a number of different accelerators within Asia Pacific, the United States, and Europe. He has also led the startup through several iterations and pivots with a variety of IoT technologies, to finally find product/market fit. Steve is a mentor and coach in university-based accelerators and incubators.

Acknowledgments

We are thankful to the founders, program managers, and entrepreneurship academics who took time out of their busy schedules to answer our lengthy questionnaires and interview questions in detail, and with full openness. We are also grateful to our supportive family and friends for accommodating our late nights and weekends spent researching and writing. Finally, we are grateful to Bill Falloon and the team at Wiley for providing us with the opportunity to research and write this book, as well as for being easy to work with and having author-friendly terms.

Preface

Accelerator programs have emerged as one of the most powerful vehicles for helping entrepreneurs to learn rapidly, create powerful networks, raise money, build their startups, and do this at speed and at scale. Since Y Combinator brought accelerators into the public consciousness in 2005, the number of accelerator programs have exploded around the world; spawning successes such as Airbnb, DropBox, Reddit, Stripe, Zenefits, Pillpack and Uber—many with billion-dollar valuations. But the number of accelerators, the global catchment area of accelerators, and differences in the benefits and costs of different startup ecosystems around the world make choosing the right accelerator a challenge. Choosing the wrong accelerator can be costly, as can failing to get into the right one. With the stakes so high, entrepreneurs need to consider their options carefully. Getting into the right accelerator is also no easy feat, since many of the best accelerators have very low acceptance rates. Once in an accelerator, founders need to take care to make the most of what the accelerator has to offer; and to ensure they don't neglect their business operations while in the accelerator. Written by entrepreneurs for entrepreneurs, this book provides entrepreneurs with an insider look into the inner workings of different accelerator programs around the world. It outlines how accelerators help startups, what the different startup accelerators around the world offer, what it takes to get into them, how to prepare accelerator applications, what to do during accelerator programs, how to raise money during accelerators, and what to do after an accelerator program ends.

The book is a one-stop resource packed with insightful data and the real-life case studies and reflections of startups going through accelerator programs, program managers operating accelerator programs, entrepreneurship educators teaching entrepreneurship, and entrepreneurship researchers researching entrepreneurship education. While the book is designed to efficiently provide entrepreneurs with critical information they need on accelerators, it is also an insightful read for accelerator program managers, entrepreneurship educators, entrepreneurship education researchers, and investors considering investment in a company coming out of an accelerator; as well as policy makers seeking to unpack the role of accelerators in the entrepreneurial journey and in entrepreneurial ecosystems.

Startups are usually pursuing opaque opportunities with closing time windows and fleeting entry points. Yet there is often an avalanche of work that must be done in order to seize the opportunity. Therefore, it is imperative that they limit how much time they waste on potential time vacuums such as engaging with the wrong type of startup support institution for a particular startup evolution stage, engaging with the wrong types of coaches/consultants/startup networks, spending time on trivial activities at the expense of critical ones, engaging in avoidable trial-and-error activities, reviewing unnecessary startup information, developing unnecessary startup know-how, accessing necessary startup information—but at the wrong time, and engaging in avoidable rework. Now more than ever, there is a proliferation of information and institutions offering support to startups—this trend is only expected to amplify. The startups likely to make it simply don't have the time to siphon through and decipher all the information on the different types of institutions supporting startups, the networks of those institutions, the offerings of those institutions, and the benefits and shortcomings of their offerings. Should startup founders undertake this arduous task with reliable rigor, within each institution type there is a proliferation of offerings. The aim of our book is to unpack the accelerator institution for entrepreneurs in a structured, simple, practical, yet rigorous way. In doing so, we hope to save entrepreneurs the costs of misunderstanding accelerators, using them in the wrong way, missing out on their key benefits, going through poor quality accelerators, or choosing accelerators not optimally suited to their particular startup.

Research for This Book

The research for this book was undertaken in five stages. In stage 1, we undertook a review of the relevant and seminal academic research on startup accelerators, incubators, and other entrepreneurial eco-system institutions. The purpose of this stage was to understand the unique role startup accelerators play in entrepreneurial ecosystems, their unique value to entrepreneurs, and the stages of the startup evolution process at which accelerators are of most value. In stage 2, we reviewed key practitioner literature on startup accelerators—focusing on the value offerings of different accelerators, their functioning, and achievements. The aim of this stage was to understand the unpacked value offering, functioning, and effectiveness of different types of startup accelerators. In stage 3, we undertook a comprehensive review of primary and secondary data on accelerator programs in general, and the different startup accelerators around the world in particular. In this review, we focused on the prevalence and verifiable effectiveness of accelerator programs. In stage 4, we drew on our experience, personally applying for and entering a number of different accelerators, incubators, and government startup support programs in different parts of the world. Through this fourth stage, we drew on first-hand experience of what it takes to get into accelerators, and to make the most of them—both during and after the program. Finally, in stage 5, we collected primary and secondary data on the experiences and reflections of founders going through different accelerator programs, around the world, program managers operating different accelerators programs and university entrepreneurship educators teaching entrepreneurship and researching entrepreneurship education (in particular, regarding the latter, we focused on educators at universities teaching entrepreneurship programs and operating accelerator programs).

How to Use This Book

This book is made up of nine chapters which can be viewed as six parts. Part 1 (Introduction and Chapter 1) explores the driving need, emergence, and ascendance of the accelerator phenomenon. This part will be of value to founders and aspiring founders, as it unpacks the key startup evolution stages and the challenges faced by founders along those stages. Part 1 will be of value to entrepreneurship educators, entrepreneurship ecosystem researchers, and policy makers as it unpacks the value of accelerators to startup journeys and therefore the role of accelerators in entrepreneurial ecosystems. Part 2 (Chapters 2–4) discusses what happens in an accelerator, how to know if a startup is ready for an accelerator, and how to prepare the accelerator application. Part 3 (Chapters 5–7) discusses how to choose an accelerator, how to handle the accelerator interview, and whether to give up equity to get into an accelerator. Part 4 (Chapters 8–9) discusses how to get the most out of an accelerator, what to expect after the accelerator, and what to do after the accelerator ends. Part 5 (Appendices) is a resource directory organized into three subparts. The first subpart provides case study reflections of the experiences of founders who have been through accelerator programs. Subpart 2 provides case study reflections of accelerator program managers who operate accelerator programs and university entrepreneurship educators who teach entrepreneurship and research entrepreneurship education. We hope these three very different reflections offer insight into the thinking and challenges faced by these accelerator institution and entrepreneurship education stakeholders. We chose to make these reflections anonymous, so participants could be fully honest, without risking their reputations or those of their organizations. Finally, in subpart 3 we have curated key resources that founders can draw on for different aspects of the accelerator experience. For example, they can find curated information for evaluating accelerators, for navigating different aspects of the accelerator process (e.g., preparing accelerator applications, preparing for interviews, starting the accelerator, networking, preparing for demo day, etc.). They can also find curated tips and advice from a range of founders who have gone through accelerators on how to approach almost all aspects of the accelerator experience. Finally, for each region of the world (Asia, North America, Europe, Africa/Middle East, South America, Oceania), we list some of the most popular accelerators, their focus, and their notable alumni startups.

The book is organized to enable efficient access to relevant information as and when needed. Thus, for example, a reader attempting to prepare an accelerator application can scan the table of contents to find Chapter 4 and go straight to that chapter. Or, for example again, a reader can scan the table of contents to locate where in the book they can find the top accelerators in their country, or the mentors in a particular accelerator. Each chapter is written to stand on its own and does not require a reader to first read the preceding chapters—although readers may benefit more from a cover-to-cover reading. At the end of most chapters, we provide a real-world case study of the chapter content in practice by a range of different founders in different accelerators around the world. For example, Chapter 4 on how to prepare the accelerator application provides case studies of the real-world applications of startups to different accelerators, and identifies those that got in and those that did not get in. Thus, a reader that finds reading theory difficult can go straight to the case study for that chapter to learn from the real-world case study. And if they have a query about a particular part of the case study, they can visit the specific theory section within that chapter. We have used endnotes to corroborate key assertions made in the book, and we encourage entrepreneurs to go to those sources for even deeper insights.

Introduction

In the startup world, you're either a genius or an idiot. You're never just an ordinary guy trying to get through the day.
Marc Andreessen, co-founder, Andreessen Horowitz

For every Facebook, WhatsApp, or Airbnb, a staggering number of startups don't make it. If we define "making it" as mere survival, rather than reaching the soaring heights of a Facebook or Airbnb, the numbers are still sobering. For example, up to 20% of startups don't survive the first year alone.[1,2] Up to 50% are no longer alive by year 5, and up to 90% ultimately fail.[3,4,5] If we define "making it" as achieving the level of success of a Facebook or Airbnb, the number of startups that don't make it grows dramatically. Consider, for instance, how many Facebooks emerge out of more than 6 million entrepreneurs that start a new business in the United States every year.[6] Or consider that top venture capitalists, whose specialist job is identifying and backing the most promising companies, only invest in about 20 of every 3,000 startups they evaluate.[7] And consider that out of these 20, only one or two ultimately earn the majority of the money that venture capital firms earn in return.[8] Irrespective of the definition of success used, the startups that make it often do so against the odds. There is a proliferation of often conflicting opinions on why this is the case; and a number of researchers and practitioners have identified different challenges, dilemmas, and pitfalls faced by startups. Melissa Cardon, a University of Tennessee professor, found that failures among entrepreneurs were commonly blamed on the mistakes and or misfortunes made and or experienced by them.[9] These range from having a product with no market need, running out of cash, not

1

having the right team, being blindsided or outdone by competitors, getting pricing wrong, poor marketing, not listening to customers, losing focus, conflicts within the founding team or with investors, failure to make the right pivots, mismanaging geographic expansion, growing too fast, failing to attract sufficient funding, getting into legal trouble, not effectively using a support network, lacking sufficient passion, and burnout of founding team members.[10] And this list is just the tip of the iceberg. Startup accelerators help startups deal with many of these issues. Before we explore just how they help startups deal with these issues, it is important to first unpack the stages a startup evolves through—so we can better understand when it may face particular challenges, dilemmas, or pitfalls. This will help clarify what stages of a startup's evolution accelerators are of most value to founders and exactly how they are of value (see Figure I.1).

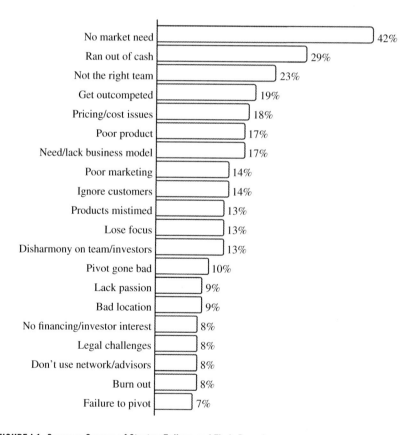

FIGURE I.1 Common Causes of Startup Failure and Their Prevalence
Source: Adapted from Sweetwood (2018).[11]

The Stages of Startup Evolution

Several researchers, entrepreneurs, and investors have unpacked, framed, and reframed the obstacles and dilemmas faced by startups to get more granular about the underlying causes; or to organize the avalanche of information about these obstacles into meaningful formats that entrepreneurs or other stakeholders within startup ecosystems can digest easily. For example, University of Southern California entrepreneurship professor and former Harvard Business School associate professor Noam Wasserman framed some of these challenges as prefounding dilemmas, founding dilemmas, and exit dilemmas.[12] Prior to founding, entrepreneurs need to know when it is right to found a startup. If they found too early, they may not have enough relevant skills, knowledge, and resources; or the market may not yet be ready for their ideas. This may result in inadvertently placing the startup in checkmate, before it has even really begun. But on the other hand, if they wait too long they may find themselves unfit for founder life, handcuffed by career and family issues. Or they may find that someone else has already seized their ideas. Once entrepreneurs decide to found a startup, they have to decide whether to have co-founders or not, who to bring on as co-founders, and how to split equity in the startup.[13] Wasserman argues that getting these early decisions wrong can result in perverse incentives and disincentives, irreconcilable friction between co-founders, or the eventual inability to raise funding—making subsequent efforts to build the startup moot. If entrepreneurs get these early decisions right, they face challenges making the right first hires and incentivizing them appropriately, so they don't become problem employees or engage in actions that undermine the startup. On the one hand, entrepreneurs want to attract professional, high-skilled employees—yet they are not able to offer the pay levels, professional management, or other intangibles offered by established brands. On the other hand, if they hire unprofessional or low-skilled employees at low pay, they may doom their startup to mediocrity or sloth. While these co-founder and employee issues may rarely be mentioned as obstacles, Noam Wasserman found that such people issues account for up to 65% of startup failures.[14] At some point, the startup may need external finance, and face dilemmas such as whether to raise capital early but give up a lot of equity and control; or whether to wait, give up less equity and control, but risk failure in the meantime.

While Wasserman explores the challenges startup founders face from a prefounding dilemmas, founding dilemmas, and exit dilemmas perspective, Andreessen Horowitz partner and Netscape co-founder Marc Andreessen explores the challenges from a before product/market fit (BPMFT) and after product/market fit (APMFT) perspective.[15] Defining product/market fit as being in a great market with a product that can sustainably satisfy that market, he argues that the only thing that matters for BPMFT startups is finding a great market, and a product that can sustainably satisfy that market. Except in rare cases, spending time on any other challenge is most likely a waste of valuable time and resources. That is, before product/market fit, nonproduct/market fit challenges are not that important to making it as a startup. Which is not to say that they don't matter at all, but rather, that startups can screw up many of these things and still make it—as long as they succeed at finding product/market fit. In contrast, startups that screw up product/market fit are more often than not doomed to failure— no matter how well they succeed at other things. Andreesen cites numerous examples of companies that have built seemingly great teams, raised money from top tier VCs, got all the legal right, listed on prestigious stock exchanges, and looked slick in every way— only to come crashing down, because they did not take the time to get the product right and the market right. U.S. healthcare technology startup Theranos Inc. is a good case in point. Theranos Inc. was heralded by the media as having made a breakthrough in the $70 billion diagnostic lab industry. It raised more than $600 million from investors, assembled a stellar board and stellar strategic partners,[16] and was valued at over $10 billion. By most accounts, it looked like the epitome of a successful startup—only to end in insolvency and fraud and conspiracy charges, when it was subsequently discovered that Theranos' product could not do for customers what it purported to do. Theranos Inc. did not have product/market fit because, although it had a great market, it did not have a validated product that could truly satisfy that market— only the promise of such a product. Marc Andreessen's delineation of startup challenges into BPMFT and APMFT challenges is a critical one, as it provides important guidance for entrepreneurs about when particular challenges and dilemmas matter the most as a startup evolves.

Silicon Valley entrepreneur, investor, and Stanford adjunct professor Steve Blank unpacks Marc Andreessen's BPMFT and APMFT delineations, and frames startup challenges into four stages: Customer Discovery, Customer Validation, Customer Creation, and Company Building.[17,18] In the Customer Discovery stage, there are three challenges. The first challenge is to validate that a big enough and painful enough problem exists for a large enough group of people, that a specific solution will solve that problem, and that the specific solution can solve the problem to such a degree that those people will buy it. The second challenge is to build a minimum viable product (MVP), or a minimum form of the complete product/service, that solves the problem. This MVP can then be tested on real-world customers in the target group. The target group may either love the MVP or provide valuable feedback about its shortcomings. This may lead to subsequent iterations of the MVP, and even to revising the original problem/solution fit assumptions. Finally, thorough interviews, surveys, usage analytics, and other approaches, the startup must identify its sales and marketing funnels. These are the key stages in the customer buying process and the activities that must be undertaken to move prospective customers through that process in a viable way. For example, a software startup may determine that the majority of its prospective customers go onto an online search engine to search for software, and that these prospective customers typically look at the top five search results within a specific software category, then check the credibility of companies developing that software and the existing customer feedback on that software, then check the pricing, and, finally, send through an email inquiry or pick up the phone and make an inquiry that may lead to a closed sale. Having discovered this buying process, the startup may configure its marketing and sales activities to ensure that it maximizes how many email or phone inquiries it receives and that it economically converts as many of those inquiries as possible into actual sales. In the process of mastering these first three challenges (validated problem/solution fit, the MVP, and sales and marketing funnels), the startup may find product/market fit. A startup has product/ market fit when customers have tried its product, accepted the product, trust the product, and want more of the product (e.g., the product does the job well it purports to do, it can be trusted to be of good quality, it can be delivered in a timely manner, it poses no risk to the organization, and it is of better value than competing and substitute products). In the Customer Validation stage, the proposed MVP, the sales and marketing roadmap and the business model are validated. Validation of the MVP involves understanding the core value the MVP provides to customers and confirming that customers are passionate about it. Validation of the sales and marketing road map involves understanding the relevant market and optimizing its conversion funnel from initial awareness of the product, to purchase of the product, to referral of the product to other customers. And validation of the business model involves proving that the relevant market can scale to sustain the business, and that the lifetime value of a customer exceeds the cost of serving that customer. In the Customer Creation stage, end user demand is created to scale sales. And in the Company Building stage, the company transitions from a startup focused on learning to a fully-fledged business.

Princeton University professor of entrepreneurial leadership and iSuppli founder Derek Lidow frames startup challenges into Customer Validation, Operational Validation, Financial Validation, and Self-Sustainability stages.[19] Customer Validation is concerned with proving the product idea with potential customers, investors, employees, and others. At the end of this stage, startups will have a product that actual customers commit to buying repeatedly. In the operational validation stage, startups put in place the capabilities to find more customers, and to produce and deliver the product to these customers so as to truly satisfy them. For example, this may require ensuring the startup can be relied on to manufacture and deliver products to customers on time, to quality and service expectations, with easy payment and after-sales support services, and with minimal risks to customers. Once a startup has confirmed that customers want to buy its product on an ongoing basis and that it has the operational capabilities in place to get new customers, deliver the product to them, and do so in such a way as to satisfy them, it is ready for the third stage—financial validation. The objective of financial validation is to reconfigure or put in place processes that are flexible enough to handle significant growth and changes in demand, but with minimal financial and key person risk. Finally, in stage 4, startups put in place an effective innovation process. This process enables them to create a consistent stream of new products and new customers that can replace customers and products that are no longer a source of profitability. For example, Amazon's first product was an online bookstore platform, but it since then put in place an innovation process that has delivered a consistent stream of products including Kindle, Amazon Web Services, Amazon Prime, Alexa, Amazon Publishing, Amazon Robotics, and many more.

Integrating and building on the insights from Noam Wasserman, Marc Andreessen, Steve Blank, and Derek Lidow, we propose that startups evolve through a six-stage iterative process as depicted in Figure I.2. Startups evolve from Insight/Opportunity Recognition

Stages of Startup Evolution

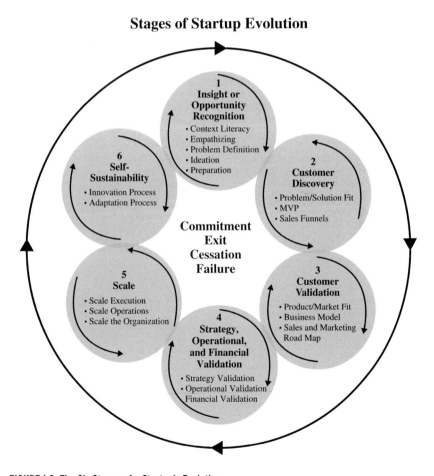

FIGURE I.2 The Six Stages of a Startup's Evolution

to Customer Discovery, then Customer Validation, then Strategy/
Operational/Financial Validation, then Scaling, then finally, Self-
Sustainability. Each stage is depicted as a continuous process of iteration to a minimum viable point, at which the startup can move onto
the next stage.

The process in Figure I.2 does not suggest or imply that startup
evolution is neat, linear, and sequential. Rather, startups can move
forward once the minimum viable point of a stage is reached, or
backwards if they discover that some of their earlier hypotheses and
assumptions were incorrect. For instance, a startup may pivot by
moving from Customer Validation back to Customer Discovery, in
order to refine problem/solution fit and develop a different MVP.
At any stage, startup founders may decide to maintain or escalate
their time and other resource commitments ("Commitment") or
they can decide to de-escalate their commitment to the point of
ceasing pursuit of the startup opportunity ("Cessation"). They may
also make certain decisions or be subject to certain unfavorable
external situations that lead to the startup being forced into discon-
tinuing ("Failure"). For example, a startup may get into so much
legal trouble that it is unable to disentangle itself in an economic
way, so as to remain a going concern. Alternatively, the founders
may exit the startup ("Exit"). For example, they may exit by selling their shares to existing shareholders or new investors, by having their startup acquired, or being forced out of the startup by
other investors. A startup may eventually make its way through all
the stages to self-sustainability and become an Amazon, Google, or
Microsoft.

In Figure I.2, Steve Blank's Customer Discovery and Customer
Validation stages are incorporated as steps 2 and 3, with the objectives of each stage included as dot points. Figure I.2 shows that a
startup can move from Customer Discovery to Customer Validation, and pivot back to Customer Discovery continuously, until
it finds product/market fit. In incorporating these stages, Marc
Andreessen's BPMFT and APMFT insights are also implicitly
incorporated.[20] Step 4 of the process incorporates Derek Lidow's
Operational Validation and Financial Validation stages.[21] Based
on our research, we have added Strategy Validation to reflect the
importance of startups making validated strategic choices (e.g., see
Joshua Gans, Erin Scott. and Scott Stern's *Harvard Business Review*

article on strategy for startups)[22] and ensuring they can execute those choices (e.g., see Richard Busulwa, Matthew Tice and Bruce Gurd's book on strategy execution and complexity).[23] Noam Wasserman's findings on prefounding, founding, and exit dilemmas[24] are reflected in step 1 and also in the center of the circle. In step 1, entrepreneurs need to build context literacy (e.g., domain/industry/market and product expertise), get an appreciation for customer issues and pain points, and clarify or better define customer or market problems to arrive at a product/service/solution insight or to recognize a startup opportunity. If they knew they wanted to become an entrepreneur prior to opportunity recognition, they may have already undertaken step 1 activities as part of their preparation for startup life. Alternatively, if the product/service idea is driving them into entrepreneurship, they may still need to go through preparation. It is in preparation that many of the prefounding dilemmas Wasserman identifies are resolved.[25] Step 1 also incorporates empathizing, defining, and ideation insights from design thinking[26]—although these may occur tacitly or by chance for some entrepreneurs. Step 5 of the process incorporates Steve Blank[27,28] and other entrepreneurs' insights into the process of scaling entrepreneurial ventures.[29] Finally, step 6 incorporates Derek Lidow's Self-Sustainability stage.[30] We drew on insights from organization adaptation research to also add the need for an effective adaptation process to maximize self-sustainability.[31] That is, in addition to having an innovation process that can create a consistent stream of new products and new customers,[32] self-sustainability requires having in place an adaptation process that can ensure the organization has the right capabilities and resources at the right time to respond to opportunities and threats in its external environment.[33,34,35]

Having identified the stages startups evolve through, we can now categorize the challenges, dilemmas, and pitfalls startups go through by evolution stage. This will enable us to, then, consider at which stages startups may need accelerators, and how helpful accelerators can be to startups at these different stages. Table I.1 categorizes some of the earlier discussed startup challenges, dilemmas, and pitfalls by evolution stage. Knowing the key objectives and the key challenges, dilemmas, and pitfalls, we will be better positioned to discuss at which stages startups need the services provided by startup accelerators and what specific objectives, challenges, dilemmas, and pitfalls accelerators address at those stages of startup evolution.

TABLE I.1 Example of Some of the Challenges, Dilemmas, and Pitfalls Startups Face Organized by Stage of a Startup's Evolution

Evolution Stage	Objectives	Example Challenges, Dilemmas, and Pitfalls Reframed as Questions
1. Insight or Opportunity Recognition	Finding an idea or problem worth pursuing. Being adequately prepared to pursue an idea or problem.	Is this an idea or problem worth pursuing?
		Is now the right time to pursue a startup, or should I (or we) wait?
		How do I (or we) know when I (or we) have sufficient skills, knowledge, and resources to be ready for startup? Will I (or we) miss the opportunity, or will I (or we) find myself (ourselves) handcuffed by career and family issues?
		Do I seek out co-founders now or go at it alone until a certain point?
		How should I (or we) approach early equity splits?
		Should I (or we) take on family/friend co-founders or not?
		When should I (or we) raise money and get investors on board? How do I (or we) do it? How much equity should I (or we) give away?
		How do I (or we) make sure we don't run out of money?
		Who should be the CEO of the startup?
2. Customer Discovery	Finding problem/solution fit.	How do I (or we) test for and find problem/solution fit?
	Building the MVP	How incomplete can my (our) MVP be? Will testing an incomplete product get my (our) startup a bad reputation? How much MVP feedback is enough? How many times should I (or we) iterate before throwing in the towel?
	Identifying and validating sales funnels.	
		What are sales funnels? How do I (or we) identify my (our) sales funnels? How do I (or we) know when I (or we) have got sales funnels right?

Evolution Stage	Objectives	Example Challenges, Dilemmas, and Pitfalls Reframed as Questions
3. Customer Validation	Finding product/ market fit. Validating the business model. Validating the sales and marketing roadmap	What is product/market fit? How do I (or we) find product/market fit? How do I (or we) know when I (or we) have product/market fit? What is a business model? How is a business model different from a revenue model, an operating model, or a strategy? How do I (or we) know when I (or we) have the right business model? What is a sales and marketing roadmap? How do I (or we) build the sales and marketing roadmap? How do I (or we) know if the conversion funnel is optimized?
4. Strategy, Operational and Financial Validation	Strategy validation. Operational validation. Financial validation	What is a strategy? Do startups need a strategy? How do I (or we) validate the strategy? How do I (or we) do operational and financial validation? What if I (or we) don't do strategy, operational, or financial validation?
5. Scaling	Scaling execution. Scaling operations. Scaling the organization	What is scaling? How do I (or we) know if my startup is ready to scale? What are the risks of scaling, and how do I (or we) manage them? Can I (or we) scale too early? How much money does it take to scale safely? What is the difference between scaling execution, scaling operations, and scaling the organization? How do we scale execution, scale operations, and scale the organization?
6. Self-sustainability	Implementing an effective Innovation Process. Implementing an effective Adaptation Process	Do startups need an innovation process? What makes an effective innovation process? How do we put in place an effective innovation process? How do we know if we have got the innovation process right? Why would we need an adaptation process? How do we put in place an adaptation process? How do we know if we have got the adaptation process right?

How Accelerator Programs Can Help Startups

Startup accelerators are fixed-term educational and mentorship programs run for a cohort of early-stage, growth-driven companies to help them circumvent startup challenges, dilemmas, and pitfalls so as to improve their odds of making it.[36,37,38] Accelerators compress years' worth of learning by doing insights into rapid, intense, and immersive learning programs of approximately three to six months.[39,40,41] The aim of the programs is to accelerate the speed with which startups progresses through the stages of startup evolution, and to significantly improve their odds of ultimately making it. Although the benefits of accelerator programs differ from one accelerator to the next, our research revealed seven key benefits: accelerated evolution, accelerated learning/skills development, funding/investment readiness/fundraising, networks, professional business services, strategy, and ongoing advice/hands-on support. The first benefit, accelerated evolution, relates to the speed with which startups make progress while in the accelerator (and thus advance through one or more stages of startup evolution). The second benefit, accelerated learning/skills development, usually occurs through education/training delivery and coaching/mentoring elements built into accelerator curriculums. The third benefit, funding/investment readiness/fundraising, usually comprises one or more of the following: cash investments in cohort companies in exchange for equity, a living stipend for the period that founders are participating in the accelerator, helping startups understand and do what is required to be attractive to investors, and linking startups to a network of investors for potential future fundraising. The fourth benefit, networks, usually comprises access to the accelerator's network of investors, entrepreneurs, professional business service providers, specialist advisors, corporate partners, and other stakeholders. This network can be a great source of potential clients, potential strategic partners, potential investors, potential cofounders, potential employees, and a broad range of intangible opportunities. The fifth benefit, professional business services, is usually comprised of free or discounted access to accelerators' in-house business service providers such as legal advisors, business model strategists, corporate communication advisors, financial advisors, and many more. Startups that are not part of an accelerator might find the cost of such specialist professional services prohibitive—that's assuming they can find such startup-focused specialist services to begin with. The sixth benefit, getting the strategy right, usually involves accelerators helping founders to think through and make the right short-, medium-, and long-term strategic choices. These choices may, for instance, involve issues such as should we spend all our money on having solid patents or just try to be first? Should we manufacture ourselves or should we license? Should we partner with distributors or do it ourselves? Should we choose a particular technology standard or hedge our bets?[42] The seventh benefit, ongoing advice/hands-on support, involves ongoing access to the accelerator organizers and advisor networks for advice regarding any number of issues that might come up during or after the accelerator program. Sometimes entrepreneurs need a trusted advisor or a sounding board, particularly someone who has experience helping other startups to successfully get through a similar challenge. As well as the advice, accelerator organizers can sometimes roll up their sleeves and hold founders' hands to navigate them through particular challenges. Such challenges might include, for example, negotiating fundraising rounds, negotiating an acquisition deal, structuring a strategic partnership agreement, or going through a stock exchange listing process. Accelerator organizers will likely have been through these challenges with other cohort companies, and also have people who can offer hands-on help to founders, albeit this may come at a cost. Although not specifically articulated in the literature we reviewed, an additional theme coming from our case study interviews is the ability of accelerators to hone entrepreneurs' professionalism and confidence in dealing with prospective hires, investors, customers, strategic partners, the media, and other stakeholders. Figure I.3 depicts some of the key benefits of accelerator programs.

As well as there being diversity in the different types of accelerators, within each type of accelerator there can be a difference in focus. For example, there are noncorporate accelerators, corporate accelerators, government accelerators, NGO/NFP accelerators, and many others. Noncorporate accelerators usually follow the original Y Combinator accelerator model, offering the seven benefits discussed earlier in exchange for equity investment—although not all accelerators take equity. Corporate, government, NGO/NFP, and other accelerators are usually run by or on behalf of corporations, governments, and NGO/NFP organizations for a range of different strategic reasons. Such reasons can include stimulation of innovation,

FIGURE I.3 Key Benefits of Accelerator Programs

finding a new competitive edge, learning commercialization skills, economic development, and many more. For example, there is a Barclay's accelerator focusing on Fintech startups and a Comcast NBC Universal LIFT Labs Accelerator focusing on media startups. Within accelerator types, accelerators may focus on a particular industry, a particular part of the value chain, a particular technology, a particular stage of startup evolution, a particular customer segment, a combination of one or more of these areas, or another area altogether. While most startups are likely to choose noncorporate accelerators, a startup may participate in one of the other types of accelerators because those types of accelerators can give it the best access to particular types of clients, funding providers, strategic partners, acquisition opportunities, or other benefit it is seeking.

Accelerators versus Incubators, Investors, Government Programs, and Other Startup Ecosystem Institutions

Accelerators are one of many institutions offering help to startups. Alternate sources of help include incubators, government support programs, universities, investors, and entrepreneurship organizations/associations and collectives. Incubators are facilities set up to nurture entrepreneurs very early on in the startup evolution process[43] (typically stages 1 to 4 in Figure I.2). Researchers have advocated the use of business incubators for improving the extent and rate of success of startups.[44] The OECD has developed a typology of incubators and classified them into three main types: general/mixed-use incubators (whose goal it is to promote economic and industry growth regionally through general business development), Economic Development Incubators (whose aim is to stimulate economic objectives in particular locations), and Technology Incubators (whose goal is to stimulate the development of technology-based firms).[45]

The European Commission provides the below definition of a business incubator:[46]

> *An organization that accelerates and systematizes the process of creating successful enterprises by providing them with a comprehensive and integrated range of support, including: Incubator space, business support services, and clustering and networking opportunities. By providing their clients with services on a "one-stop-shop" basis and enabling overheads to be reduced by sharing costs, business incubators significantly improve the survival and growth prospects of new startups.*

Thus, incubation facilities are usually set up to provide affordable space, shared business services, hands-on training, and general commercialization support. They differ from accelerators in that they are not cohort-based, are not offered on a fixed time frame, generally do not invest in startups, and are usually of a not-for-profit nature. Incubators may be run by universities seeking to support researchers to commercialize their discoveries, by government entities seeking to stimulate economic development, by companies wanting a commercialization arm, or by investors seeking early access to proprietary ideas. Although not as competitive as accelerators, most incubators are still quite selective. That is, they usually only accept entrepreneurs and ideas that are promising and fit specific criteria.

Most national, state, and local government institutions will usually operate startup support programs, especially in locations where the entrepreneurial ecosystem may not have much in the way of private or not-for-profit support institutions. Government support programs can provide support ranging from government operating incubators startup funding grants, startup advisory/coaching/mentoring services, and education programs to supporting workshops and conferences, establishing or operating government-financed angel/venture capital investment bodies, and much more. Some government programs are ongoing, and others are established to fill a particular ecosystem void for a period of time, for example, until private/NGO and NFP institutions can replace them—at which point those government programs may be shut down. Government support programs are usually free and can result in startups that meet certain criteria receiving millions of dollars in finance without giving up any equity.

In most national, state, and local geographical areas, there will usually be a range of entrepreneurship organizations, entrepreneurship associations, and entrepreneurship groups or collectives that exist to provide support to entrepreneurs on a profit or not-for-profit basis. Some of them are global organizations with reach in almost every country in the world. Many achieve this global reach through digital platforms. Examples of such organizations include the Entrepreneur's Organization (EO), Young Entrepreneur Council (YEC), Social Enterprise Alliance, Startup Grind, Vistage, Entrepreneur. com, and Ashoka. These organizations will usually offer education through content creation, hosted conferences, facilitated peer support groups, and other avenues. For example, Entrepreneur.com provides entrepreneurship education through a range of specialist content addressing common issues faced by startups. And Vistage facilitates peer support groups, mentoring, workshops, and conferences for founders and their key executives leading operational businesses. These organizations will usually also provide access to unique and varied networks. For instance, Vistage and the Entrepreneur's Organization plug members into a global network of business founders, strategic leaders, and thought leaders.

Investors are also able to provide significant support to select entrepreneurs, although this is usually restricted to firms they have invested in, and especially those with the most potential. While they may not provide professional services or working spaces, investors often provide funding, can significantly accelerate entrepreneurs' learning, and can help significantly with strategy, ongoing advice, and hands-on support. They also often have invaluable networks. Finally, there are entities that may bring together different combinations of features from incubators, accelerators, investors, government programs, and entrepreneurship organizations/associations/ collectives. See Figure I.4 for a summary of the key features and benefits of the different types of institutions that support startups. In Figure I.4 we have used the terms "early stage" and "late stage"

		Incubators	Angel Investors	Accelerators	Hybrid	Venture Capitalists	Governments Programs/Grants	Entrepreneurship Organizations/Associations/Collectives
Features	Duration	1 to 5 years	Ongoing	3 to 6 months	3 months to 2 years	Ongoing	Variable	Ongoing
	Stage of Evolution	Early or late	Early	Early	Early	Early or late	Early or late	Early or late
	Business Model	Rent; nonprofit	Investment	Investment or nonprofit	Investment or nonprofit	Investment	Nonprofit	Membership; content; conferences; nonprofit
	Selection	Noncompetitive, selective	Competitive, ongoing	Competitive, cyclical	Competitive, ongoing	Competitive, ongoing	Noncompetitive, selective	Features
	Cohorts	No	No	Yes	No	No	No	Features
	Location	On-site	Off-site	On-site	On-site	Off-site	Off-site	Features
	Accelerated Learning	Moderate	Moderate	Rapid	Moderate	Rapid	Low	Low
	Funding	No	Yes	Yes or No	Yes	Yes	Yes or No	No
	Networks	Yes	Yes	Yes or No	Yes	Yes	Yes	Yes
	Professional Business Services	Yes	No	Yes or No	Yes	No	No	No
	Strategy	Yes	Yes	Yes	Yes	Yes	No	Yes
	Ongoing Advice	Yes	Yes	Yes	Yes	Yes	No	No
Benefits	Hands-On Support	Yes or No	Yes or No	Yes or No	Yes or No	Yes	No	No

FIGURE I.4 Types of Institutions That Support Startups
Source: Based on Hathaway (2013).[47]

to illustrate the point in a startup's evolution at which each sup-port institution typically provides support. The term "early stage" typically refers to startups at stages 1 to 4 in the startup evolu-tion process; whereas the term "late stage" often refers to stages 5 and 6. While an institution may typically help startups at a particular stage, this does not necessarily mean that it will be the most helpful to startups at that stage.

Notes

1. J. Desjardins, "Here's Why Small Businesses Fail," *Business Insider*, August 2, 2017, accessed November 7, 2018, https:// www.businessinsider.com/why-small-businesses-fail-infographic-2017-8?IR=T.
2. "Entrepreneurship and the U.S. Economy." Bureau of Labor Statistics, United States Department of Labor, April 28, 2016, accessed November 7, 2018, https://www.bls.gov/bdm/ entrepreneurship/bdm_chart3.htm.
3. J.A. Timmons, *New Venture Creation: Entrepreneurship in the 21st Century* (Homewood, IL: Irwin, 1990).
4. N. Patel, "90% of Startups Fail: Here's What You Need to Know about the 10%," *Forbes*, January 16, 2015, accessed November 7, 2018, https://www.forbes.com/sites/neilpatel/2015/01/16/ 90-of-startups-will-fail-heres-what-you-need-to-know-about-the-10/#4e63bc7a6679.
5. E. Griffith, "Why Startups Fail, According to Their Found-ers," *Fortune*, September 25, 2014, accessed November 7, 2018, http://fortune.com/2014/09/25/why-startups-fail-according-to-their-founders/.
6. G. Reader, "Around 550,000 People Become Entrepreneurs Every Month," *Entrepreneur*, August 4, 2016, accessed November 7, 2018, https://www.entrepreneur.com/article/280212.
7. B. Snyder and Marc Andreessen, "We Are Biased Toward People Who Never Give Up," Stanford Graduate School of Business, June 23, 2014, accessed November 7, 2018, https://www.gsb. stanford.edu/insights/marc-andreessen-we-are-biased-toward-people-who-never-give.
8. Ibid.

9. M. Cardon, C. Stevens, and D. Potter, "Misfortune or Mistake? Cultural Sensemaking of Entrepreneurial Failure," *Journal of Business Venturing* 26 (2011): 79–92, doi:10.1016/j.jbusvent.2009.06.004.

10. "The Top 20 Reasons Startups Fail," CB Insights Research, February 2, 2018, accessed November 7, 2018, https://www.cbinsights.com/research/startup-failure-reasons-top/.

11. Adapted from M. Sweetwood, "Infographic: The 20 Most Common Reasons Startups Fail and How to Avoid Them," *Entrepreneur*, February 7, 2018, accessed August 1, 2019, https://www.entrepreneur.com/article/307724.

12. N. Wasserman, *The Founder's Dilemmas* (Princeton, NJ: Princeton University Press, 2013).

13. Ibid.

14. Ibid.

15. M. Andreessen, "Product/Market Fit," Stanford University, June 25, 2007, accessed October 23, 2018, http://web.stanford.edu/class/ee204/ProductMarketFit.html.

16. K. Weisul, "Heavy Hitters Join Theranos Advisory Board," *Inc.*, April 7, 2016, accessed October 23, 2018, https://www.inc.com/kimberly-weisul/heavy-hitters-join-theranos-advisory-board.html.

17. S. Blank, *The Four Steps to the Epiphany* (K & S Ranch, 2013).

18. S. Blank and B. Dorf, *The Startup Owner's Manual: The Step-by-Step Guide for Building a Great Company* (K & S Ranch, 2012).

19. D. Lidow, *Startup Leadership: How Savvy Entrepreneurs Turn Their Ideas into Successful Enterprises* (San Francisco: Jossey-Bass, 2014).

20. M. Andreessen, "Product/Market Fit."

21. D. Lidow, *Startup Leadership: How Savvy Entrepreneurs Turn Their Ideas into Successful Enterprises* (San Francisco: Jossey-Bass, 2014).

22. J. Gans, E. L. Scott, and S. Stern, "Strategy for Start-Ups," *Harvard Business Review* (May–June 2018), accessed November 7, 2018, https://hbr.org/2018/05/do-entrepreneurs-need-a-strategy.

23. R. Busulwa, M. Tice, and B. Gurd, *Strategy Execution and Complexity: Thriving in the Era of Disruption* (Routledge, 2018).

24. Wasserman, *The Founder's Dilemmas*.

25. Ibid.

26. T. Ogilvie and J. Liedtka, *Designing for Growth: A Design Thinking Toolkit for Managers* (New York: Columbia University Press, 2011).
27. Blank, *The Four Steps to the Epiphany.*
28. Blank and Dorf, *The Startup Owner's Manual.*
29. J. Livingston, *Founders at Work: Stories of Startups' Early Days* (Apress, 2008).
30. Lidow, *Startup Leadership.*
31. Busulwa, Tice, and Gurd, *Strategy Execution and Complexity.*
32. Lidow, *Startup Leadership.*
33. Busulwa, Tice, and Gurd, *Strategy Execution and Complexity.*
34. R. A. Burgelman and A. S. Grove, "Let Chaos Reign, then Rein in Chaos—Repeatedly: Managing Strategic Dynamics for Corporate Longevity," *Strategic Management Journal* 28, no. 10 (2007): 964–979.
35. R. A. Burgelman, "Intraorganizational Ecology of Strategy Making and Organizational Adaptation: Theory and Field Research," *Organization Science* 2, no. 3: (1991): 239–262.
36. S. Cohen, D. C. Fehder, Y. V. Hochberg, and F. Murray, "The Design of Startup Accelerators," *Research Policy* 48 (2019): 1781–1797.
37. B. Clarysse, M. Wright, and J. van Hove, *A Look Inside Accelerators: Building Businesses* (London: NESTA, 2015).
38. S. L. Cohen, C. B. Bingham, and B. L. Hallen, "The Role of Accelerator Designs in Mitigating Bounded Rationality in New Ventures," *Administrative Science Quarterly* (July 23, 2018): 1–45.
39. Cohen, Fehder, Hochberg, and Murray, "The Design of Startup Accelerators."
40. Clarysse, Wright, and van Hove, *A Look Inside Accelerators.*
41. Cohen, Bingham, and Hallen, "The Role of Accelerator Designs."
42. J. Gans, E. L. Scott, and S. Stern, "Strategy for Start-Ups," *Harvard Business Review* (May–June 2018), accessed November 7, 2018, https://hbr.org/2018/05/do-entrepreneurs-need-a-strategy.
43. *Technology Incubators: Nurturing Small Firms* (Paris: OECD, 1997).
44. N. Callegati, S. Grandi, and G. Napier, *Business Incubation and Venture Capital: An International Survey on Synergies and Challenges* (Rome: IPI, 2005).

45. *Technology Incubators: Nurturing Small Firms.*
46. European Commission, *Benchmarking of Business Incubators* (Kent: Centre for Strategy & Evaluation Services, 2002).
47. This model builds on I. Hathaway, "What Startup Accelerators Really Do," *Harvard Business Review* (March 1, 2016), accessed November 6, 2018, https://hbr.org/2016/03/what-startup-accelerators-really-do.

1

The Emergence of Startup Accelerators

The accelerator model has become a "graduate school" for startups.
Alex Friedman, co-founder and president, Ruckus;
Member, Forbes Councils

Emergence

In 1995 Paul Graham and Robert Tappan Morris co-founded Viaweb. They sold the company three years later to Yahoo for $49 million. Prior to founding Viaweb, Graham had received an undergraduate degree in philosophy from Cornell University, a Master of Science degree, and a PhD from Harvard University. Robert Tappan, on the other hand, had graduated from Harvard University and attended Cornell as a postgraduate student—before being suspended[1] and becoming one of the first people to receive a criminal conviction for hacking.[2] In early March 2005, almost seven years after the sale of Viaweb, Paul Graham was in conversation with Robert Morris and Trevor Blackwell (who had also been part of the Viaweb team) about possible ways of continuing to work together.[3] At that same time, Graham had been contemplating becoming more involved in angel investing. Later that week, he was discussing the venture capital business with Jessica Livingstone, a friend who was contemplating moving from investment banking to work for a Boston-based venture capital (VC) fund. In this conversation, Graham had been pointing out all the things that were wrong with the VC business and that needed to change—investors needed to make smaller investments, they needed to be funding hackers rather than suits, and they ought to fund younger founders. While walking with Jessica between Harvard Square and his house one day, the idea hit him to start an investment firm with Robert and Trevor and ask Jessica if she would work for that firm instead of the Boston VC firm she was contemplating working for. He discussed the idea with Jessica, and they decided to do it. Graham agreed to put in $100k, and he would later recruit Robert and Trevor, who each put in $50k. Their idea was to do seed funding with standardized terms. They based their model on a Viaweb investment arrangement they had in which a friend of theirs, Julian Webber, had invested $10k, provided support to set up the company, and provided them with early business education in exchange for 10% equity in Viaweb. The idea and model became Y Combinator. Y Combinator experimented with its first startup investments through summer job–style startup acceleration programs. Y Combinator soon had success from four of its first eight cohort companies, with Reddit (acquired by Conde Nast in 2006 for between $10 and $20 million) and Loopt (acquired by Green Dot for $43.4 million) being the biggest exits at the time. Y Combinator's success only improved with subsequent cohort programs.

Ascendance

Given Y Combinator's success with its first few cohorts, it's not surprising that competition soon followed. In 2006 David Cohen, Brad Feld, David Brown, and Jared Polis started the Techstars accelerator. More and more accelerators started to emerge. U.S.-based competition grew slowly to 16 accelerators within the first 3 years before starting to really take off at the end of 2008. After 2008, the number of U.S.-based accelerators grew by nearly 50% per annum before flattening out at around 170 accelerators in 2014.[4,5] Similar growth was replicated globally, so that by the end of 2016, there were 579 accelerators globally. As at that point in time, these accelerators had invested over $206 billion in 11,305 startups with 178 exits that year alone. Bart Clarysse, professor of entrepreneurship at the Swiss Federal Institute of Technology in Zurich, observed that most accelerator programs that emerged were modeled on either the Y Combinator or Techstars format.[6] (See Figure 1.1.)

Why was Y Combinator and its accelerator model such a runaway success? Without a doubt, Y Combinator needed and had an enviable founding team, with stellar education, skills, and experience;

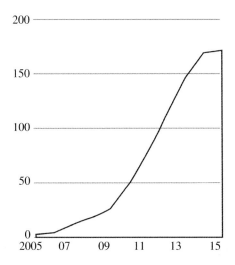

FIGURE 1.1 The Number of U.S. Accelerators Grew Dramatically between 2005 and 2015
Source: Adapted from Hathaway (2016).[7]

and the team had also previously founded and exited multiple startups. But while this may explain part of Y Combinator's success, it does not fully explain the runaway global success of their model. Other factors and trends that may explain some of the model's success include growing availability of access to capital globally, growing number and success of digital technology companies, and growing government interest in entrepreneurship globally. Although these parallel trends explain some of the model's success, our research suggests that Y Combinator did two critical things that, in the main, ensured the success of its model. First, it addressed a major gap in the support available to startups in entrepreneurial ecosystems. This gap is best conceptualized by Figure 1.2, which maps a start-up's evolution (on the *x* axis) against its funding needs[8] (on the *y* axis). Figure 1.2 also depicts the risk faced by a startup as it goes through the six stages of startup evolution, and the types of entities that are typically a source of funding and funding related support. Between stages 1 and 2 (the Ideation/Preparation and Customer Discovery stages), founders usually fund the startup themselves or receive funding from family and friends (as Y Combinator founders Paul Graham and Robert Morris did for both Y Combinator and for their earlier startup, Viaweb). From stages 2 to 3 (the

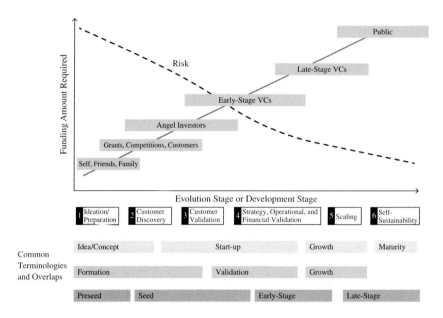

FIGURE 1.2 Startup Evolution and the Introduction of "Smart" Money

Customer Discovery and Customer Validation stages), startups may also source funding from grants (e.g., government or philanthropic grants), competitions (e.g., business planning competitions), and prospective customers (e.g., the problem a startup is solving may be so important to a customer that the customer funds the startup to develop the solution). More recent funding vehicles such as crowd funding and initial coin offerings (ICOs) also fall into this category; notwithstanding that these now offer entrepreneurs the opportunity to raise significantly greater amounts of money, and often without having to give up equity. From stages 3 to 4 (the Customer Validation and Strategy/Operational/Financial Validation stages), startups can usually successfully access angel investment (i.e., investment from high-net-worth individuals who invest their own money, along with their time and expertise, directly into private companies in which they have no family connection, in the hope of financial gain).[9] And from stage 4 (Strategy/Operational/Financial Validation) onwards, startups can usually access early-stage and late-stage venture capital funding (venture capital funds come from sources such as pension funds, banks, and foundations—there is a duty of care for how these funds are invested which may influence when VC firms can invest).[10] Of course, there are exceptions to the accessibility of each type of funding—depending on the founders, the nature of the startup, and the nature of the funding environment. And, needless to say, there are many overlaps—or points at which more than one funding source can be accessed. Below the startup evolution or development stages, we show other terminology often used to describe these stages and the overlaps within this terminology. For example, stage 1 (Ideation/Preparation) can also be referred to as the *Idea/Concept* stage or the *Pre-seed* stage. The term *startup* is sometimes used to describe the activities between Customer Discovery and Strategy/Operational/Financial Validation. Other times it is used to describe the full journey from stage 1 to stage 6. The term *growth* is sometimes used to describe the *Scaling* stage. Stages 1 to 2 can sometimes be referred to as *Formation*, and stages 3 to 4 can sometimes be referred to as *Validation*. Stages 2 to 4 can sometimes be referred to as the *Seed* stage, with stages 4 to 5 often referred to as the *Early* stage, and stages 5 to 6 as the *Late* stage. The overlapping terminology can often create confusion, so we clarify it here prior to further unpacking the startup support gap addressed and the success of Y Combinator's accelerator model at addressing it.

As Figure 1.2 shows, "smart" money (funding that also comes with the expertise critical to helping entrepreneurs maximize startup development speed, scale, and odds of success), is usually accessible from stage 3 onwards. It is usually from this stage that more sophisticated angel investors can be attracted, followed by early-stage and late-stage VCs between stages 4 and 5. Paradoxically, founders face the highest risk of failure and perhaps the greatest need for "smart" money support before they are able to access "smart" money. The Y Combinator model provided an effective solution to this paradoxical problem and support gap within entrepreneurial ecosystems. It provided a highly effective proof of concept for the idea that providing early "smart" money support could both help entrepreneurs and, at the same time, be of commercial value. The success of the model meant that "smart" money investors would have improved investment opportunities (i.e., greater quantity and quality of startups making it to the "smart" money stages). It also meant that existing companies would have improved acquisition opportunities (more startups to buy/better quality startups to buy), and public markets would also have improved IPO opportunities (more/better startups making it to IPO stage). Governments and communities would

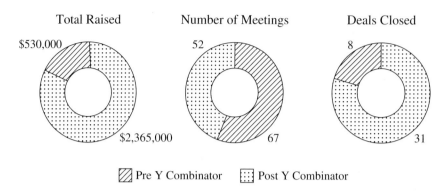

also have improved innovation, economic development, and job creation opportunities from the greater number of startups succeeding, or at least surviving longer. Essentially, the accelerator model supercharged entrepreneurial ecosystems and provided tangible and intangible benefits to most ecosystem entities and stakeholders (e.g., see Figure 1.3.) We believe the problem the accelerator model solved, and the benefits it provided to entrepreneurial ecosystem entities and stakeholders, made its global adoption irresistible.

Expansion

As the number of accelerators grew, they began to differentiate their offerings and branch out into different niches. For example, some accelerators started to differentiate themselves on location, on cohort sizes, on global reach, on the nature of their networks, on accelerator size, on sector, on industry, on value chain area, on technology type, on customer type, and so on. Thus today, there are a large number of different types of accelerators. These include, for example, non-corporate accelerators, corporate accelerators, government accelerators, NGO (nongovernment organization)/NFP (not-for-profit) accelerators, university accelerators, specific industry accelerators (e.g., defense, healthcare, media, etc.), specific technology accelerators (e.g., IoT, blockchain, fintech, etc.), and many others. As we noted in the introduction, noncorporate accelerators usually follow the original Y Combinator accelerator model, offering the seven benefits discussed earlier in exchange for equity investment, although not all accelerators take equity. Corporate, government, NGO/NFP, and other accelerators are usually run by or on behalf of corporations, governments, or NGO/NFP organizations for a range of different strategic reasons. Such reasons can include stimulation of innovation, enhancing adaptive capacity, learning commercialization skills, stimulating economic development, and many more. For example, there is a Barclay's accelerator focusing on Fintech startups, and a Comcast NBC Universal LIFT Labs Accelerator focusing on media startups. Other examples include the United Arab Emirates' Government Accelerator Program, which, through a range of different accelerator programs, brings together people across government to rapidly address government challenges.

Accelerators have also started to differentiate themselves by stage of startup evolution. That is, to focus exclusively on earlier or later stages of startup evolution. Early on, accelerators invested less money, and took on more ideation/preparation and customer-discovery stage startups. As they have grown in size and competition has intensified, many accelerators have begun to invest much more money and take more developed startups with greater exit certainty and better return multiples. For example, many of the original accelerators that initially focused on cohorts at the customer-discovery stage now mostly take startups that have found product/market fit (part of the customer validation stage). As a result, the odds of getting into some of these accelerators is now almost commensurable with the odds of getting venture capital investment. But while these accelerators have shifted their focus to more developed startups, several new programs have sprung up with an exclusive focus on the ideation/preparation and or the customer-discovery stages. For example, programs such as Startup Weekend bring together people interested in being part of a startup (e.g., developers, business managers, aspiring entrepreneurs, marketing gurus, designers, and more), and facilitate a program to help them derive startup ideas, form startup teams, and leverage these teams to translate the ideas into minimum viable products (MVPs) or working prototypes. Other programs, branding themselves as pre-accelerators, focus exclusively on the stages that are too early for most accelerators. These programs focus on supporting aspiring entrepreneurs or other people with startup involvement intentions to accelerate advancement to the stage where most accelerators are ready to accept a startup. For example, Startup Boost supports aspiring entrepreneurs by providing them with one-on-one mentorship as well as experienced entrepreneur, investor, and industry connections to help them move as fast as possible from intention to being ready to enter an accelerator such as Techstars. Newer types of programs, sometimes referred to as "germinators," amalgamate some of the benefits of accelerators and incubators, and even go beyond these benefits, to play part of the confounding role for a temporary or contingent timeframe. For example, in addition to the accelerator benefits, such programs may also provide product development as a service-type infrastructure. This infrastructure may be in the form of software development teams (in the case of potential software product startups), or labs (in the case of potential biotechnology startups). Examples of these programs include Biotechandbeyond, which provides lab space, shared resources, and other support to make it easy for science startups. The accelerator types and the nature of their offerings continue to evolve to accelerate the efficiency and success rate of startups.

Impact

The impacts and implications of accelerators are best understood by exploring the role they play in entrepreneurial ecosystems, how they impact different ecosystem actors, and how they impact the system as a whole. Exact definitions of what an ecosystem comprises of are scarce.[12] Some researchers view an entrepreneurial ecosystem as a conceptual framework designed to foster economic development via entrepreneurship, innovation, and small-business growth.[13] Others view an entrepreneurial ecosystem as a set of interdependent actors and factors coordinated in such a way that they enable productive entrepreneurship.[14] For the purpose of this book, we draw on the different definitions and use the term to describe the configuration and interaction of the different entities, actors, and stakeholders that influence the rate and extent to which startups emerge and succeed. The actors or entities within entrepreneurial ecosystems are diverse and include accelerators (providing mentoring, curriculum-based experiential learning programs, funding, investor networks, hands on support, professional services, etc.), incubators (providing working spaces, discounted professional services, etc.), and venture capital firms/angel investors/other investors (providing funding, accelerated evolution, etc.). They also include government entrepreneurship support organizations (providing ecosystem strategic leadership as well as nurturing actors/entities to fill temporary ecosystem gaps or filling these gaps until such actors can, providing incentives and disincentives, etc.), startup and business planning competition entities (providing early concept development direction, concept validation and funding, etc.), and startup service providers (providing startup focused services). They extend to also include entrepreneurship education organizations (e.g., those providing formal entrepreneurship education programs), entrepreneurship research organizations (e.g., those finding solutions to entrepreneurship issues or explaining the dynamics of entrepreneurial ecosystems), and small business support entities (providing early and later generic business support). Extending even further, they include entrepreneurship and startup associations (providing community/belonging, peer support, peer-based learning and peer collaboration opportunities for entrepreneurs and aspiring entrepreneurs, etc.), established businesses (who may be potential customers, investors, acquirers, competitors of entrepreneurial businesses, etc.), and the wider community (e.g., community attitudes towards entrepreneurs may shape government entrepreneurship policy and investment, treatment of entrepreneurs and therefore entrepreneurial intentions, etc.).

Startup accelerators play a unique role in entrepreneurial ecosystems that includes but is not limited to, closing the "smart" money gap, sharing startup acceleration best practices, raising the bar of other entrepreneurial ecosystem entities through competition, expanding the supply of startup-ready entrepreneurs, upgrading and expanding the network of mentors and advisors available to founders, improving community know-how of startup evolution and of the entrepreneurial process, improving the link between founders and corporates, as well as improving the link between founders and government institutions. By playing this unique role, accelerators increase the number of startups making it to smart money, and ultimately succeeding. As a part of this, they increase the number of entrepreneurs and investors successfully exiting startup deals. In doing so, they may indirectly expand the competition for startups as an investment product (e.g., see Figure 1.4). They also lead to more and better-quality startup investment opportunities being available to "smart" money investors, more and bigger startup success stories, and therefore faster economic development and job creation. Thus, in the same way startup accelerators accelerate startups, they also supercharge and accelerate the development, efficiency, and effectiveness of entrepreneurial ecosystems.

Future

Since coming into the public consciousness in 2005, accelerators have become one of the most powerful vehicles for helping entrepreneurs to learn rapidly, connect with powerful networks, raise money, and build their startups at speed and scale. In doing so, they have supercharged entrepreneurial ecosystems and demonstrated their potential to accelerate economic development, expand job creation, and enhance economic competitiveness. All this has occurred in just over 10 years. Based on the impact over this term, the impact of accelerators on entrepreneurship and the entrepreneurial process over the next 10 to 20 years may be more comparable to the impact of the internet on business. Irrespective of the size of the impact, we believe accelerators will continue to further unpack startup evolution challenges, illuminate the causes, and make solving the challenges more of a science.

We anticipate that accelerators will continue to specialize and differentiate themselves on the types of startup evolution challenges they help entrepreneurs solve, the types of skills they help founders develop, and the types of support services they provide founders. We anticipate that with time, there will be a proliferation of corporate and government accelerators as large institutions start to fully understand the benefits of accelerators for solving complex problems, driving innovation needs, and enabling adaptation to environmental change. At present, accelerators are largely the domain of investors or entities with access to large amounts of money. But we expect to see more and more entrepreneurs start contemplating just why they shouldn't start their own accelerators. We expect this will intensify competition among accelerators leading to more diverse and hands-on help being available to founders. We also expect

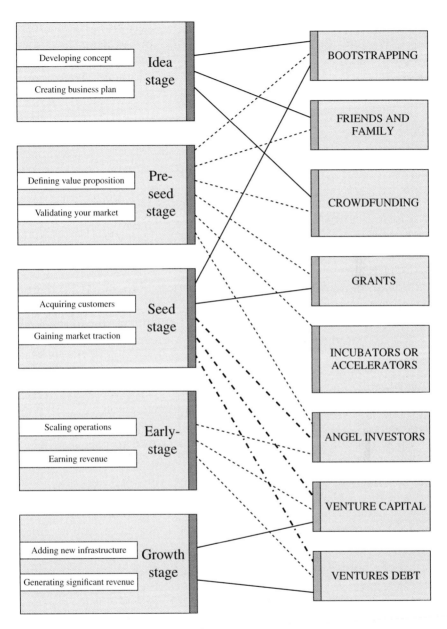

FIGURE 1.4 Expanding Funding Options Now Available to Entrepreneurs at Different Stages
Source: Adapted from Jumpstart (2018).[15]

startup evolution to become more scientific, entrepreneurial ecosystems to become more efficient and effective, and economic development and job creation to accelerate in the regions that embrace and invest in accelerators.

Notes

1. J. Markoff, "Cornel Suspends Computer Student," *New York Times,* May 25, 1989, accessed July 31, 2019, https://www.nytimes. com/1989/05/25/us/cornell-suspends-computer-student.html.
2. E. Fuchs, "How the 'Computer Wizard' Who Created the First Internet Virus Got Off without a Day of Jail," *Business Insider,* January 22, 2013, accessed July 31, 2019, https://www.business insider.com.au/why-robert-morris-didnt-go-to-jail-2013-1?r=US&IR=T.
3. YCombinator, accessed July 31, 2019, https://www.ycombinator .com/.
4. I. Hathaway, "Accelerating Growth: Startup Accelerator Programs in the United States," Brookings Institution (2016).
5. I. Hathaway, "What Startup Accelerators Really Do," *Harvard Business Review,* March 2016.
6. B. Clarysee, M. Wright, and J. van Hove, *A Look Inside Accelerators: Building Businesses* (London: NESTA, 2015).
7. Adapted from I. Hathaway, "What Startup Accelerators Really Do," *Harvard Business Review,* March 1, 2016, accessed August 1, 2019, https://hbr.org/2016/03/what-startup-accelerators-really-do.
8. Ciarán Mac an Bhaird and Brian Lucey, "An Empirical Investigation of the Financial Growth Lifecycle," *Journal of Small Business and Enterprise Development* 18, no. 4 (2011): 715–731.
9. C. Mason, "Business Angel Investing," in *The Handbook of Personal Wealth Management: How to Ensure Maximum Investment Returns with Security* (Kogan Page, 2005), 169–175.
10. Ibid.
11. J. Streebin, "Was Y Combinator Worth It?" *TechCrunch,* February 15, 2014, accessed August 1, 2019, https://techcrunch.com/2014/ 02/15/was-y-combinator-worth-it/.
12. D. B. Audretsch, J. A. Cunninghman, D. F. Kuratko, E. E. Lehmann, and M. Menter, "Entrepreneurial Ecosystems: Economic, Technological and Societal Impacts," *Journal of Technology Transfer* 44 (2019): 313–325.

13. T. Mazzarol, "Growing and Sustaining Entrepreneurial Ecosystems: What They Are and the Role of Government Policy" (white paper WP01-2014, Small Enterprise Association of Australia and New Zealand (SEAANZ, 2014)), www.seaanz.org.

14. E. Stam, "Entrepreneurial Ecosystems and Regional Policy: A Sympathetic Critique," *European Planning Studies* 23, no. 9 (2015): 1759–1769.

15. "Understanding Funding: The Stages of a Typical Startup Company & Its Funding Options," JumpStart, April 23, 2018, accessed August 1, 2019, https://www.jumpstartinc.org/understanding-funding-stages-typical-startup-company-funding-options/.

2

What Happens in an Accelerator

Learning-by-doing is vital to the process of scaling ventures, and the point of accelerators is to accelerate that process. In this way, founders compress years' worth of learning into a period of a few months.
Brad Feld, co-founder, Techstars;
co-founder, Foundry Group

Accelerator Programs

Being fixed-term, cohort-based learning and support programs, accelerator programs usually occur over a period usually ranging from three months to six months.[1,2] In this period, all the accelerated evolution, education, mentorship, coaching, connections, advice, hands-on support, strategy, and investment readiness preparation occurs—culminating in a public pitch event known as "demo day."[3,4] Each accelerator program usually has a curriculum, occurs at an accelerator space (or co-working space), is operated by program managers, and has advisors/mentors.[5,6,7] Participant startup companies are typically referred to as "cohorts," rather than individual companies.[8] Most accelerators also have a network of active investors and other entrepreneurial ecosystem stakeholders whom they invite to "demo day."[9,10,11] Investors can make investments before demo day, on demo day, after demo day, or not at all—if none of the cohort companies meet their investment criteria.[12,13] In the rest of this chapter, we unpack the different elements of accelerator programs in more detail (see Figure 2.1 for common elements) and provide a case study at the end of the chapter of a startup's experience going through an accelerator program and interacting with the common elements of an accelerator program.

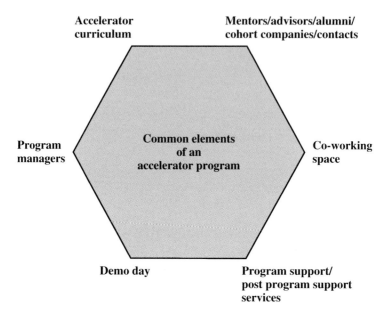

FIGURE 2.1 Common Elements of an Accelerator Program
Source: Adapted from Pauwels et al. (2016).[14]

Accelerator Curriculums

Most accelerators share a similar curriculum, delivery structure, or "pattern of learning,"[15] that is typically organized into months. Month 1 is usually focused on customer discovery or customer validation—digging deep to find out if each cohort startup's idea has legs. That is, is the idea going to be a success? Are customers actually going to pay money for the idea? How many of these customers are really out there? Is the idea scalable? How much money can be made from the idea? Does the startup have product/market fit? And, has the startup validated the business model? According to most founders, month 2 is often the *"prepare for investors/get the product ready/get traction/ write a business plan"* month. Traction is "Quantitative evidence of market demand" or evidence that the idea actually works in the real world.[16] You may hear most accelerators and investors say that traction trumps everything else that people may think of the idea.[17] This usually refers to the belief that, even if people don't understand the idea or like it, they can't ignore great traction data. For example, many people thought Gabriel Weinberg was nuts when they heard his idea of building a search engine to compete with Google.[18] Two years later, when Union Square Ventures saw the number of monthly searches for his search engine and the visits to his website, they invested in DuckDuckGo saying, "*We invested in DuckDuckGo because we became convinced that it was not only possible to change the basis of competition in search, it was time to do it.*"[19] Traction can take the form of a range of measures including, but not limited to, sales revenue, profitability, active users, clients, partnerships, site traffic, and search engine searches.[20] Month 3 typically involves preparing for "demo day,'" the day when cohort teams pitch their business concepts to a live audience made up of local and international investors as well as other entrepreneurial ecosystem stakeholders, for between 5 and 10 minutes. As a part of this process, cohort companies will prepare PowerPoint presentations, write and rehearse investor pitches, and go through public speaking training. The audience on demo day may be as small as 10 to 20 people for some accelerators, and as large as 500 or more people for more popular accelerators like Techstars and Y Combinator.[21]

Sometimes the accelerator will break the curriculum into weeks, with each week focusing on a certain theme or topic. For example, startups may have a "sales week" in week 4, a "marketing week" in week 8, and a "financial projections week" in week 10. The agenda/schedule may be shared prior to the program, or cohorts may only find out what they are doing at the start of each week. There are usually good reasons for either approach. For example, an undisclosed agenda may allow program organizers the flexibility to deliver particular modules when a cohort is ready for those modules—this can vary depending on the strengths and weaknesses of different cohorts.

Accelerator Co-Working Spaces

Accelerator programs are usually held in a large space referred to as "accelerator spaces," "labs," "co-labs," or "co-working spaces." These spaces can be critical to the effectiveness of the accelerator program.[22] Spaces are built or chosen to suit the delivery of the particular accelerator program. The spaces will typically have booths or large and long desks grouped by participating team; they will also typically have fast internet connections, printers, photocopiers, lunch rooms, meeting rooms, storage space, and maybe even table tennis tables and pool tables. So, while startups may not have their own private office, they will usually have booths or large tables for the team to work at. For private meetings, there are usually meeting rooms available that are shared between cohort companies on an as-needed basis.

Accelerator Mentors

For many weeks of the accelerator program, startups will have what arc called *mentoring sessions* with the accelerator program mentors.[23,24,25,26] These mentoring sessions involve spending time one-on-one (or one-on-team) with highly experienced founders (successful entrepreneurs) and or investors (venture capitalists, angel investors) or professional business services specialists (e.g., lawyers, accountants, media experts, public speaking experts, business model experts).[27,28] Typically, these sessions can range from 15 minutes to a few hours at a time. Some of the mentors may be there in person, and some of them may video conference in from different parts of the world. In either case, the best program organizers seek out and pull in some of the best experts from around the world.[29,30] These mentors come to the program to share their knowledge, experiences, and wisdom with program participants in return for an opportunity to invest in the ideas they like, to extend their networks, to promote their profile, to get insight into emerging innovations, or simply for the pure joy of helping others and giving back to the community (see Figure 2.2 for data on the impact of a top mentor on startup success).

As a member of a cohort team, you will likely attend anywhere between 2 and 50 mentoring sessions throughout the program. For example, some programs build in up to 20 or more compulsory mentoring sessions focused on particular issues. This can be in addition to specific mentoring sessions you may organize yourself. Other programs leave it up to you to arrange the meetings you want with the mentors that interest you and to arrange the location and format of these meetings as suits you. If it is left up to you, you can arrange these mentoring sessions at the accelerator space or let them happen informally over drinks or at a restaurant. In place of mentoring sessions, some accelerator programs simply curate

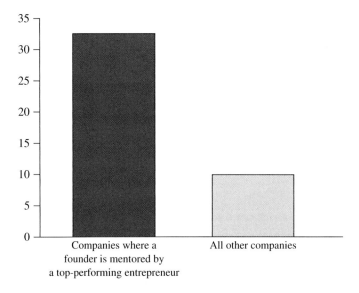

FIGURE 2.2 Proportion of Top-Performing Companies Where the Founders Were Mentored by a Top-Performing Entrepreneur, Based on Analysis of New York Tech Firms Founded between 2003 and 2013

Source: Adapted from Morris (2015).[31]

and deliver essential advice via lectures to all participants in the program at once. It all depends on the accelerator program. During mentoring sessions, some mentors might sit with you for up to four hours at a time, advising you on every aspect of your business. They may stay involved in the accelerator for the duration of the program, or they may just attend the program for a couple of hours and leave as soon as their mentoring sessions are over. If they stay involved for the duration of the program, they might turn up to the accelerator lab space two or three times a week and want to have coffee with you every time. You might develop wonderful lifelong friendships with some mentors, and you might find it a challenge to develop a rapport with others. Some may give you advice that changes everything about your idea and your business plan. Others may offer generic insights. Yet others may seem to offer no useful insights at the time, but this may be because you just don't get what they are talking about yet. At some point, their advice may start to make sense.

Accelerator Program Managers

Before you apply for an accelerator, it's important to understand the role, motivations, and pressures of accelerator program managers so you can work with them effectively and make the most of what they have to offer. Program managers are usually the ones who make the final decisions about who gets into an accelerator program. Sometimes they may consult with the program sponsors or mentors about who should be shortlisted for interviews and who ultimately gets selected. Either way, the program managers have great influence on who gets into accelerators. The role of the program managers is similar to that of film or play producers. There are usually two to five of them, and they generally organize everything for the "show" while constantly trying to bring the best out of you and your team. The program managers will have a variety of other roles too, from looking after the mentors (for example, organizing for them to be picked up from the airport if they are coming in from out of town), through to all the other nitty-gritty details that keep the program going. By nitty-gritty, we mean things such as booking rooms for presentations in the shared office space, organizing/paying for dinners, organizing program and mentoring schedules, introducing the daily mentor lectures, organizing cohort accommodation (if required), preparing reports for sponsors and investors, and much more. During the accelerator, the program managers might also hold regular meetings with the mentors and investors to discuss the progress and investment readiness of each cohort company. The list of program managers' responsibilities goes on and on. It even includes doing press releases, speaking to journalists, promoting demo day in the local community, consulting with investors and venture capitalists regularly, advising cohort founders on demo day presentation styles, and helping founders prepare business and financial plans.

Program managers are usually available in the accelerator offices from at least 9 a.m. to 5 p.m. most days. Despite the many things they do, they usually have an open-door policy, and are usually open to you approaching them for any kind of advice, at any time. Most program managers are successful entrepreneurs who have developed at least one idea into a successful company at some point. In addition to this, they have usually seen many companies come and go through accelerator programs with varying outcomes. They will likely have seen many companies making the most of the accelerator offering and going on to great success, as well as many companies letting their "know it all" attitude make them persona non grata to the accelerator network. Program managers are usually also well connected and well resourced. They usually have access to lawyers, accountants, professors, marketing experts, and CEOs of large companies. They will typically have "*templates*" for anything you need to complete during the accelerator. These templates may range from business plans, Excel-based financial plans, sales/marketing funnels, shareholder agreements, joint venture agreements, and licensing agreements. Further, each program manager will usually have a specialized skill set (e.g., board building, traction building, social media, sales, marketing, legal, graphic design, IT, project management, business development, etc.). Program managers are usually much more hands-on than mentors and advisors. They are usually also quite down-to-earth for people of so much experience, and in such a position of authority. They may become an invaluable resource and advocate, depending on the effort you make to engage with them.

What really drives these program managers? If they are successful entrepreneurs, you may ask, "*Why are they wasting their time in an accelerator when they can be sitting on their giant yacht in the Bahamas or kite surfing every day in the Virgin Islands?*" Their motivations usually vary. Often, program managers may get shares in accelerator program companies through seed investment opportunities or through a share of the equity the accelerator owns. For example, there might be an arrangement whereby a program manager receives up to 2% of the equity that the accelerator program acquires in exchange for providing cohort companies seed capital and a spot in the program (see Figures 2.3 and 2.4 for examples of seed capital investment amounts and equity taken by accelerators in U.S. and U.K. accelerators). Some program managers may not receive any equity but do the job for other reasons such as extending their networks, getting insider insight into possible investment opportunities, promoting their profile, or giving back to the community. In any case, the best way for program managers to remain in their role is to keep the accelerator going. That is, for each cohort to do so well that the next accelerator will happen, and the next one, and the next one after that. Therefore, most program managers will do whatever they can to make each accelerator a success, to attract sufficient funding, and to attract the best sponsorship for the next program. For example,

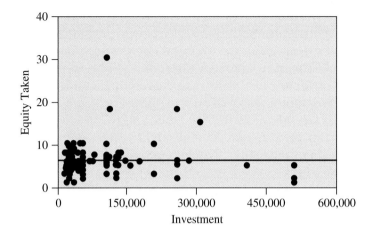

FIGURE 2.3 Equity Taken (%) versus Investment Amount (USD$): Distribution of U.S. Accelerators (circa 2015)
Source: Adapted from Rowley (2016).[32]

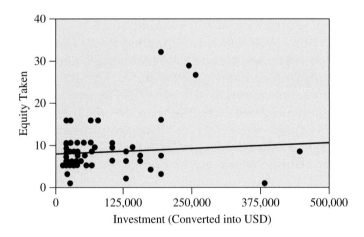

FIGURE 2.4 Equity Taken (%) versus Investment Amount (USD$): Distribution of UK Accelerators
Source: Adapted from Rowley (2016).[33]

program managers may need to find funding for the next program from corporations, sponsors, politicians, local/state/federal governments, past cohort investments exits, or donations. They may also need to attract top startups to the next program. Continuing to attract the funding, mentors, advisors, and startups requires building a track record of success and a good reputation. For example, with quality startups joining each program, press coverage will come easier and corporate sponsors will look better in the local media. If the sponsors look "good" in the local community, then their brand credibility and earnings may improve.

We have focused on accelerator program managers and their staff in this chapter, as they are the primary stakeholders cohort companies interface with. But for other important accelerator stakeholders it may be of benefit for founders to include program sponsors, program directors, partners, investors and alumni, or portfolio companies.[34] Sponsors fund accelerators and could be corporations, private investors (e.g., angel investors, venture capitalists, and public or semipublic organizations such as universities and government agencies). Directors are the general managers or executive directors responsible for the strategic decision making and for overseeing managers of day-to-day operations. Partners are individuals or organizations that offer services and products to accelerators or their portfolio companies for free or at a discount. Typical partners would be mentors, professional services or technology companies, pre-accelerators, incubation entities, key customer networks, and so on. Investors provide the follow-on funding for accelerated ventures and could be angel investors, VCs, or large corporations. And lastly, portfolio companies are all the active startups that have ever graduated from the accelerator.

Accelerator programs are not cheap to run. Some estimates of the running costs (in $USD) of a single cohort three-month program range between $300,000 and over $1 million. For example, startup accelerator researchers Paul Miller and Kirsten Bound reviewed the operations of The Difference Engine—an accelerator operating in Sunderland and Middleborough in the UK. The costs associated with running one cycle of the program was £250,000 (USD 300,000). This did not factor in any potential returns on the equity stake that the program took in the companies it supported.[35] If you consider the facilities and human resource requirements of a typical accelerator alone, you can see how quickly the costs can add up. For example, there is rent for the offices for the cohort teams, there is food and drink for events, fees for guest speakers, airfares, and accommodation for mentors visiting from out of town. And of course, there are the wages for the program managers, both during the event and in the lead-up to the event. If there are four program managers, each one may be paid $3,000–$5,000 a week. That's around $140,000 alone for a 12-week program. There is usually a month or two in between each program, too, where the program managers need to be paid for preparation work—so you can begin to see how it all adds up. That's before including the seed capital investment that accelerators make into each company (i.e., the $10,000 to $250,000 equity investment). For a cohort of 10 startups, that investment will require an extra $100,000–$2.5 million. Given these costs, a common objective of program managers is to make the accelerator program self-funding from past alumni investment exits. At that stage, the accelerators won't need to rely on attracting new corporate sponsors' money for every program. Usually, for the program to cash in on the 4–10% equity in accelerator companies, there needs to be an exit event such as a sale of the company, an IPO, or an investor buyout. The program managers will do everything they can to help accelerator companies achieve the best and fastest exits. This is usually also in the interest of accelerator company founders, as the longer it takes for an exit to occur, the more likely it is that the company may become one of the great majorities that don't make it.[36]

Accelerator Weekly Check-In Sessions

Every week, the program managers will usually ask the team's CEO to report in on the team's latest achievements. This may be done in a formal workshop or informally during conversations. Some accelerators call the formal workshops the weekly check-in, or CEO check-ins, or CEO weekly updates. These workshop sessions usually happen at a set time each week. They may be held over lunches or dinners. These check-ins could be held in the accelerator workspace, or they could be held at a mentor's house or in a restaurant. Often, these sessions run for 30 minutes to one hour, with each team's CEO talking for 5 to 10 minutes. The mentors and program managers often use these CEO check-ins as an opportunity to assess your startup's progress and to determine whether you are getting closer to be being "investment ready." They may check what weekly achievements you are making, what you have remaining to achieve, and what you may need to do differently. They will also check how your communication skills are developing. Being able to communicate your business idea clearly and simply is a critical outcome of most accelerator programs.[37] If you want to convince investors to invest in your company, you need to be able to clearly articulate what your business or product is all about. You need to be able to convince investors why your idea will be a success, and how much money it is likely to make them. Often, teams with tech-heavy products/ services, and with the co-founding team made up of engineers/ software developers, can struggle with communication due to issues like introversion, technical jargon, or a negative attitude towards the business side of their technology.[38]

Accelerator Advisors

Often, it is beneficial to have at least one of the accelerator program mentors, or an influential/powerful friend of one of the mentors, join your team as an advisor. For example, this special person might join your advisory board or perhaps join your board of directors or become your chairperson.[39] A particular mentor may be encouraged to approach you to potentially join your team, or they may wait for you to approach them with a proposal.[40] Some mentors may not be aware of the possibility of them or their friends being able to join your team—so you may have to suggest it to them. Either way, you want to headhunt the right mentor to join your team as an advisor. Perhaps someone operating or having operated in the industry or market that you are targeting. Perhaps someone who has built the same type of business as yours. Some accelerators have advisor agreements ready to go, and they may encourage you and your advisor to sign one as soon as possible after starting the program.

Throughout the program, you will have many different mentors. Before you start with each new mentor, you should know in advance from the program managers who the mentors are, their background, and what value they could offer your team as an advisor. You can research each of the different mentors before you meet with them. You can get online and look for information about them on platforms such as LinkedIn or news outlets or company websites. When you meet the mentors in person, you can complement the secondary information you have gathered about them with in-person observations. For example, you can ask them questions through informal discussions to dig deeper about their background, skills, and work experience. Ideally, you want to see if their background and capabilities align with your company's needs and that you are able to effectively work with them. For example, if you are a healthcare product company, you may not want a mentor from a lock hardware manufacturing background to join your team. Alternatively, you may find a mentor with adequate healthcare product commercialization experience, but their style may not suit your company. Ideally, you want the right mentor or mentors to join your advisory board. Some mentors may want a small percentage of equity in return for becoming an advisor, given that you may not be able to pay the types of fees they may charge. This equity can range from 0.5% to 5% but may be more, depending on the value of your company, how much input you require from the mentor, and the profile of the mentor. The accelerator program managers have legal agreement templates that you can use to formalize an agreement with your chosen advisor. They may also be able to provide advice about the amount of equity that is reasonable to give up. The level of equity you provide to a mentor may influence their commitment to help you succeed.

If you don't raise funding during an accelerator, or shortly afterwards, then getting a high-profile advisor to join your team can be equally valuable. The right advisor can guide your company, help attract other high-profile people, and be critical to future fundraising efforts. For example, Swinburne University associate professor Naomi Birdthistle notes that the founder of Quitch, a spin-out from Swinburne University of Technology, which was founded by Grainne Oats, had Oji Udezue (former Head of Product for Communications Tools at Atlassian) as a director and Jane Hewitt, founder of Unilodge, as an advisor. The two high-profile people were considered invaluable in the startup's fundraising efforts and for customer/ strategic partner credibility. The right advisor can also open many doors for your company. For example, they can introduce you to their connections who may become critical customers, strategic partners, or acquirers. Alternatively, they may allow you to use the product development, marketing, or sales resources at their companies. The right advisor might get you distribution deals in big supermarkets, in national chain hardware stores, or they could get you a deal with behemoth like Amazon. The right advisor could get you interviews with leading tech journals that can result in 500,000 downloads of your app on launch. The right advisor might even take your phone call in the middle of the night, if you're having a breakdown about cash flow, legal, or people problems. Even if they do nothing else, a high-profile advisor brings their established reputation to your company, giving your startup valuable credibility. For example, imagine if you managed to get Bill Gates on your advisory board. Even if he did nothing but sign the advisor agreement, the brand credibility and the opportunities that will suddenly open up may surprise you. If he were available as a sounding board, his advice could give your startup the ultimate unfair advantage. If he were to call on his network to assist your startup, you may be catapulted into startup royalty. For instance, consider how Bill Gates' support of Khan Academy catapulted that startup.[41] Figure 2.5 presents some data on the relationship between having an advisor and amount of funding raised.

The right advisor's experience can be extremely important to you once the program finishes. You may be surprised by the number of issues that come up and are a challenge to solve without all the accelerator program resources at your fingerprints. However, at that point, you won't be able to rely on the program managers to support you. Sure, you should keep in touch with the program managers and ask them for help, but the program managers will most likely be occupied with running or preparing to run the next program. They typically won't have the time to support you or other past accelerator

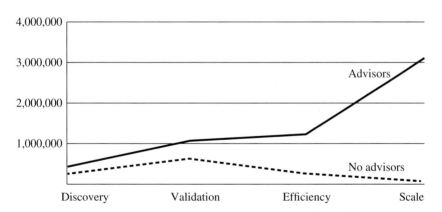

FIGURE 2.5 Average Funding Raised ($USD) at Different Stages of Startup Evolution by Startups with Advisors versus Those without Advisors; the Stages Can Be Approximated to Our Stages of Startup Evolution as Follows: Discovery = Customer Discovery, Validation = Customer Validation, Efficiency = Strategy/Operational/Financial Validation, Scale = Scale).
Source: Adapted from Dwyer.[42]

companies the way they did during the accelerator program. If you sign on a mentor as an advisor during the accelerator, they may be happy for you to tell the world about it. In this case, you may be able to update your website; update your social media accounts; blog about it; do press releases; and name-drop during partner, client, and investor meetings.

By the end of the accelerator there are typically nine key things your startup should have completed to investable standard. First, you should have a clear business plan, marketing plan, and financial plan for the next three to five years (this may be in written form or just clarified in team members' minds). Second, you should have completed an Investor Memorandum/Executive Summary to give to potential investors. Third, you should have a professionally registered company with the right registration documents and proper shareholder agreements signed by you and your team. Fourth, you should have a fully professionalized website and other forms of online presence relevant to your company (e.g., social media). Fifth, you should have prepared a professional pitch deck or PowerPoint presentation for demo day, and for sending to prospective investors. Sixth, you should have prepared and fully rehearsed a professional 5–10-minute investor pitch that you can deliver in your sleep. Seventh, you should have developed a set of relationships that you can draw on for advice/mentoring/coaching, access to customers, access to strategic partners, and access to investors after the accelerator. Eighth, you should have raised seed funding from the accelerator and possibly from the accelerator network. Ninth and finally, you should have achieved investable traction/progress. It is common for the accelerator curriculum to be designed around the deliverables in Figure 2.6. Some accelerators may prioritize particular deliverables over others.

Demo Day

The climax of most accelerator programs is called demo day.[43] Demo day is when all the teams pitch their startups on stage to an audience typically made up of investors, in the hope of getting investment.[44] The lead-up to demo day can be pressure filled, as most companies in the cohort know that this may be one of their best opportunities to get investment. The intense buildup of demo day pressure may begin

Common Objectives/Outcomes of an Accelerator

Business Plan Have a business plan, marketing plan, and financial plan for the next three to five years	**Investable Traction/Progress** Advance rapidly through a stage or from one stage to another (e.g., Progress from Customer Discovery to completion of Customer Validation)
Legal Structure Have an appropriately registered company with professional registration documents, shareholder agreements, and other legal documents that can pass due diligence	**Investor Memorandum** Write an investable investor memorandum/executive summary
	Professional Online Presence Designed/modified/published a professional website for your business that attracts customers and investors
Networking Have a developed a set of relationships that you can draw on for support with a range of issues (e.g., advice, hands-on support, peer support, customer access, strategic partner access)	**Pitch Deck** Have a professional PowerPoint presentation/pitch deck for demo day and to give to interested investors
Fundraising Raise seed funding from the accelerator, the accelerator network, and your own network	**Pitch** Have a prepared/rehearsed investment-ready pitch that you can almost deliver in your sleep

Investment Readiness/Accelerated Evolution Readiness

FIGURE 2.6 Common Deliverables of Cohort Companies Prior to Demo Day

from the moment you step foot into the accelerator on day 1. Following this, program managers usually take every opportunity to remind you of demo day's importance throughout the program. For example, the program managers might tell you at the start of a week, *"... you have less than three weeks until demo day, and you have so much work to do."* Many things done within the accelerators are aimed at maximizing your performance on demo day (see Figure 2.6 for an example of common deliverables of cohort companies prior to demo day). For example, the program managers might introduce each week's mentor by saying, *"This mentor will help with your body language for the demo day presentation,"* or *"This mentor will help you prepare your financial projections graph for your demo day presentation."* The program managers want you to understand the importance of demo day to your business. If you get investment on that day, you are likely to significantly improve your chances of success. Correspondingly, your success may improve the accelerator program's chance of success in the long run. If you are the sort of person who thrives on pressure and getting things done against a deadline, you are likely to be at home in the accelerator environment. On the other hand, if you don't like pressure and anxiety, then you may have to come up with your own strategies for dealing with the aggressive deadlines.

Whether they refer to it as demo day or not, at the end of the program all accelerators will have some sort of graduation event. But the size and focus of this event may differ from accelerator to accelerator. For example, Techstars' demo days have been held in large halls (often concert venues), and invitees have included investors, press, and industry insiders. The accelerator has also hosted a large party to mark the closure of each cohort.[45] Bart Clarysse, professor at the Swiss Federal Institute of Technology in Zurich, notes that on demo day MIT's DeltaV accelerator has filled its Kresge Auditorium with over 1,500 attendees including local alumni, investors, and the entrepreneurial community. Following the program, most accelerators usually maintain close relationships with portfolio companies (i.e., alumni companies, or companies that have graduated from their program). Some accelerators will run alumni events or invite alumni to share their experiences with current cohort companies. The equity that accelerators have in alumni startups usually provides them with added incentive to continue supporting alumni startups to succeed.[46] Accelerator stakeholders have started to explore which of the different accelerator program elements and support services cohort companies value the most (e.g., see Figure 2.7).

In Case Study 1, the lead founder of a startup going through an accelerator discusses his experience taking a startup through an accelerator program. Specifically, he discusses his startup's experience of the accelerator program elements (e.g., the accelerator co-working space, the accelerator curriculum, the accelerator program managers, the accelerator mentors/advisors, the accelerator demo day, and the post accelerator phase).

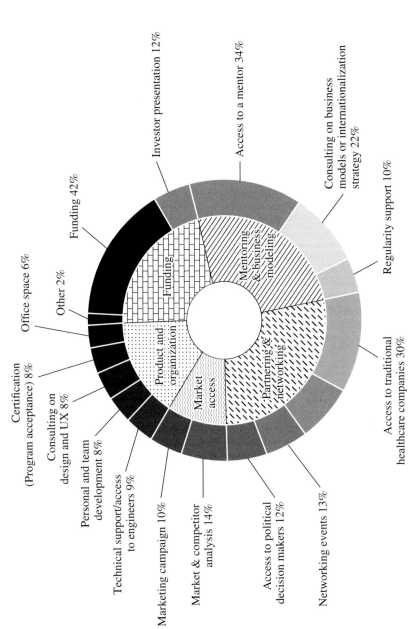

FIGURE 2.7 Accelerators Services Valued the Most (%) by Members of the Global Digital Healthcare Community (i.e., the greater the % the higher that service was valued).
Source: Adapted from Jahns (2018).[47]

Case Study 1: LEAPIN Digital Keys and the H-Farm Deutsche Bank IoT Accelerator Program (Italy)

In the winter of 2016–2017, LEAPIN Digital Keys (LDK) was a startup offering a complete end-to-end Narrowband Internet of Things (NB IoT) smart access control solution that included NB IoT smart locks, digital key apps, and smart lock management software. Looking to accelerate its evolution, LDK was exploring different accelerators and came across the H-Farm Deutsche Bank IoT Accelerator. Given the accelerator's niche focus on IoT startups, the fact that LDK had recently received a funding grant from the European Commission and the fact that LDK had recently signed a partnership with Vodafone Spain to support the delivery of LDK's product in the European market, LDK reasoned it was ready to apply for the H-Farm Deutsche Bank IoT Accelerator in Italy. The accelerator was to be held at an innovation hub called "H-Farm," which was in a farming and winery district on the outskirts of Venice. A farming and winery district in Venice was far removed from LDK's location adjacent the sandy, sunny beaches of the Gold Coast in Australia. Still, the startup had been gaining traction for its product offering with many potential customers across Europe and was working in partnership with SAG, a German lock manufacturing company. So, it was looking to relocate from Australia to Europe to be close to its partners and customers there. Also, relocating to Europe made flights from Europe to the United States and Asia, where LDK's other customers and manufacturing partners were, much shorter and less expensive relative to flying from Australia. LDK had, in fact, been considering and actively seeking out European accelerators on www.f6s.com for a couple of months prior to applying and being accepted into the H-Farm IoT accelerator. LDK had submitted four applications to European accelerators on f6s.com. It had received interviews for two of them and offered a place in the H-Farm IoT accelerator. LDK saw the IoT accelerator located in Venice, close to an international airport, with flights to most of Europe being only one to two hours away and costing less than 100 euros, as the perfect launching ground for its new European strategy. Prior to applying for the accelerator, LDK had read journal articles discussing H-Farm alumni who had relocated to the shared office spaces on-site after the program had finished. Also, some alumni were offered nearby affordable accommodation owned by H-Farm. LDK was attracted by this possibility, and the fact that many H-Farm accelerator alumni had raised investment capital. It was also attracted by the fact that for some international startup co-founders, H-Farm had sponsored permanent Italian living visas.

The Accelerator Program

LDK's research into the H-Farm accelerator revealed that the accelerator was founded in 2005 and had developed a reputation for being one of Europe's leading accelerator programs running three-month programs two to three times a year. H-Farm was a unique establishment in Europe, often referred as an innovation hub, since it included an incubator, office spaces for about 15 companies, a school, a university, accommodation, and restaurants. It educated more than 1,000 students annually. Since its founding, H-Farm had invested 25 million euros to support the development of 105 innovative startup companies. H-Farm also operated like a consultancy firm; it was listed on the Italian Stock Exchange, and had helped over 100 of the most important international brands take advantage of the opportunities made possible by digital transformation.

H-Farm had seven successful exits in the last ten years of running accelerator programs, including H-ART, LogoPro, and Wishpot, which had been acquired by companies such as WPP and Lockerz. More recently, H-Farm had a partial exit which generated a cash return of close to 12 times their initial investment, when they sold their stake in a tourism startup called Travel Appeal to a Dutch investment firm for 900,000 euros. H-Farm had built a great base of international mentors/advisors that regularly returned from overseas for each program. In addition, it ran a consistent curriculum program and had good follow-up investments and top-class program managers. H-Farm invested 20,000 euros into cohort startups for 5% equity. The program also provided free accommodation and free food for the duration of the program (through its facilities and restaurant managed on-site). It offered many other perks to accelerator participants (e.g., free Amazon Web Hosting fees paid for a full year).

The focus of accelerator programs held every year at H-Farm varied considerably. For example, in the last two years, H-Farm had, in addition to running the Deutsche Bank IoT accelerator program, held a blockchain accelerator program, a health/wellness accelerator program, a food/agricultural tech accelerator program, a tourism accelerator program, and a Fintech accelerator program. Each program was sponsored by large companies such as Deutsche Bank, Cisco, ING, Technogym, and a large Chinese Investment firm called QWOS. Due to the wide variety of its accelerator programs, H-Farm attracted high-quality and well-established startups from all over Europe and around the world. H-Farm liked to include at least one local Italian startup in each program, to show its support for the local startup ecosystem, but it could not guarantee this, as the quality of applications from startups all over Europe was usually very high. Like most accelerators, H-Farm began advertising for IoT accelerators around three months prior through local and international networks and through the European startup ecosystem. Advertisements for the program were placed on one of the world's largest startup founder platforms, f6s.com. The application form for the IoT accelerator was typical of most accelerators around the world, with around 15 to 20 questions asked via the online form on f6s.com. The IoT accelerator program aimed to take between 5 to 10 teams that made it through a rigorous selection process composed of the application form, a first interview, a pitch, a second interview, and final selection.

(Continued)

The Application Process

LEAPIN Digital Keys, like one other team in the Deutsche Bank IoT accelerator, had already completed an accelerator program in another country. So the founders had a good understanding of what to include in the f6s application form. LDK also had an advantage in knowing what to expect before, during, and after an accelerator. Steve had learned in a previous accelerator program to "*have well-rehearsed, direct, short, and to-the-point answers*" to all questions about his startup. This also applied to the accelerator application form and any question ever asked by a potential investor or a potential customer. Steve reflected on how one of the unstated outcomes of an accelerator is being able to effectively communicate or sell the startup. That, although this might sound simplistic, if you ask a startup to describe their product before the accelerator and then again after the accelerator, you would see a world of difference in the answer. He recalled his early challenges not making it through the application process until he learned to communicate the startup value proposition succinctly. On acceptance of LDK's application, the founders were invited to an interview to be held on the H-Farm site. Steve, along with other international applicants, was offered the option of a video conference interview and pitch. His interview, pitch deck, and pitch were well received, and he was later accepted into the program without a second interview. The entire application process from application form to invites for the interview, to conducting of interviews and to final offer or rejection took around three to four weeks. At the end of this period, Steve received a phone call and an email offer to participate in the program. He also received relevant term sheets and legal paperwork. LDK was one of only five teams selected to participate in the accelerator.

The Accelerator Curriculum

The Deutsche Bank IoT accelerator was held in conjunction with a Food accelerator sponsored by Cisco, with five startups participating in each of the programs. Steve found the running of two completely different themed accelerators, with two different groups of contrasting startup teams in the same space, was an unusual approach. He was surprised to learn that H-Farm commonly delivers its accelerators this way, and that this is a formula that seems to have worked for them over the last ten years. Thus, the two accelerator programs started at the same time, and shared the same curriculum, the same mentors and coaches, the same co-lab working spaces, and the same scheduling. Each program had two program managers specific to it.

The IoT program started in early November. The first part of the program involved intense mentoring sessions with up to four different mentors each week over six weeks. It also involved preparing for a networking event in week 2 with the program sponsors. The accelerator then had a break for two weeks over Christmas and New Year. Since H-Farm closed over this period, most people returned to their homes to celebrate the festive season. Steve got on a flight back to Australia to spend Christmas with his wife and two kids. The other co-founder participating in this accelerator with him remained in Europe over that period. Steve flew back from Australia to Italy when the program reconvened in the new year. When the program resumed, there was a new focus on getting the PowerPoint presentations, business plans, five-year financial projections, and pitch presentations ready. This time, the mentoring schedules were not as intense as the first six weeks of the program. Instead of two to four mentors coming in each week in the first six weeks, now only one mentor would come in on a weekly basis in the second half of the program. The resumed part of the program was also far less structured, with many teams travelling all over Europe at different times to meet with interested customers, partners, or investors. During this part of the program, the co-working space was usually only half full. The teams were often left to themselves most of the week in the co-working space to work on getting traction, on the PowerPoint presentations for demo day, on the business plan, on the financial projections, or on preparing the pitch for demo day. The program managers would come around every couple of hours to have a look at the progress in these activities and, in addition, to offer advice and course correct people who were going down the wrong path. In Steve's opinion, one of the most valuable sessions of the IoT accelerator was the "Intro to Capital Markets Presentation" delivered over three hours by an experienced corporate investment banker. The presentation discussed in detail issues such as how to develop an effective story for fundraising, how to approach the investment community, ideal funding and growth roadmaps, go-to market strategies in the context of fundraising, types of investors to target, and the funding market landscape. Steve found the session extremely valuable, not necessarily for learning new groundbreaking content, but for getting the nuances and distinctions from an Investment banker with over 30 years' experience. The investment banker had spent years and years investing in startups and companies around the world on behalf of Deutsche Bank. Steve noted that this was the type of learning he could not have derived from a textbook.

The Weekly CEO Check-Ins

As the IoT accelerator only had five teams, with many of the teams constantly travelling, CEO check-ins were held only periodically during special events. For example, in week 2, the CEOs had to do a presentation to all the program sponsors for a large event. And in week 4, many university students and lecturers from H-Farm University were invited to a special event at which each of the cohort company CEOs delivered a presentation. In week 6 a Christmas break-up event was held, and the cohort company CEOs delivered an update on what they had achieved since starting the program. In the new year, in around week 9, another large event was organized with all the sponsors. It was a condition for

(Continued)

all cohort teams that the cohort company CEOs attend and deliver an overview of their company, as well as any new developments since the sponsors last gathered (in week 2).

The Mentors

Each week for the first six weeks of the IoT accelerator, two to four new mentors, who were experienced and successful entrepreneurs, were flown in from the United States, Israel, Italy, or other parts of Europe. The mentors were housed in on-site accommodations for the week. The mentors usually began each Monday morning by delivering a one- to three-hour presentation, supported by PowerPoint slides. These presentations were delivered to all the co-founders grouped together in a lecture-type theatre room. The mentors discussed their backgrounds, the key challenges they faced, the mistakes they had made, and the things they had learned on their entrepreneurial journey. They organized these presentations in a format that enabled them to pass on their best advice. The formal presentation session was usually followed by a one-hour interactive question time or discussion forum. In this forum, co-founders asked questions of each mentor and of the program managers facilitating the interactions. Each mentor usually had unique strengths, experiences, and valuable advice to offer all the co-founders. For example, in the third week there was a mentor who was an expert in social media. Other mentors were experts in startup strategy and selling software to corporate customers, or they had worked with big IoT companies. Following lunch on the Monday, each mentor's schedule for the week was drawn up on the whiteboard in the co-working space so that all ten teams could book in time with the mentor for two-hour one-on-one or one-on-team deep-dive sessions. In the first few minutes of these deep-dive sessions, Steve did a presentation on the LDK startup. This was followed by mentors asking incisive questions of the co-founders and offering advice. Often during the week, different mentors would organize a catch-up with LDK at a nearby restaurant or bar or club, to relax and talk in an informal environment.

The Program Sponsors

For the IoT cohort, H-Farm organized a number of events with sponsors and invited senior managers from Deutsche Bank to come and meet the co-founders. As well as meeting the co-founders, the sponsors came to see if there were any synergies and possibilities to work together for a common goal. In addition to Deutsche Bank, other sponsors included Sigfox (an IoT company), STMicroelectronics, and Enel—Italy's largest energy company. In week 2 of the program, each company sponsor flew in between one to five representatives for a big introductory demo night, where each startup delivered a five-minute PowerPoint pitch, followed by dinner, drinks, and networking in the on-site restaurant. If there were synergies between the sponsors and startups, then the company representatives came back to the farm every few weeks to meet and further develop relationships or joint products or services. For example, Deutsche Bank helped one of the startups from the IoT program, throughout the course of the program, to build a data analytics platform by offering developers from the bank and advising on the platform architecture and design. LDK had developed great synergies with all the program sponsors, and discussed many business opportunities; however, no formal agreements or partnerships eventuated.

The Accelerator Co-Working Space

The accelerator was held in a large open space, similar in size to a basketball stadium. Each team had a large table that could hold around eight members. There were three meeting rooms, which surrounded the large open space table areas. One meeting room was large and like a lecture-theater, while the others were of normal size. A makeshift wall of bookcases separated the space into two sides, with the IoT program on one side of the makeshift wall and the Food program on the other side. The space was purposefully built for the H-Farm accelerator programs. At times during the second half of the program, the co-working space would be very quiet, as each team worked hard on the tasks set, or many teams were away traveling on business. But at other times, the co-working space was loud and chaotic, as co-founders jostled over meeting rooms for phone meetings, Skype meetings, and team meetings. The co-founders often talked to each other, helping each other out with the tasks they had been set. For example, co-founders from different teams would work together to determine the best way to do projections in the financial plan. There never seemed to be enough private meeting rooms on-site, and the co-founders often joked among themselves that the lack of meeting rooms was deliberate. That accelerator program managers wanted companies to work together. And that program managers wanted to be able to overhear the phone and Skype meetings and observe how the co-founders were interacting with potential customers, partners, and investors—this way, they could intervene to offer advice for improvement if necessary. The ongoing joke was that the program managers were like spies listening in to see if the startups were investment ready; and if everything the co-founders were describing was "real" (e.g., partnerships with large companies). Some joked that the program managers, by listening in on phone meetings, Skype meetings, and team meetings, were carrying out due diligence. Steve found a rarely used 3m x 2m photocopy/printer/storage room, which he used as his backup office for skype meetings. The downside to his plan was that he often had to climb over brooms, mops, and buckets to make his regular ongoing phone calls; and to get out the way as other people came into the room to use the photocopier/printer.

(Continued)

The Program Managers

The two program managers for the IoT accelerator program supported LDK in a variety of ways. The support ranged from advising on how to prepare the pitch presentation to driving three hours north of the accelerator site to meet with a lock manufacturer interested in partnering with LDK. The program manager also organized client and partner introductions and meetings through H-Farm connections. The program managers also organized sightseeing visits and oriented the LDK team to the city of Venice. They surprisingly attended many LDK evenings out at restaurants and local bars.

Demo Day

The IoT accelerator demo day experience was different from Steve's past demo day experiences. This was in part because Steve did not deliver the pitch for this demo day—another team member agreed to deliver the pitch. This meant that Steve was able to avoid a lot of the pressure and practice sessions to concentrate on developing the product, corresponding with potential customers, engaging with potential partners, and not neglecting operations. For the last week of the accelerator, at least two hours per day was taken up by private pitch coaching sessions with one of the most experienced program managers. Many sessions were held in the larger lecture theatre space that held over 300 people, so that the co-founders could get used to presenting in the space. On demo day, around 250 people attended the event, including local angel investment groups, groups from the program sponsor companies (e.g., Deutsche Bank sent 12 people), representatives from venture capital groups, and local business community stakeholders. Although LDK had a lot of interested investors, the startup did not ultimately get investment on the day. On reflection, Steve notes that from product development, traction, and cofounding team perspectives, LDK was not quite investor ready at that time.

After the Accelerator

A short while after the accelerator, a number of success stories from the alumni started to emerge and get announced. These included one company raising $20 million in a blockchain Initial Coin Offering (ICO) and another startup executing a successful crowdfunding campaign that raised over 300,000 euros. Yet another company was accepted into a leading global accelerator. Shortly after the program, LDK completed the build of a new product and began taking bulk orders from a customer in Europe with significant revenue. The LDK team returned to Australia. LDK remained in contact with the accelerator program managers, often seeking their advice or referral to contacts via email. Although the accelerator was located overseas, this was no barrier to the program managers being accessible and responsive.

Notes

1. I. Hathaway, "What Startup Accelerators Really Do," *Harvard Business Review*, March 2016.
2. S. Cohen, D. C. Fehder, Y. V. Hochberg, and F. Murray, "The Design of Startup Accelerators," *Research Policy* 48 (2019):1781–1797.
3. Ibid.
4. B. Clarysse, M. Wright, and J. van Hove, *A Look Inside Accelerators: Building Businesses* (London: NESTA, 2015).
5. S. Cohen, "What Do Accelerators Do? Insights from Incubators and Angels," *Innovations* 8, nos. 3–4 (2013): 19–25.
6. Cohen, Fehder, Hochberg, and Murray, "The Design of Startup Accelerators."
7. Clarysse, Wright, and van Hove, *A Look Inside Accelerators.*
8. P. Miller and K. Bound, *The Startup Factories: The Rise of Accelerator Programs to Support New Technology Venture* (London: NESTA, 2011).
9. Cohen, "What Do Accelerators Do?"
10. Cohen, Fehder, Hochberg, and Murray, "The Design of Startup Accelerators."
11. Adapted from Clarysse, Wright, and van Hove, *A Look Inside Accelerators*; and S. L. Cohen, C.B. Bingham, and B. L. Hallen, "The Role of Accelerator Designs in Mitigating Bounded Rationality in New Ventures," *Administrative Science Quarterly* (2018): 1–45.
12. P. Andrus, "What to Look for in an Accelerator Program," *Entrepreneur* (January 2013).
13. Miller and Bound, *The Startup Factories.*
14. C. Pauwels, B. Clarysse, M. Wright, and J. Van Hove, "Understanding a New Generation Incubation Model: The Accelerator," *Technovation* 50–51 (2016): 13–24.
15. L. Deering, M. Cartagena, and C. Dowdeswell, *Accelerate: Founder Insights into Accelerator Programs* (FG Press, 2014).
16. G. Weinberg and J. Mares, *Traction: How Any Startup Can Achieve Explosive Customer Growth* (Penguin, 2015).
17. G. Weinberg, "What Taking on Google Taught Me about Startup Traction," *Fast Company*, September 29, 2015.

18. Weinberg and Mares, *Traction.*
19. B. Burnham, "DuckDuckGo," Union Square Ventures blog, 2011, accessed October 2, 2014, https://www.usv.com/writing/2011/10/duck-duck-go/.
20. Weinberg and Mares, *Traction.*
21. A. Roy, "For Many Tech Investors in Silicon Valley, This Is the Most Important Event of the Year," CNBC, March 21, 2017.
22. J. Ericson, "Space Matters: Why Is Startup Accelerator Space Important?" 500 Startups, December 9, 2010.
23. Deering, Cartagena, and Dowdeswell, *Accelerate.*
24. B. Feld and D. Cohen, *Do More Faster: TechStars Lessons to Accelerate Your Startup* (Hoboken, NJ: John Wiley & Sons, 2010).
25. S. L. Cohen, C. B. Bingham, and B. L. Hallen, "The Role of Accelerator Designs in Mitigating Bounded Rationality in New Ventures," *Administrative Science Quarterly* (2018): 1–45.
26. Pauwels, Clarysee, Wright, and van Hove, "Understanding a New Generation Incubation Model."
27. Deering, Cartagena, and Dowdeswell, *Accelerate.*
28. Feld and Cohen, *Do More Faster.*
29. Deering, Cartagena, and Dowdeswell, *Accelerate.*
30. Feld and Cohen, *Do More Faster.*
31. R. Morris, "Mentors Are the Secret Weapons of Successful Startups," *TechCrunch*, March 22, 2015, accessed August 1, 2019, https://techcrunch.com/2015/03/22/mentors-are-the-secret-weapons-of-successful-startups/.
32. J. Rowley, "How Much Does Pre-Seed Equity Really Cost?" Mattermark, May 20, 2016, accessed August 1, 2019, https://mattermark.com/whats-price-curve-pre-seed-equity/.
33. Ibid.
34. L. Vandeweghe and J. Fu, "Business Accelerator Governance," in *Accelerators: Successful Venture Creation and Growth*, edited by M. Wright, and I. Drori (Edward Elgar Publishing, 2018).
35. Miller and Bound, *The Startup Factories.*
36. N. Wasserman, *The Founder's Dilemmas: Anticipating and Avoiding the Pitfalls That Can Sink a Startup* (Princeton, NJ: Princeton University Press, 2012).
37. S. Revzin, "3 Things to Know before Joining a Startup Accelerator," *Forbes,* January 23, 2018.

38. H. Batista, "Are You a Technical Founder? Here's How to Get Better at Communicating Your Vision," *Entrepreneur,* October 1, 2018.

39. B. Bernthal, "Who Needs Contracts? Generalized Exchange within Investment Accelerators," *Marquette Law Review* 100 (2017): 997–1061.

40. Miller and Bound, *The Startup Factories.*

41. L. Calhoun, "Bill Gates and 20 Million More Smart Folks Use This Learning Platform—Should You?" *Inc.,* July 14, 2016, accessed August 1, 2019, https://www.inc.com/lisa-calhoun/bill-gates-uses-this-tool-to-teach-his-kids-should-you.html.

42. Adapted from J. Dwyer, "The Complete Guide to Forming and Managing an Advisory Board," *Digital Intent,* accessed August 1, 2019, https://digintent.com/advisory-boards/.

43. A. Roy, "For Many Tech Investors in Silicon Valley, This Is the Most Important Event of the Year," CNBC, March 21, 2017.

44. Deering, Cartagena, and Dowdeswell, *Accelerate.*

45. Clarysse, Wright, and van Hove, *A Look Inside Accelerators.*

46. Ibid.

47. R. Jahns, "Health Accelerators Must Adjust Their Offerings to Meet the Needs of Start-Ups," R2G, 2018, accessed August 1, 2019, https://research2guidance.com/health-accelerators-must-adjust-their-offerings-to-meet-the-needs-of-start-ups-what-health-start-ups-expect-from-accelerators-global-survey-results/.

3

Is Your Startup Ready for an Accelerator?

Startups get distracted by fake work. Fake work is both easier and more fun than real work for many founders.

Sam Altman, co-founder of Loopt, venture investor and
president of Y Combinator

What It Takes to Get into an Accelerator

Getting accepted into a top tier accelerator, like 500 Startups or Techstars, can be a game changer for any startup.[1] For a start, it often comes with instant credibility (e.g., with prospective customers, future employees, and investors). It also usually comes with access to world-class mentors and networks, access to big-time investors, as well as a great opportunity to get startup strategy right. Perhaps even more important, it comes with a great opportunity to get the execution right (for example, by receiving hands-on help to initiate and close mission-critical partnerships and deals). Not surprisingly, the entry criteria for such accelerators can be steep. With reported acceptance rates of 1% to 2%, some have contended that it is easier to get into Ivy League universities like Harvard and Princeton[2,3] (who have acceptance rates of around 5%), than it is to get into a top-tier accelerator. But not all accelerators have such steep entrance hurdles. Our observation was that the acceptance rates and impact of accelerators on startup success roughly follow a normal distribution, as depicted in Figure 3.1. In this figure, the quality tier or effectiveness or success of accelerators increases as we move from left to right on the *x*-axis. And the number of accelerators operating at that level increases as we go up the *y*-axis.

The bell curve shows that mid-tier accelerators make up the majority of accelerators (say up to 80% of accelerators). As we move from left to right along the x-axis, the odds of acceptance would correspondingly decrease. Thus, we can see that the odds of getting into a mid-tier accelerator would be similar to the odds of getting into a non–Ivy League university. But, although easier to get into, the speed, scale, and success rate of startups in these accelerators are usually not as high as that of startups participating in a top-tier accelerator. Similarly, although almost any startup can march into a bottom-tier accelerator, in most cases, the probability of that startup making it will be very slim. This is both due to higher-tier accelerators taking the most promising startups, and also due to their having more tangible and intangible resources to leverage (e.g., greater access to seed funding, more high-profile networks, greater startup success track record, etc.). Yael Hochberg and Susan Cohen, entrepreneurship professors at Rice University and the University of Georgia, who run the US Seed Accelerator Rankings Project, unpack the accelerator tiers we propose in Figure 3.1 into Platinum Plus, Platinum, Gold, Silver, and Bronze[4] tiers. They base accelerator rankings on criteria such as number of exits, mean valuations, fundraising success, startup survival, alumni network size, and founder satisfaction. At the time of writing this book, Y Combinator and Angelpad were among those considered Platinum Plus; Techstars and MuckerLab were among those considered Platinum; and 500 Startups was among those considered Gold. These rankings fluctuate from year to year (e.g., due to annual changes in number and size of exits, changes in mean valuations, and fundraising success rates). Relative to Figure 3.1, we believe that the US Seed Accelerator Rankings mainly rank top-tier accelerators, and that the great majority of accelerators (mid-tier plus bottom-tier) probably lack the type of data needed to make it into the rankings.

Accelerator Acceptance Criteria

Given the differences in the quality of accelerators, and in the competition to enter them, it follows that what it takes to get into an accelerator largely depends on the accelerator. This is because different accelerators may look for or emphasize different things in their program aims, design, and, therefore, acceptance criteria.

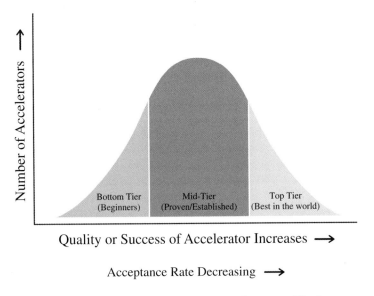

FIGURE 3.1 Accelerator Acceptance Rates versus Accelerator Success and Number of Accelerators

What is considered nonnegotiable for one accelerator may be of low priority to another. This is as it should be, since we would expect, for example, most accelerators looking at a very-early-stage Google to see it as a great opportunity and want to accept it—but no accelerators would consider themselves as having the capability to help a nascent Google make it. Thus, a nascent Google may not have been accepted by every accelerator. Despite differences in accelerator acceptance criteria, there are still some common criteria that all accelerators look for. The type of criteria that would result in most accelerators seeing a nascent Google as a great investment opportunity, even if not for them. We found the most common of these criteria to include the team, the product, the market, and the startup's progress. We discuss each of these in more detail below. Many of these common criteria also happen to be important elements of the selection criteria used by angel investment and venture capital firms. Again, this is as it should be—since a common aim of accelerators is to help cohort companies become investment-ready. That is, to prepare portfolio companies to meet angel and venture capital investment criteria.

The Team

Startups that make it often work through significant challenges, demanding workloads, unrelenting time pressure, and stress to build their companies and succeed against the odds. Doing so usually requires a talented, well-functioning, and adaptive team[5]—even though at times the media may focus on the hero entrepreneur narrative. William Gartner, Distinguished Professor of Entrepreneurship at Babson College, proposed that the "entrepreneur" in entrepreneurship is more likely to be plural rather than singular.[6] This is echoed by Thomas Cooney, professor of entrepreneurship at Technological University Dublin, who says that despite the somewhat romantic notion of an entrepreneur as a lone hero, the reality is that successful entrepreneurs either build teams or are part of entrepreneurial teams from the beginning.[7]

Founding team shortcomings are one of the most common causes of startup failure. For example, founding team members may not have the credibility to convince prospective early customers, investors, and employees to take a chance on them. Alternatively, it is common for co-founders to not be able to put aside their egos, default working habits, or interpersonal issues with other founders to make startup success the priority. This can result in team dysfunction, co-founder separation, and unnecessary additional complexity that can lead to the team missing critical opportunity windows. It is also not uncommon for co-founders to fail to meet the requirements of critical challenges, required workload, or necessary sacrifices such as lower salaries and unfair co-founder contributions. Thus, accelerators are first and foremost looking for the most talented, committed, well-functioning, and adaptive teams. Although a good team isn't all it takes to succeed, without it the odds of making it can be greatly compromised. Relative to talented solo founders, talented founding teams usually have (among team members) deep knowledge of industries and products relevant to them, have the technical expertise necessary to successfully build their product/service, are able to learn quickly and make smart decisions, and often have greater external validation of their talent (e.g., past startup or industry successes, qualifications, startup milestones, etc.).[8,9,10] Talented founding teams also usually demonstrate extraordinary determination and the ability to convince prospective customers, investors, and employees to take a chance on them.[11,12,13,14,15] Another critical, although little discussed, component of talented teams is their lead founder or lead entrepreneur.[16] The lead founder has final accountability for fielding the best team, having the right approach to strategy and ensuring that the team works together in an optimal way to efficiently realize startup strategy. This can be a challenge for startup teams in which roles and responsibilities are not yet well defined,[17] collective norms about how to make decisions and work together are not yet established,[18] ownership and employee roles are blended, and fit between contribution and compensation is difficult to pin down.[19] Marc Andreessen contends that three qualities are important in a lead entrepreneur—he or she should be a great product innovator, have great entrepreneurial skills, and have the capacity to be an effective CEO.[20] While different accelerators may emphasize different qualities, most look for a talented lead founder as a critical foundation of any startup team. Figures 3.2 and 3.3, taken from Airbnb's $600,000 seed round pitch deck and LinkedIn's Series B Pitch to Greylock, contrast two different teams and the evidence provided of how talented, well-functioning, and adaptive the teams were.[21,22,23] As can be seen, Airbnb's pitch deck team slide emphasizes prior product/service successes, work experience, and academic successes. Although the team's experience was limited,

Team

Joe Gebbia User Interface and PR
Entreprenuer and designer. Holds a patent for this product Critbuns. A graduate of the Rhode Island School of Design (RISD), has dual BFAs in graphic design and industrial design.

Brian Chesky Business Development and Brand
Founder of Brian Chesky Inc. industrial design consultant. A graduate of Rhode Island School of Design (RISD), has a BFA in industrial design.

Nathan Blecharcyk Developer
Created Facebook Apps, "Your neighbours" (75,000 users) and "Rolexdextrous"; recently launched "Identified hits." A graduate of computer science Harvard, Nate has worked at Microsoft, OPNET Technologies, and Bastiq.

FIGURE 3.2 The Airbnb Team from Their $600k Seed Funding Pitch Deck
Source: Reproduced from Dias (2017).[24]

Business and Tech Team Has Strong Track Record

Reid Hoffman, CEO
- Former EVP and Founding Board Member, Paypal
- Investor in Friendstar, Ironport, Six Apart, Vendio et al

Sarah Imbach, Chief of Staff and VP
- Former SVP Operations, Paypal

Allen Blue, VP of Product
Former Director of Product Design, SocialNet.com

Jean-Luc Valliant, VP of Engineering
- Former Director of Engineering and Software Development, Logitech, Spotilife

Konstantin Guericke, VP of Marketing
- Former VP of Marketing, Presenter Blaxxun

Eric Ly, CTO
- Founder and former CTO, Netmosphere (sold to Critical Path)

Matt Cohler, Director of Corporate Development
- Former top ranked analyst at McKinsey, marketing at Asiainfo, published in HBR

Technical team with experience at Apple, Cisco, Hotwire, Citigroup, Sprint, TIBCO, VERITAS et al

FIGURE 3.3 The LinkedIn Founding Team from Their Series B Pitch Deck
Source: Reproduced from Hoffman (2014).[25]

their academic successes, combined with the milestones the company had achieved to date at that time, provided corroborating evidence of their ability to learn and to adapt quickly. In contrast, the LinkedIn team pitch deck slide emphasizes the team's prior industry leadership experience, combined with the milestones the LinkedIn team had achieved.[26]

The Product

Despite any statements to the contrary, your startup's product is usually the first thing most accelerators will evaluate. In evaluating it, accelerators are usually evaluating four key product dimensions: progress along the customer discovery and customer validation stages, potential product risks, and the products' competitive barriers. Along the customer discovery stage, accelerators want to know if a startup has found problem/solution fit, has developed an acceptable minimum viable product (MVP),[27] and has a product line growth path. Specifically, with regard to problem/solution fit, accelerators are looking for two things. First, they want to see if there is validated evidence of a specific, big enough, and painful enough problem existing for a large enough group of people. Second, they want to see validated evidence that the startup's proposed product solves the problem to such a degree that those people will buy the product at a premium price.[28] For the MVP, accelerators are first looking to see whether the startup has built an MVP that actually solves the problem. And second, that this MVP has been tested on real-world customers in the target group who have provided valuable feedback to iterate the product to an acceptable level for that target group.[29] For product line growth path, accelerators want to know whether the product has related services and spinoffs that can add significant profitability to the future firm or whether it is a limited product. For example, a startup with a product that is a core technology or platform applicable to lots of industries and for lots of different uses would be far more attractive than a startup with a product limited to a very niche part of a single industry. Along the customer validation stage, accelerators want to know if the startup has found product/market fit and if it has a validated business model.[30] For product/market fit, accelerators want to know if the startup's product is in a great market with target customers who have tried the product, accepted the product, trust the product, and want more of the product. For the business model, accelerators want to know if a startup can produce and distribute the product profitably and at scale. Cloud-based software platform products, for example, often offer nearly unlimited scale and significant profitability. Along the product risk dimension, accelerators want to ensure that the product has no significant limitation, safety, or liability issues. Examples of such issues are abundant. For example, when St. Joseph's® Children's Aspirin was first introduced, studies came out suggesting it could cause Reye's Syndrome and thus could be dangerous to children—the product immediately lost its main market share.[31] Product development or manufacturing process–related safety and liability issues can be common for startups, depending on where and how they are getting their products manufactured or developed. Finally, on the competitive barriers dimension, accelerators are looking for a product that is going to have zero to minimal competition (the more of a monopoly a startup has the better).[32] For example, the startup could have a product unique enough so that it cannot be easily duplicated through extensions of existing product lines.

Or the startup may be so far ahead with its product development and commercialization, that it would take a miracle for competitors to catch up. Alternatively, the startup could have a product that has secure intellectual property (IP) owned by the startup. If there is no secure IP, it is usually not long before competitors emerge. If there is IP but it is not owned by the firm, this can be a significant limitation to the ability of the firm to adapt its business model. Secure IP can take the form of patents, algorithms, code, or a secret sauce that is just too difficult to reverse engineer. For example, after all these years, KFC's secret sauce is still secure and a significant competitive barrier. Table 3.1 provides a summary of the criteria and best-case scenarios accelerators are typically looking for along the different product dimensions. Except for top-tier accelerators, it is rare for accelerators to find startups that tick off the best-case scenario for all criteria. More often, they will find startups that have real potential to meet these criteria, particularly with help from the accelerator.

The Market

Accelerators want to understand the market for a startup's products. That is: who is going to be using the product? How valuable is it to them? How much are they willing to pay for the product? And how many of these potential customers are out there? In the best-case scenario, they want a startup that is in a big and rapidly growing market (or what Andreessen Horowitz co-founder Marc Andreessen refers to as a "great market"). Andreessen describes a "great market" as one with lots of real potential customers. That is, a market with a large number of real potential users, high growth in number of these real potential users, and ease of user acquisition. In such a market, the customers need or want the product so much that they literally pull the product out of the startup.[33] He proposes that when this is the case, the product doesn't even have to be great; it just has to basically work. That is, it only has to basically do the job it is meant to do for the customers in that market. For example, in the early days of the internet search engine market, the first search engines just needed to enable the customer to get the information they wanted in an acceptable time frame, as opposed to being up to the standards of the Google search engine today. Andreessen contends that in the best of great markets, customers need or want the product so

TABLE 3.1 Key Product Dimensions, Criteria, and Best-Case Scenarios Sought by Accelerators[34,35,36,37,38]

Product Dimension	Criteria	Best-Case Scenario
Customer discovery	Problem/solution fit	There is validated evidence of a specific, big enough, and painful enough problem existing for a large enough group of people.
		There is validated evidence that the startup's proposed product solves the problem to such a degree that those people will buy the proposed product at a premium price.
	MVP	The startup has built a minimum viable product (MVP), or a minimum form of the complete product, that solves the problem.
		This MVP has been tested on real-world customers in the target group who have provided real and valuable feedback to iterate the product to an acceptable level for the target group.
	Product line growth path	This product/service has related services and spinoffs that can add significant profitability to the firm.
Customer validation	Product/market fit	The startup is in a great market.
		The target customers have tried the product, accepted the product, trust the product, and want more of the product.
	Business model	The startup can produce and distribute the product profitably and at scale.
		The production and distribution risk associated with the product is acceptable.
Product risk	Product safety	The product/service is completely safe, and there is no likelihood of injury or damage to the environment.
	Limitations	There are no limitations to the product/service. There will be many applications in various environments.
	Product liability	There are no liabilities that are created by this product/service.
Competitive barriers	Product differentiation	Duplicability of the product through relatively immediate extension of product lines of existing competitors is very difficult.
	Intellectual Property	The product has novel intellectual property (IP). This IP is secure and owned by the firm.

bad that they are "knocking down your door to get the product." In such a situation, "the main goal is to actually answer the phone and respond to all the emails from people who want to buy."

In contrast, customers are elusive in a bad market. Startup founders may break their backs in a bad market for years, trying to find customers for their "great product" who don't actually exist. Eventually, founders may run out of money or get demoralized. Yet, it is not uncommon for startups to cite great markets with great growth rates as evidence of how great the startup's prospects are. For example, an IoT (Internet of Things) startup may argue in its pitch to an accelerator or potential investor, "*We're in the $157 billion IoT market, which is growing at an annual compound rate of 28% and is projected to grow to $457 billion by 2020.*" While there is verifiable proof of the market size and growth rate, there is no verifiable proof that the startup is actually in this market. That is, there is no verifiable proof that the startup has a product or service that can adequately satisfy an important need of customers in that market, and there is no verifiable proof that those customers have tried the product and want more of the product. Thus, as well as looking for startups in big and growing markets, accelerators look for customer validation and market validation. In other words, they look for compelling evidence that potential customers really want the product, that they are willing to pay a premium for it, and that there are lots and lots of these potential customers.[39,40]

Progress

There is a lot of uncertainty in entrepreneurship. For example, uncertainty about whether intended customers will really want the proposed product, uncertainty about how many of these customers are really out there, uncertainty about what substitute products may already exist, and uncertainty about the founding team's ability to execute and seize the market opportunity. As a result, accelerators are usually very interested in a startup's progress to date, as a gauge of how likely it is that a startup has the right product, for the right market, and has the right team to execute in that market.[41]

A startup's progress towards having the right product for the right market (or finding product/market fit), is often referred to as "Traction."[42,43] As we noted in Chapter 2, traction is often defined as "quantitative evidence of market demand" and can often trump everything else accelerator decision makers may think of your start-up's product/service.[44,45,46] Whatever they think of you or your product, they can't ignore great traction data. We noted earlier that many people thought Gabriel Weinberg was nuts when they heard his idea of building a search engine to compete with Google.[47] But when Union Square Ventures saw the number of monthly searches for his search engine and the visits to his website, they invested in Duck-DuckGo saying, "*We invested in DuckDuckGo because we became convinced that it was not only possible to change the basis of competition in search, it was time to do it.*"[48] Traction measures can vary depending on the product, the market, and even the startup.[49] They can include diverse measures such as number of active users, number and types of clients, number and types of partnerships, sales revenue, sales volume, profitability or margins, web traffic, number of search engine searches, and many more (see the traction slide shown in Figure 3.4).[50]

Marc Andreessen proposes that the number-one killer of startups is lack of market. That is, lack of enough buyers who have tried a company's product, are actually satisfied with it, want more of it, and are willing to pay a premium price for it. He proposes that before finding product/market fit, nothing else that startups do really matters. Thus, startups can be sure that their progress towards finding product/market fit, and how compelling their data is at demonstrating this progress, are elements of their accelerator application that accelerators will be most interested in.

Accelerators will also be interested in other important startup milestones, as evidence of founder/market fit[51] and founding team capability.[52,53] Such milestones could include, for example, securing

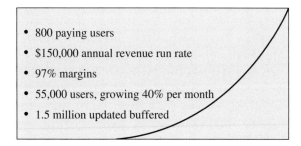

- 800 paying users
- $150,000 annual revenue run rate
- 97% margins
- 55,000 users, growing 40% per month
- 1.5 million updated buffered

FIGURE 3.4 The Traction Slide from Buffer's Pitch Deck Used to Raise a $500k Seed Round (Buffer is a social media management platform)
Source: Adapted from https://pitchdeckexamples.com/startups/buffer-pitch-deck.[54]

industry leading hires, securing enviable clients and strategic partners, securing funding, securing critical intellectual property protection, achieving critical marketing or publicity wins, and many more.
Milestones like these demonstrate the talent within the founding
team, and also its ability to work together efficiently and effectively to
execute startup strategies. To the extent that the milestones require
industry know-how to be achieved, they also demonstrate the likely
fit of the founding team with the particular industry. Milestones
like these can trump traditional founding team talent indicators
such as prior startup success, university degrees, work experience,
startup location, industry experience, and whether a startup product
has intellectual property protection or not. Thus, if your founding
team's resumes are lacking in traditional startup success indicators,
you can make these shortcomings less and less relevant with the progress or milestones your startup is able to achieve since its founding.

In Chapter 1 (Figure 1.2), we demonstrated that the risk of failure is highest at the earliest stages of startup evolution and that this
risk gradually reduces as founders progress within a stage, and from
one stage to the next. So, for example, the risk associated with a
startup reduces the further into customer discovery it gets. And risk
reduces as a startup advances from ideation/preparation to customer discovery, customer validation, strategy/operational/financial
validation, scaling and, finally, self-sustainability. It follows then, that
startup progress is also an indicator of how much risk is still inher-
ent within a startup, and how much has already been removed. For
example, a founding team that is still at the customer discovery stage
remains with all the uncertainty associated with this stage, as well
as all the uncertainty associated with the remaining stages it is yet
to go through. At the customer discovery stage, the founding team
may be unable to find problem/solution fit. If they find it, they may
not be able to build the MVP. If they manage to build the MVP, the
target customers may not care much for it—even after several iterations and pivots. If the founding team iterates to an MVP that target
customers care about, the team may not be able to find a viable way
to move prospective customers through the buying process. Eventually, the startup may not find product/market fit. Or the startup may
end up in a terrible market. Alternatively, the startup could end up
with a great product in a great market but lose the opportunity due
to team dysfunction and terrible decisions. At any point along the

startup evolution process, the founding team may quit. Given all of this uncertainty, the more relevant progress a founding team has made, and the further it is along the startup evolution process, the less risky it is that an accelerator's time, money, and energy invested in that startup will be wasted (i.e., not produce an acceptable return or result in a loss of invested capital, effort, and reputation). Further, there is an opportunity cost to investing in your startup from the investor or accelerator's perspective. Investing in your startup often means saying no to another startup that may have yielded a great return. So, progress matters—a lot. But it has to be the right progress. The more progress your startup has made in areas critical to startup success, the less risky your startup is to an accelerator and its investor network; and the more attractive your startup is for accelerator acceptance.

What Matters More: The Team, the Product, the Market, or Progress?

In his seminal articles on the importance of product/market fit,[55,56] Marc Andreessen makes the compelling argument that the market matters the most—since it is the market that will buy or ignore what a startup is selling. He argues that in a terrible market, a startup can have the best product in the world and an absolutely killer team—but none of that will matter. The startup will most likely hack away for years, break its back, and eventually die with various degrees of indignity. Therefore, he contends, the market is the number one killer of startups. In contrast, in a great market, a startup can have an average team and an average product. The market won't care, it needs the product, must have the product, and will take the first viable product that comes along[57]—so long as it is able to do the job the market wants done at an acceptable level.[58] Andreessen goes on to argue that once a startup is in a great market with a product that customers have tried, accepted, and want more of, it is remarkably easy to upgrade the team on the fly. As we noted in the introduction chapter, Andreessen follows by contending that getting into a great market with a product that can sustainably satisfy that market is the only thing that matters for startups that are not there yet. And if they spend time on any other challenge, it will more than likely be a waste of valuable time and resources. Non–product/market fit challenges are not that important to making it as a startup, he adds.[59] Which is not to say that they don't matter at all, but rather, that startups can screw up many of these things and still make it—as long as they succeed at finding product/market fit. In contrast, startups that screw up product/market fit are more often than not doomed to failure— no matter how well they succeed at other things. He proposes that if you have no product, then the purpose of a team is to develop a product to a baseline level of quality that a great market will accept; and then get it to that market. And a team is great to the extent it can do that. Alternatively, a great team may create a product that is so transformational that it creates a huge new market that never existed before. For example, VMWare's product was so transformational it created the operating system virtualization market—which turned out to be a "monster" market.[60] If you have a viable product, a team is great to the extent that it can find you a great market that wants your product on an ongoing basis, and where the provision of that product can be monetized in a viable way.

What about progress? If finding product/market fit is what matters most to preproduct/market fit startups, then progress matters to the extent that it demonstrates progress towards finding product/ market fit. So, accelerators may look for traction data demonstrating a startup's progress towards finding product/market fit. This data may signal that the startup has made sufficient progress to be on the cusp of finding product/market fit. Or, even better, that it has found product/market fit. For example, DuckDuckGo founder Gabriel Weinberg presented traction data (monthly searches for his search engine and visits to his website) to demonstrate that his startup had made significant progress towards finding product/market fit. What about after product/market fit startups? For such startups, progress along the remaining startup evolution stages will then start to matter.

Common Accelerator Turnoffs[61,62]

As well as there being common criteria that accelerators look for, there are also common things that turn them off. Such turnoffs can result in an accelerator not accepting a startup in spite of it satisfying most of the common criteria we have discussed. We have curated the common turnoffs here below and provide brief explanations of how they turn off accelerators. We have focused on ones that are not simply the opposites of common criteria accelerators look for.

Incomplete, Error-Laden, Inconcise, or Vague Applications

The more popular an accelerator is, the more applications it is likely to receive. This can result in program managers having to go through hundreds or even thousands of applications, each with a potentially different product, industry, market, team, and story.[63] Adding to the challenge, program managers are usually under significant time pressure to get through these applications in time for the accelerator program start date. As a result, accelerator applications that are incomplete, or don't follow the guidelines, start off on the wrong footing—if these are even considered at all.[64] The same goes for applications full of errors, applications that dance around rather than directly address key questions, and applications that use the accelerator application as an encyclopedic information dump. Besides disrespecting the time of program managers, these applications can reflect badly on your startup team. For example, a program manager may take your effort in the application as an indicator of the effort you are likely to have put into developing your product, hiring your team, and operating your startup. Or they may take it as an indication that you are not really serious about the accelerator opportunity and would likely not work hard if you get into the accelerator. If you are such a person, accelerators would typically not want anything to do with you. They would anticipate that you would have a negative effect on other startups in your cohort, that you are unlikely to make the most of the accelerator experience, and that you are unlikely to achieve the type of success accelerators want for their portfolio companies.

Too Early[65]

Startups can apply for some accelerators too early.[66] That is, they can submit an accelerator application before they are at a stage where they can be accepted or where they can really benefit from that accelerator. Typically, these startups will still be between stage 1 (ideation/opportunity recognition) and stage 2 (customer discovery), or they may be at the start of stage 3 (customer validation). As a result, they won't satisfy many accelerator acceptance criteria, particularly product and market criteria. From a product criteria perspective, startups that are still in these early stages of startup evolution will commonly not have found problem/solution fit, not have an MVP that has been tested or can be tested on real-world customers. Sometimes startups have great products but are too early for their market. For example, Airware was too early for the drone market. And Loudcloud had a great product in the early 2000s for what is today the monster cloud computing market; but back then it was too early for that market.[67,68] Having a product that is too early for a market can turn off accelerators, who may be more interested in you later, when the timing becomes right.

No Product/No Market or Bad Product/Bad Market

If the only thing that matters to BPMF (before product/market fit) startup founders is having a great market accept the product, trust the product, and want more of the product—then it follows that accelerator applications of startups with no product or no market will turn accelerators off. We found that it is more common for unsuccessful accelerator applicants to have a product and no market (i.e., no customers that accept the product, trust the product, and want more of it). Until a good market is found or the startup shows real promise of finding product/market fit, the possibility of a startup hacking away for years, breaking its back, and eventually dying is very real. Given this, it is clear why accelerators are likely to be turned off from a startup with a product and no market. Alternatively, a startup may be in a great market, but it may have a bad product for that market (e.g., the product may only superficially satisfy the need of that market, or the product may have fatal safety and liability issues, or the product may not really be that differentiated from competing products and substitutes). Again, this would turn accelerators off—particularly if these issues are not fixable. Finally, a startup may have a great product but be in a bad market. A bad market may be too small, or too competitive, or too risky, or be lacking in some other way that will constrain long-term profitability and likelihood of a meaningful exit for the accelerator.

Solo Founder/Inability to Lead

Several accelerators hold the view that startups are far more likely to make it if they have more than one founder.[69] A common reason cited is that different founders bring unique strengths to a startup. For example, Steve Jobs brought sales and business savvy to Apple, while Steve Wozniak brought technical leadership. Other examples include Bill Gates and Paul Allen (Microsoft), Larry Page and Sergey Brin (Google), Jerry Yang and David Filo (Yahoo), Ben Cohen and Jerry Greenfield (Ben & Jerry's), and William Procter and James Gamble (Procter & Gamble). Aside from missing out on the benefits of different strengths, Y Combinator co-founder Paul Graham argues that being a solo founder can signal a vote of no confidence in the founder.[70] That is, it can signal that he or she was not able to convince anyone of the benefits of the startup or of the benefits of partnering with him or her.[71] If this is the case, how can the founder convince potential customers, investors, strategic partners, or potential star hires? That aside, Graham observes that startups are just too hard for one person.[72] Who is the founder going to bounce ideas off? Who will talk the founder out of crazy ideas and show them their blind spots? Who will uplift the founder's morale during dark periods?[73] For these reasons and more, the first piece of advice Graham usually provides solo founders is to go get a co-founder.[74] When Dropbox co-founder Drew Houston's application was received by Y Combinator, Graham loved the product but specifically told, then solo founder, Drew Houston, that he needed to find himself a co-founder or YC wouldn't consider his application further.[75] Drew went out and got Arash Ferdowsi within two weeks; and he played an invaluable co-founder role in Dropbox's growth. Although solo founders can sometimes make it into accelerators, accelerator program managers have to find them extraordinarily good at product development, sales/marketing, and management/leadership. But it's rare for one person to be so good in all these areas. Even if they are, their time is limited and looking after sales/marketing well, for example, may come at the expense of product development or maintaining productive working relationships. Given all the drawbacks associated with solo founders, it is understandable why many accelerators would be turned off by solo founder applications. However, solo founders seem to do better at raising funding from investors and even making it to successful exit than their counterparts. (See Figures 3.5 and 3.6.)

Prohibitive Location

Startups are known to prosper in startup hotspots like Silicon Valley, Boston, and Denver because these locations have some of the best

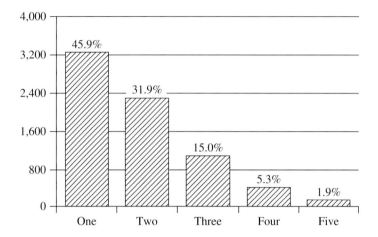

FIGURE 3.5 Number of Startups Raising More than $10 Million (USD) in Funding (*y*-axis) and Corresponding Number of Founders on Startup Team* (*x*-axis)
Source: Adapted from Kamps (2016).[76]
*Although accelerators may not be attracted to solo founders, they represent nearly half of startups that raise more than $10 million in the United States.

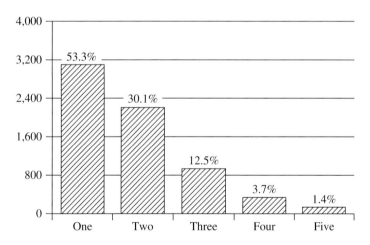

FIGURE 3.6 Number of Startups That Raised More than $10 Million (USD) in Funding and Went onto a Successful Exit (*y*-axis) and Corresponding Number of Founders on Startup Team** (*x*-axis)
Source: Adapted from Kamps (2016).[77]
**Similarly, being a solo founder does not seem to result in diminished success at exit time.

experts in the world, highly competitive standards, highly skilled potential hires, supporting industries, access to significant resources, and an abundance of people who are most supportive of startups' efforts.[78] In such locations, startups with a good product, in a good market, and with a good team often have little trouble signing global customers, raising large amounts of funding, building enabling relationships with world-class experts, scaling their businesses globally, and making big exits.[79] But not all locations are like this.[80,81] In some locations, access to large amounts of funding or to particular types of customers and employees may be nearly impossible. Even with the right product for the right market, a startup may hack away for years trying to access the right resources to seize the opportunity—only to miss the opportunity window. Or a startup may access much of what it needs, but just not at the same scale as a competitor in a startup hotspot. As a result, the competitor may move much quicker and build an unbeatable first mover advantage. The right or best location will differ from startup to startup, depending on the startup's product, industry, target customers, target workforce, and required professional services. A software startup may thrive best in locations like Silicon Valley and Denver, where industry-leading customers, potential star hires, and world-class professional services and funding opportunities have been argued to reside. In contrast, a petroleum startup may thrive best in locations like Norway or Dubai. Even where co-founders are willing to enter an accelerator in the right location, co-founders' inability to relocate for the long term, or until the startup succeeds, may make their startup less attractive to accelerators. The challenge for founders is twofold: finding the optimal location for their startup and committing to being in that location for long enough. We are not proposing that founders will not make it just because of their location;[82] rather, we're saying that in the right location their odds of making it are improved significantly.[83] Accelerators are aware of this and may consider a startup's intended operating location very seriously in any acceptance decision. (See Figure 3.7.)

Lying and/or Questionable Values

Almost all founders are against lying in theory. But in reality, many practice it to some degree—although they may think of it more as "stretching the truth" or "playing the game."[84] Some accelerators and investors see through this and overlook it.[85] Perhaps because much of the time, founders actually believe their assertions are the truth, for example, assertions about startup progress, product readiness,

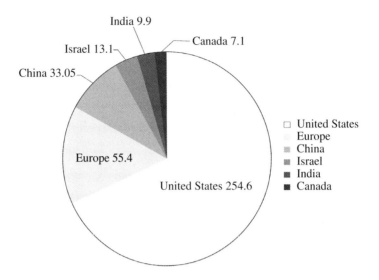

FIGURE 3.7 Proportion ($USD billions) of the World's Total Venture Capital Investment between 2006 and 2013 ($373 billion) Occurring in Different Parts of the World
Source: Based on data from "Top Countries for Total Venture Capital Invested."[86]

sales projections, etc. We did not find much writing on the issue arguing one way or the other whether these lies or half-truths harm or benefit entrepreneurs.[87,88] Nevertheless, there are many accelerators and investors who will be turned off by a startup completely when they come across obvious lies.[89,90] And most lies will be obvious to them. Lying in an accelerator application may signal that founders cannot be trusted to be honest with accelerator program managers. If founders cannot be honest about where their startup is at and the real problems it is facing, accelerator advisors may not be able to actually help it resolve the real problems. For example, advisors may prioritize helping a startup to address one issue when, unbeknownst to them, the startup is facing a more fatal issue that founders have not disclosed—perhaps because of an earlier lie. Lying in the application may also signal that founders will be dishonest with the accelerator's advisor and investor network—this may reflect poorly on the accelerator, especially if some advisors and investors work with and fund accelerator companies because they trust the accelerator brand. Thus, accelerators may be weary of startups whose lies may put the accelerator's reputation at risk. If founders lie and get into an accelerator, going through the accelerator may be of little value to them, as the accelerator and its network may be hesitant to trust anything the founders say after discovering the lie. In extreme cases, word about the startup's values may spread within the accelerator network and outside it—limiting the startup's opportunities. 500 Startups partners Marvin Liao and Elizabeth Yin warn that founders lying in their application shouldn't even bother applying.[91] She notes that such applicants will usually be caught out in the interview or due diligence stages. But if they are somehow missed, they can later be kicked out of the accelerator. While lying is one signal of questionable values (i.e., values that may turn off others from wanting to work with that startup, partner with it, buy from it, or invest in it), there are many others. Examples of other questionable values include lack of openness or transparency, lack of ethics, being too stubborn to change, not being coachable, irresponsible spending, and more. One way to understand what may constitute questionable values is to consider the types of values/behaviors that may put you off as a potential co-founder or investor. Some accelerators will have founder principles or a code of ethics that may signal the types of founder values that turn them off. For example, Y Combinator's "Founder Ethics" discourages dishonesty with investors/partners, treating co-founders unfairly, not keeping your word, and not treating money invested in your startup with respect.[92]

Prohibitive Cap Table

Accelerators will want to know who has control of your company, what they will contribute or have contributed, how this will impact future company valuation, and what risks existing company ownership might have on their investment—should they make one. Much of this information will be found in your capitalization table (cap table). In a nutshell, this is a record of who owns what and under what terms.[93] There are some common cap table issues that can prohibit or prevent a prospective investor from investing in your company.[94] Where an accelerator is not able to help your startup from fixing these issues, those issues are also likely to prohibit it from accepting your startup. Basically, accelerators want to see a simple cap table, founders having sufficient equity to have a long-term incentive to stick with the business (especially after fundraising and stock options for future hires), straightforward fundraising negotiations, and minimal risk of equity-related disputes that may disrupt the startup (e.g., due to lengthy legal battles and cost, effects on founder morale, effects on decision making, and introduction of negative political dynamics).[95,96,97,98] A simple cap table is one without a large number of small equity holders, that does not have unique terms for each shareholder (making interpretation complex), and does not contain shareholder terms that prevent actions being taken that are actually necessary for company growth. For example, shareholders may have nondilute clauses in their agreements that make certain future investments near impossible. Accelerators want co-founders to have sufficient equity so that after future fundraising rounds (of which there may be many) and employee stock options, their commitment to the startup is not eroded. Common mistakes founders can make to compromise this include having co-founders or hires who haven't worked out but still hold significant equity (e.g., due to not having a vesting plan), giving away too much equity in early fundraising rounds and not giving away enough equity to important co-founders. Finally, cap tables for which all shareholders have clear and transparent understanding of their equity, related terms, and implications in different scenarios prevent shareholder disputes that may be fatal. For example, the last thing a startup needs when it has managed to attract an investor or acquirer is a lawsuit or risk-fraught due diligence issues. Getting cap tables right is important to future fundraising and acquisition opportunities. Not making fatal cap (e.g., unfixable) table mistakes is important to your accelerator application.

Lack of Persistence/Distraction/Half-Hearted Effort/Poor Past Decisions

Investors, and therefore accelerators, can also be put off by a startup if they see signals of distraction and half-hearted effort. Distraction can cause founders to waste time and effort on activities that don't matter to the startup's success and thus to miss important opportunity windows. Half-hearted effort can result in shoddy products and a founding team not being able to execute efficiently or effectively enough to seize an opportunity. Signals of half-hearted effort can be found in the quality of the accelerator application, the preparedness of founders in interviews and meetings, the startup's product, and interactions between founders, and other stakeholders. Poor past decisions can also be a turnoff for accelerators, as they may signal poor future decisions. For example, a founder who has made poor past hires is likely to make poor future hires. And a founding team that has made poor execution decisions in the past is likely to make poor decisions in that area in the future. Finally, a number of accelerators look for persistence in a founding team.[99] Persistence enables founders to overcome the multitude of surprises, challenges, and setbacks they will face at different stages of startup evolution.[100] Founding teams lacking adequate persistence are more likely to roll over in the face of such challenges.

When Are You Ready for an Accelerator?

Depends on the Accelerator

Whether you are ready for an accelerator or not partly depends on the specific accelerator you want to apply for. This is partly due to differences in the entry criteria and competition to get into different accelerators. Although most accelerators are concerned with the generic entry criteria we have discussed (i.e., the team, the product/service, the market, and progress), some may focus on or emphasize particular elements of those criteria and not only have those elements as non-negotiables of entry, but also require more of startups in those areas. But they may relax other criteria.[101] For example, one accelerator may place greater emphasis on progress and on product/market fit. Where this is the case, a before product/market fit startup may not be ready for such an accelerator, unless it is very close to finding product/market fit. Another accelerator may focus on startups at a particular stage of startup evolution. For example, one accelerator may focus on startups at the customer validation stage; while another focuses on startups ready to scale. A before product/market fit startup may be ready for the customer validation stage focused accelerator. But it will not be ready for the scale-ready focused accelerator. The competition to get into an accelerator can also have an effect on whether you are ready or not. All else being equal, if you are competing with thousands of startups that are more advanced along the startup evolution process than your startup, they are likely to be selected ahead of your startup (unless your startup's potential more than compensates for it being much earlier in the evolution process). This is because there is less risk associated with these startups. Where competition is so steep, you may be wasting your time applying too early in the startup evolution process. Thus, before applying for an accelerator, we recommend that founders consider the accelerator's acceptance criteria, the stage of startup evolution that most accepted companies are usually at, and the steepness of the competition to get into that accelerator. These considerations will give a good signal as to whether the startup is ready for that particular accelerator or not That being said, some accelerators explicitly say that there is no such thing as being too early; and thus startups are always ready for their specific accelerator.[102] Even where it is the case that the bar is set low, there is usually a minimum criterion worth identifying.

Depends on Your Startup

Readiness for an accelerator also depends on the specific startup. For example, does that startup meet or can it meet most of the generic and accelerator-specific acceptance criteria? Is the startup willing and able to overcome most of the accelerator turn offs we discussed earlier, or make them pale in comparison to performance in other criteria? Do the founders have the time to go through the application process and produce an application that will reflect well on the startup? If they get accepted into the accelerator, can the founders and their startup afford the three-month time commitment? If they get accepted into the accelerator, are the founders ready to give up equity, and can they afford to give up more equity if things don't work out with this particular accelerator? Finally, who are the startup's customers, and where do they reside? This may affect whether a particular accelerator is the best accelerator to help that startup. For example, a startup whose customers are in Europe may be better off entering a European accelerator than one in South America. After considering these questions honestly, and also considering issues related to readiness for a specific accelerator, the founding team ought to know whether their startup is ready for an accelerator.

Can You Be Too Early or Too Late for an Accelerator?

Some accelerators say you can never be too early or too late.[103,104] Others say you are most likely too early if you are still largely at the ideation stage, with no backable team or live product, or no market/ no customers/no revenue. And you are most probably too early if you have a great team, great product, and promising market but you are too early for the market. A potential difference between these different perspectives is that some accelerators operate a range of different programs focused on startups at different stages, while others focus on startups that have passed particular stages. Nevertheless, a startup can be in an accelerator whose focus it is not ready for (e.g., a stage 2 startup in a scaling-focused accelerator). When the accelerator's focus is not a good fit for the startup, the accelerator curriculum, accelerator investment network, accelerator professional services, and accelerator advisors may not be a good fit for the startup. For example, a late-stage accelerator is likely to have an accelerator curriculum, investor network, professional services, and advisors suited to late-stage startups. Such an accelerator may be a waste of time for an early-stage startup. Similarly, an accelerator focused on early-stage startups will have an accelerator curriculum, investor network, professional services, and advisors suited to early-stage startups. As a result, it may be a waste of time to a late-stage startup. Being too early for an accelerator or being in an accelerator whose focus is ill fitted to your startup can result in your wasting significant time, with little progress, diluting founder equity unnecessarily, and incurring significant opportunity cost (e.g., the rewards of other activities where you could have invested your time and effort).

What If You Are Not Ready?

If you judge that you are not ready for the particular accelerator you are targeting, there is a lot you can do to accelerate your readiness. For instance, you can find a suitable pre-accelerator, an entity whose focus is to get your startup accelerator ready. If you choose not to enter a pre-accelerator, you and your team can focus on making convincing progress along the generic accelerator acceptance criteria discussed earlier. For example, you can work on making breakthroughs in product/market fit, breakthroughs in revenue and number or profile of customers, and upgrading of the team. You can also work on limiting the presence of common accelerator turnoffs. You can also start to reach out to the accelerator's alumni and talk to them about what you need to do to be ready. Finally, you can invest time in identifying which accelerators are going to be best fit for you, and how to maximize your chances of getting into them and making the most of them.

Case Study 2: BroZone Inc. and the Founders Frontier Accelerator* (USA)

The Accelerator

The Founders Frontier Accelerator, based in Nashville (USA), was founded in 2011 as a mentorship-driven accelerator and investment program for tech entrepreneurs. Structurally, the Founders Frontier accelerator was founded as a collaborative partnership between the Seedling Fund (a venture capital firm), a local Nashville incubator, and other private and community organizations. After three years of operation, it had successful alumni including an entertainment app startup that had recently had an early exit, and an education app that had just closed a $3M investment round. Although the accelerator did not discourage most startups from applying, it had a focus on developing companies that played to its strengths in big data, cybersecurity, educational technology, and retail. As Nashville is an upcoming destination in the worldwide fashion industry, and the accelerator received some funds from community organizations, fashion startups were also of interest to the accelerator.

The Startup

BroZone Inc. was a men's fashion startup, designing, manufacturing, and distributing men's clothing with unique designs. BroZone also had a well-branded website with advanced e-commerce facilities. In the early 2010s, e-commerce platforms like Shopify, which make it easy for anyone to set up online stores, were only just starting to become available. BroZone's sole founder, Andrew Keenan,* was an early twenties male with a few years' experience in the fashion industry (including as an assistant buyer), as well as a few years' experience in account management and promotions. Andrew also had an undergraduate degree in marketing and a strong interest in fashion and the fashion business. At the time of BroZone's application for the Founders Frontier accelerator, the startup had been operating for just under two years, having been started part-time while Andrew worked in fashion buying and account management/promotions. Over this time period, the startup had put together a well-branded e-commerce site (this was considered hi-tech at the time), had found reliable U.S. manufacturers, and bedded down effective distribution processes. It also had some early sales. On the company website were a range of trendy shirts that sold for $40–$200.

BroZone Inc. and the Accelerator Acceptance Criteria

The Founders Frontier accelerator acceptance criteria were typical of most accelerators, which have criteria focusing on the team, the product/idea, the market, product/market fit, progress, and particular accelerator turnoffs (discussed earlier in this chapter). The key sections of the application questionnaire

---

* Startup name, founder name, accelerator name, and locations changed for confidentiality reasons.

were Company Overview, Team, Product, and Business Information. The Company Overview section asked applicants to create and submit a 3-minute video and gave the following direction:

> *In your 3-minute video submission, which will be evaluated by our pool of judges, please make sure to address the following: Convince us that the problem you are solving (or the opportunity that you are exploiting) is big and needs to be solved immediately. Convince us that your solution is THE answer to the problem and how you will create real value for your customers. What specific hurdles do you see ahead for your project, and how do you intend to overcome them? What is so unique about your team that makes you think you can solve this big problem, and why should we believe you? (Experience, interests, talents, etc.)*

The Team section asked questions about how many founders there were, whether they could all attend the program, how long they had worked together, their roles and experience, their intended startup location after the program, and their time commitments during and after the program. The Product question asked about any customer discovery or market research activities and feedback received from customers, what the market and market size were, what the most recent milestone achieved was, and what the next most important milestone the startup needed to make was. Finally, the Business Information section asked about company structure, funding raised to date, and Google analytics data. Andrew's application was well received (perhaps because his startup ticked the fashion box, or perhaps because his tech and traction were convincing at the time—relative to most of the teams that were still at the customer discovery stage). And Andrew impressed in the interview with his deep knowledge of the industry, of sales, and of e-commerce. The accelerator had particularly been impressed with how advanced his e-commerce tech was. Interviewers were concerned about him being a solo founder, but he assured them that if they accepted him, he would have a great co-founder by the time the program started. He already had some good potential co-founders in mind.

BroZone's Accelerator Experience

Early Issues

Despite promising to bring on a co-founder if he was accepted, Andrew started the accelerator without a co-founder. As a result, he participated as a solo founder in the first week, even though the accelerator activities were designed for startup teams of more than one person. The accelerator program managers reminded him of his promise to find a co-founder in the first few days. When they reminded him again in week 2 of the program, Andrew said his co-founder was coming.

(Continued)

That week, he brought into the accelerator labs a young woman, who he intro-duced to everyone as his co-founder. But when quizzed by accelerator partici-pants, mentors, and program managers, it became clear that this woman had not signed any shareholder agreement or term sheets, did not seem to know much about the fashion industry, and had little knowledge or interest in startups. And she knew nothing about the BroZone. She seemed unaware that she was there as a co-founder and seemed to have no interest in being at the accelerator lab. She was there for a few hours on a couple of occasions and came to a couple of networking events in the evenings. But other than that, she was not seen again. A rumor started circulating between other startup founders that she was actually Andrew's new girlfriend. And that, although he had not been dating her long, he had convinced her to come into the accelerator lab to pose as his co-founder.

Fatal Decisions

One of the early decisions accelerator program managers encouraged startups to consider was how to best spend the seed money the accelerator had invested into their startup. Many of the startups started to discuss this and seek out advice from accelerator advisors and mentors. When accelerator program managers checked in on Andrew, to see how he planned to spend the money, they were surprised to find he had decided to spend all the money on getting his product packaging done in bulk. The program managers and mentors advised him that spending his entire seed investment on bulk packaging would not be the best use of money, considering the stage his startup was at. They thought Andrew was reflecting on their advice, but when they next checked in on him, they were shocked to discover that he had already spent all the $15,000 seed money on purchasing his product packaging in bulk. They were at a loss for words when his thousands of well-decorated boxes arrived for storage at the accelerator labs, which were not actually set up for such storage. Program managers, mentors, and other startup founders soon became frustrated and irritated with Andrew as boxes were everywhere, cramping the accelerator lab shared areas and meet-ing spaces. People had to climb over packing to get to their desks or to meeting rooms. Common working space became too cramped. And all his boxes lying around the lab became a hazard. Andrew was asked repeatedly to remove the packaging from the lab, but he didn't seem to listen. Looking back, he probably had nowhere else to store that many boxes. He definitely didn't have the money to pay for storage. Unfortunately for Andrew, all the boxes and packaging lying around the lab became a constant daily reminder to investors, mentors, and advisors of Andrew's bad decision making and his inability to listen to advice.

Biting the Hand That Feeds

One of the program managers suggested Andrew consider following in the footsteps of the founders of an iconic apparel company that was founded in

Nashville. And that he could "*pack his clothing range and packaging into the back of a van, or trailer, and take them out to the local markets to sell and receive customer feedback.*" This, the program managers suggested, would help raise awareness of the brand in the local community, bring some sales to demonstrate demand for his product, and also lead to potentially useful customer feedback to improve designs. Program managers pointed out that the owners of that apparel company had done this. They told Andrew the exact local markets the owners had gone to when first building the brand in Nashville—which were just up the road from the accelerator labs. Since this formula had worked for them in Nashville, it might also work for BroZone—or at least help with promotion and consumer feedback. But Andrew mocked this advice publicly in the weekly CEO stand up sessions, saying that taking his fashion to the local markets would negatively affect his brand.

Alienation

By the fourth week of the program, it became clear to everyone that Andrew was not mature enough to be in the program. He seemed to be superficially participating, pretending to perform the program activities, pretending to listen, pretending to build relationships, and pretending to undertake activities to build the startup—but not actually doing those things. His attitude to the program was more like he was attending a summer camp, rather than hustling, working hard, and developing his startup. It was as if whatever was said to him went in one ear and out the other. He seemed to think he knew it all. He was running around always talking about the "importance of branding," more focused on his startup appearing big and successful than on making real progress. He was not open to taking advice, to coaching from anyone, or learning from the different speakers and advisors that came as part of the accelerator program curriculum. The other startup founders often shared humorous "*Why is he even in this accelerator?*" looks whenever advisors suggested something to Andrew—only for him to shoot it down or just do what he wanted anyway. It was as though either he didn't hear or thought they didn't know anything. He continued to go through the program activities, but the advisors and mentors pulled back and focused on the founders who were actually seeking advice, acting on it, learning from the different accelerator program events, and making real progress. Not surprisingly, Andrew got no interest from potential investors on or after demo day. Within three months of the accelerator finishing, BroZone was no longer operational. While in the program, Andrew had made a connection through the accelerator who offered him a full-time job at a top fashion brand. Andrew accepted the job and shut down BroZone.

Out of the cohort startups that went through the accelerator program with BroZone, three went on to raise capital within a few months of the program ending—one has gone on to raise over $20 million in a number of investment rounds.

(Continued)

Two of the startups eventually raised seed rounds of $250,000–$500,000. And the remaining four were still operating as of early 2019.

Reflections

Although BroZone Inc. was accepted into the accelerator, we believe it should not have been accepted, as it did not satisfy some crucial criteria we discussed in this chapter. In particular, the startup should have had a founding team and not have entered as a sole founder. We believe BroZone may have seemed suitable to accept in the accelerator due to the accelerator application missing some critical criterion or questions that, if included, would have unearthed information that would have resulted in BroZone Inc. not getting accepted. Perhaps the accelerator also had too much bias on accepting fashion design startups, because of the region's reputation and the influence of the accelerator's stakeholders in the fashion industry. When the Founders Frontier accelerator was founded, accelerators had only been in existence for a few years. So, it's reasonable to expect that the acceptance criteria had to start somewhere and then evolve as the organizers learned lessons from experience. Specifically, the accelerator criteria lacked appropriate questions to effectively assess problem/solution fit, how close startups were to finding product/market fit, startups' competition/barriers to competition, and startups' traction/progress. First, BroZone did not have validated evidence of a specific, big enough, and painful enough problem for a large enough group of people. Therefore, it had not really found problem/solution fit. As a result, BroZone was nowhere near finding product/market fit. It was possible for BroZone to somehow have designed a product that lucked out and fit a great market, but the startup did not have the sales or traction data to demonstrate this. Second, BroZone's type of product had significant competition, especially with the accelerating growth of online platforms like Amazon and Shopify (platforms that were starting to scale rapidly around the time of the accelerator—these platforms enabled customers to quickly purchase unique clothing from all around the world and even to retail their own products on these platforms). BroZone's product was just not differentiated enough. The Founders Frontier accelerator application did not ask about BroZone's competition or about BroZone's barriers to competition. As a result, this was probably not weighed heavily enough in the acceptance decision. The accelerator did ask a lot of questions about the founding team, but somehow let in a solo founder. As we discussed earlier, this is a common accelerator turnoff. However, during the interview, the founder had promised the program managers that if his startup was accepted, he would bring on a co-founder for the duration of the program.

We have included this true story as an example of what can happen if a startup gets into an accelerator before it is ready. In BroZone's case, the first problem was the lead founder. He wasn't ready, maturity-wise. He wasn't ready to take advice; he wasn't ready to be coached—he thought he knew it all. With that kind of attitude, it is difficult for an accelerator to be of optimal value. The second problem was that BroZone, while good at marketing and promotion, had not really found problem/solution fit. It was rushing off to spend money on marketing and promotion but actually needed to do customer discovery right. Further, it was in a market with intense competition, and yet it had no competitive edge. Perhaps five years earlier, before the proliferation of online e-commerce platforms like Shopify, BroZone's competitive edge would have been its e-commerce tech. But at the time the startup was emerging, it was becoming increasingly possible for anyone to easily sign up to Shopify, and other similar platforms, and within an hour or so, have an e-commerce website ready to start taking orders and payments for products. As a result, we believe Bro-Zone was accepted into the accelerator too early. That is, it should have at least had validated evidence of a specific, big enough and painful enough problem for a large enough group of people before it could be accepted. We can't help but think that if it had been ready for the accelerator, or at least if the founder had been ready, it may have persevered or pivoted its way to success.

Notes

1. M. Suprovici, "Read This Before Applying to an Accelerator," Founder Institute, August 16, 2018, accessed July 31, 2019, https://fi.co/insight/read-this-before-applying-to-an-accelerator.
2. P. Karpis, "Want to Get into a Top Startup Accelerator? Try These 3 Strategies," *Forbes*, May 30, 2017, accessed July 31, 2019, https://www.forbes.com/sites/paulinaguditch/2017/05/30/get-into-a-top-startup-accelerator/#32a5cb93725f.
3. A. Cremade, "10 Startup Accelerators Based on Successful Exits," *Forbes*, August 7, 2018, accessed July 31, 2019, https://www.forbes.com/sites/alejandrocremades/2018/08/07/top-10-startup-accelerators-based-on-successful-exits/#29e726364b3b.
4. "Seed Accelerator Rankings Unveiled at SXSW | MIT Sloan," MIT Sloan Office of Media Relations, March 17, 2015, accessed July 31, 2019, https://mitsloan.mit.edu/press/seed-accelerator-rankings-unveiled-sxsw.

5. T. Cooney, "What Is an Entrepreneurial Team?" (Editorial), *International Small Business Journal* 23, no. 3 (2005): 226–235.
6. W. B. Gartner, K. G. Shaver, E. Gatewood, and J. A. Katz, "Finding the Entrepreneur in Entrepreneurship," *Entrepreneurship Theory and Practice* 18, no. 3 (1994): 5–10.
7. Cooney, "Editorial: What Is an Entrepreneurial Team?"
8. S. Chowdhury, "Demographic Diversity for Building an Effective Entrepreneurial Team: Is It Important?" *Journal of Business Venturing* 20, no. 6 (2005): 727–868.
9. M. G. Colombo and L. Grilli, "On Growth Drivers of High-Tech Start-Ups: Exploring the Role of Founders 'Human Capital and Venture Capital,'" *Journal of Business Venturing* 25, no. 6 (2010): 610–626.
10. A. C. Cooper and C. M. Daily, "Entrepreneurial Teams," in *Entrepreneurship 2000*, edited by D. L. Sexton and R.W. Smilor (Chicago: Upstart Publishing Company,1997), 127–150.
11. Chowdhury, "Demographic Diversity for Building."
12. Colombo and Grilli, "On Growth Drivers of High-Tech Start-Ups."
13. Cooper and Daily, "Entrepreneurial Teams."
14. T. Lechler, "Social Interaction: A Determinant of Entrepreneurial Team Venture Success," *Small Business Economics* 16 (2001): 263–278.
15. L. Schjoedt and S. Kraus, "Entrepreneurial Teams: Definition and Performance Factors," *Management Research News* 32, no. 6 (2009): 513–524.
16. A. de Jong, M. Song, and L. Z. Song, "How Lead Founder Personality Affects New Venture Performance: The Mediating Role of Team Conflict," *Journal of Management* 39, no. 7 (2013): 1825–1854.
17. Ibid.
18. Ibid.
19. N. Wasserman, *The Founder's Dilemmas* (Princeton, NJ: Princeton University Press, 2013).
20. D. Baer, "Do You Have the 3 Qualities Marc Andreessen Wants in a Founder?" *Fast Company*, May 15, 2013, accessed July 31, 2019, https://www.fastcompany.com/3009768/do-you-have-the-3-qualities-marc-andreessen-wants-in-a-founder.

21. R. Hoffman, "LinkedIn's Series B Pitch to Greylock: Pitch Advice for Entrepreneurs," accessed August 1, 2019, https://www.reidhoffman.org/linkedin-pitch-to-greylock/.
22. Suprovici, "Read This before Applying to an Accelerator."
23. J. Hannah, "The Team Slide: You Had Me at Hello," accessed August 1, 2019, https://www.forentrepreneurs.com/team-slide/.
24. D. Dias, "What YouTube and Airbnb Included in Their Pitch Decks When They Were Searching for Investors," *SmartCompany*, accessed August 1, 2019, https://www.smartcompany.com.au/startupsmart/advice/startupsmart-growth/young-entrepreneurs/check-out-the-pitch-decks-of-youtube-linkedin-and-airbnb-when-they-were-growing-startups/.
25. Hoffman, "LinkedIn's Series B Pitch to Greylock."
26. N. Hutheesing, "Corporate Inter-Face-Time," *Forbes*, March 22, 2004, accessed August 1, 2019, https://www.forbes.com/best/2004/0322/002_print.html.
27. D. R. Moogk, "Minimum Viable Product and the Importance of Experimentation in Technology Startups," *Technology Innovation Management Review* (March 2012): 23–26.
28. S. Blank and B. Dorf, *The Startup Owner's Manual: The Step-by-Step Guide for Building a Great Company* (K & S Ranch Consulting, 2012).
29. E. Reiss, *The Lean Startup: How Constant Innovation Creates Radically Successful Businesses* (New York: Crown Business, 2011).
30. A. Osterwalder and Y. Pigneu, *Business Model Generation: A Handbook for Visionaries, Game Changers and Challengers* (Hoboken, NJ: John Wiley & Sons, 2010).
31. Kauffman Foundation, "Address Your Limitations and Reduce Your Liabilities," January 17, 2007, accessed August 1, 2019, https://www.entrepreneurship.org/articles/2007/01/address-your-limitations-and-reduce-your-liabilities.
32. P. A. Thiel and B. Masters, *Zero to One: Notes on Startups, or How to Build the Future* (Broadway Business, 2014).
33. M. Andreessen, "The Only Thing That Matters," *The Pmarca Guide to Startups*, accessed August 1, 2019, https://pmarchive.com/guide_to_startups_part4.html.
34. S. Blank, *The Four Steps to the Epiphany* (K & S Ranch, 2013).
35. Blank and Dorf, *The Startup Owner's Manual*.

36. Adapted from J. Craig and N. Lindsay, "Quantifying 'Gut Feeling' in the Opportunity Recognition Process," *Frontiers of Entrepreneurship Research* (2001): 124–137.
37. J. Hall and C. W. Hofer, "Venture Capitalists' Decision Criteria in New Venture Evaluation," *Journal of Business Venturing* 8, no. 1 (1993): 25–42.
38. I. C. MacMillan, R. Siegel, and P. S. Narasimha, "Criteria Used by Venture Capitalists to Evaluate New Venture Proposals," *Journal of Business Venturing* 1, no. 1 (1985): 119–128.
39. Reiss, *The Lean Startup.*
40. Blank and Dorf, *The Startup Owner's Manual.*
41. D. Cohen, "What Investors Look for in Startup Projects—with Techstars Founder David Cohen," Codementor, May 26, 2015, accessed August 1, 2019, https://www.codementor.io/startups/tutorial/investors-look-startup-projects-open-qa-TechStars-founder-david-cohen.
42. H. Greenstein, "How to Show Market Traction," accessed August 1, 2019, https://www.inc.com/howard-greenstein/how-to-show-market-traction.html
43. A. Maurya, "Traction Is What Investors Are Looking for When You Present Your Plan," accessed August 1, 2019, https://www.entrepreneur.com/article/279391.
44. G. Weinberg and J. Mares, *Traction: How Any Startup Can Achieve Explosive Customer Growth* (New York: Penguin, 2015).
45. G. Weinberg, "What Taking on Google Taught me about Startup Traction," *Fast Company,* September 29, 2015, https://www.fastcompany.com/3051613/what-taking-on-google-taught-me-about-startup-traction.
46. S. Cohen and Y.V. Hochberg, "Accelerating Startups: The Seed Accelerator Phenomenon," March 30, 2014, https://ssrn.com/abstract=2418000 or http://dx.doi.org/10.2139/ssrn.2418000.
47. Weinberg and Mares, *Traction.*
48. B. Burnham, "Duck Duck Go." Union Square Ventures blog, accessed October 2, 2014, https://www.usv.com/writing/2011/10/duck-duck-go/.
49. J. Mares and G. Weinberg, *Traction: A Startup Guide to Getting Customers* (S Curve Publishing, 2014).
50. Weinberg and Mares, *Traction.*

51. C. Dixon, "Founder/Market Fit," cdixon blog, June 20, 2011, accessed August 1, 2019, http://cdixon.org/2011/06/20/foundermarket-fit/.

52. S. Efti, "Everything You Need to Know to Get into a Top Startup Accelerator—And More," *Fast Company*, July 9, 2014, accessed August 1, 2019, https://www.fastcompany.com/3032763/everything-you-need-to-know-to-get-into-a-top-startup-accelerator-and.

53. G. Chilton, "4 Things Startup Leaders Need to Know About Accelerators," *Entrepreneur*, February 23, 2017, accessed August 1, 2019, https://www.entrepreneur.com/article/287910/.

54. Buffer (Angelpad accelerator Alumni) Pitch Deck Traction Slide, accessed August 1, 2019, https://pitchdeckexamples .com/startups/buffer-pitch-deck.

55. M. Andreessen, Product/Market Fit: "The Only Thing That Matters Is Getting to Product Market Fit," Stanford University, June 25, 2007, accessed October 23, 2018, http://web.stanford .edu/class/ee204/ProductMarketFit.html.

56. T. Griffin, "12 Things about Product-Market Fit," Andreessen Horowitz, February 18, 2017, accessed March 6, 2019, https://a16z.com/2017/02/18/12-things-about-product-market-fit/.

57. Ibid.

58. C. Christensen, T. Hall, K. Dillon, and D. Duncan, "Know Your Customers' 'Jobs to Be Done,'" *Harvard Business Review*, September 2016, accessed March 6, 2019, https://hbr.org/2016/09/know-your-customers-jobs-to-be-done.

59. Griffin, "12 Things about Product-Market Fit."

60. Andreessen, Product/Market Fit: "The Only Thing That Matters."

61. W. Thompson, "Why Your Accelerator Rejected You," 500 Start-ups, July 15, 2016, https://500.co/why-accelerator-rejection/.

62. A. Iskold, "10 Reasons to Join (and Not to Join) an Accelerator," August 19, 2014, accessed August 1, 2019, https://alexiskold .net/2014/08/19/top-10-reasons-to-join-and-not-to-join-an-accelerator/.

63. Cremades, "10 Startup Accelerators Based on Successful Exits."

64. Iskold, "10 Reasons to Join (and Not to Join) an Accelerator."

65. Thompson, "Why Your Accelerator Rejected You."

66. Ibid.

67. "Crank It Up," *Wired,* August 2000, https://www.wired.com/2000/08/loudcloud/.
68. G. Venkat, "Loudcloud: Early Light on Cloud Computing," Cnet, March 23, 2009, accessed August 1, 2019, https://www.cnet.com/news/loudcloud-early-light-on-cloud-computing/.
69. Cooney, "Editorial: What Is an Entrepreneurial Team?"
70. P. Graham, "The 18 Mistakes That Kill Startups," October 2006, accessed August 1, 2019, http://paulgraham.com/startupmistakes.html.
71. Ibid.
72. Ibid.
73. J. Bruder, "The Psychological Price of Entrepreneurship," *Inc.,* September 2013, accessed August 1, 2019, https://www.inc.com/magazine/201309/jessica-bruder/psychological-price-of-entrepreneurship.html.
74. J. Mangalindan, "Y Combinator's Paul Graham: Get a Co-Founder," *Fortune,* February 25, 2014, accessed August 1, 2019, http://fortune.com/2014/02/25/y-combinators-paul-graham-get-a-co-founder.
75. B. Upbin, "Paul Graham, Dropbox and the Single Founder Exception," *Forbes,* October 18, 2011, accessed August 1, 2019, https://www.forbes.com/sites/bruceupbin/2011/10/18/paul-graham-dropbox-and-the-single-founder-exception/#468b46434fa2.
76. H. Kamps, "Breaking a Myth: Data Shows You Don't Actually Need a Co-Founder," *TechCrunch,* August 26, 2016, accessed August 1, 2019, https://techcrunch.com/2016/08/26/co-founders-optional/.
77. Adapted from H. Kamps, "Breaking a Myth: Data Shows You Don't Actually Need a Co-Founder, *TechCrunch,* August 26, 2016, accessed August 1, 2019, https://techcrunch.com/2016/08/26/co-founders-optional/.
78. Graham, "The 18 Mistakes That Kill Startups."
79. P. S. Cohan, *Startup Cities: Why Only a Few Cities Dominate the Global Startup Scene and What the Rest Should Do About It* (New York: Apress, 2018).
80. Ibid.
81. S. Jones, "Does the Location of Your Startup Determine its Success?" *Inc.,* September 23, 2013, accessed August 1, 2019, https://www.inc.com/scott-jones/does-startup-location-determine-success.html.

82. W. Craig, "Why Location Does (and Doesn't) Matter for Entrepreneurial Success," *Forbes,* January 16, 2015, accessed August 1, 2019, https://www.forbes.com/sites/williamcraig/2015/01/16/why-location-does-and-doesnt-matter-for-entrepreneurial-success/#40d17f544bf6.

83. Graham, "The 18 Mistakes That Kill Startups."

84. D. Isenberg, "Should Entrepreneurs Lie?" *Harvard Business Review,* April 2010, accessed August 1, 2019, https://hbr.org/2010/04/is-it-ok-for-entrepreneurs-lie.

85. J. Feifer, "Should Entrepreneurs Lie? It's a Tricky Question," *Entrepreneur,* October 31, 2018, accessed August 1, 2019, https://www.entrepreneur.com/article/321494.

86. "Top Countries for Total Venture Capital Invested—Share of Total Venture Capital Invested 2006–2013 $billions," accessed August 1, 2019, https://www.weforum.org/agenda/2015/07/which-countries-have-the-most-venture-capital-investments/.

87. Isenberg, "Should Entrepreneurs Lie?"

88. Feifer, "Should Entrepreneurs Lie? It's a Tricky Question."

89. Thompson, "Why Your Accelerator Rejected You."

90. M. Rosoff, "Marc Andreessen Just Gave Loads of Advice to Start-Up Founders," CNBC, July 13, 2017, accessed August 1, 2019, https://www.cnbc.com/2017/07/13/marc-andreessen-advice-for-start-up-founders.html.

91. Thompson, "Why Your Accelerator Rejected You."

92. Ycombinator.com, "Founder Ethics," accessed August 16, 2019, https://www.ycombinator.com/ethics/.

93. A. Johansson, "5 Cap Table Management Issues Every Business Owner Faces," *Inc.,* May 1, 2017, accessed August 1, 2019, https://www.inc.com/anna-johansson/the-5-biggest-problems-with-cap-table-management.html.

94. M. Grof, "12 Rules Entrepreneurs Must Know about Cap Table Management," *Entrepreneur,* September 13, 2016, accessed August 1, 2019, https://www.entrepreneur.com/article/281445.

95. J. Maher, "4 Things Investors Secretly Look For in Your Cap Table," *Startup Grind,* 2016, accessed August 1, 2019, https://www.startupgrind.com/blog/4-things-investors-secretly-look-for-in-your-cap-table/.

96. Ibid.

97. Johansson, "5 Cap Table Management Issues Every Business Owner Faces."

98. Thompson, "Why Your Accelerator Rejected You."

99. B. Snyder, "Marc Andreessen: 'I'm Biased Toward People Who Never Give Up,'"*Inc.*, June 30, 2014, accessed August 1, 2019, https://www.inc.com/bill-snyder/marc-andreesen-why-failure-is-overrated.html.

100. R. Ebrahimi, "5 Things I Learned About Entrepreneurship from Y Combinator's Paul Graham," *Fast Company*, March 23, 2012, accessed August 1, 2019, https://www.fastcompany.com/1825877/5-things-i-learned-about-entrepreneurship-y-combinators-paul-graham.

101. D. Cohen, "Ask David Cohen: When Is the Right Time to Apply to an Accelerator?" Techstars, September 15, 2016, accessed August 1, 2019, https://medium.com/TechStars/ask-david-cohen-when-is-the-right-time-to-apply-to-an-accelerator-854fc1296a86.

102. D. Cohen, "How Early Is Too Early?" TechStars, March 25, 2008, accessed August 1, 2019, https://www.TechStars.com/content/blog/how-early-is-too-early/.

103. Ibid.

104. D. Cohen, "You're Never Too Far Along for TechStars," Tech-Stars, January 17, 2012, accessed August 1, 2019, https://www.TechStars.com/content/accelerators/cape-town/youre-never-too-far-along-for-TechStars/.

CHAPTER

4

How to Prepare the Accelerator Application

Whatever you have to say, give it to us right in the first sentence, in the simplest possible terms. If there's a simple one-sentence description of what you're doing that only conveys half your potential, that's actually pretty good. You're halfway to your destination in just the first sentence.

Paul Graham, co-founder, Y Combinator;
co-founder, Viaweb

Accelerator Acceptance Criteria versus the Accelerator Application

In the previous chapter, we discussed the common elements of accelerator acceptance criteria. In particular, we identified elements such as the founding team, the product/idea, the market, and progress as important common elements of accelerator acceptance criteria. We also identified common accelerator turnoffs such as incomplete/error-laden/inconcise or vague applications, being too early, having no product/no market or a bad product/bad market, being a solo founder or being a lead entrepreneur who is unable to lead, having a prohibitive location, lying and/or having questionable values, having a prohibitive cap table, lacking persistence, getting distracted, putting in halfhearted effort, and poor past decisions. We bring these up again because they have an important relationship with the accelerator application questionnaire (the initial questionnaire you fill in to apply for entry into an accelerator). Essentially, the accelerator application is a set of questions an accelerator asks applicants to gauge whether they meet the different elements of the accelerators' acceptance criteria; and to what extent accelerator turnoffs are present. Often, the questions may be accompanied by requests to include supporting resources such as a company intro video, product demonstration, company website, founding team member resumes, etc. Although the set of questions and supporting resources may differ from accelerator to accelerator, all the questions are usually aimed at collecting information about the extent to which each startup meets the acceptance criteria and does not have unacceptable accelerator turnoffs. Thus, as founders fill in answers to accelerator application questions, it is beneficial to keep in mind what criteria each question is attempting to assess, so the founders can succinctly demonstrate whether they meet that criteria or not. Where they do not meet the criteria, advance knowledge of the criteria can enable founders to undertake the right preparation to meet that criterion.

The Accelerator Application Process

The accelerator application process is typically a four- or five-step process—depending on the accelerator. Step 1 usually involves registration, signup, or account creation. In this stage, the founders provide their names/contact details and set up usernames and passwords. In doing so, they create a secure account for their application that they can log back into as needed to update their application until it is complete. Most accelerators require this first step to be completed before startups will be able to access the accelerator application questionnaire. Step 2 involves filling out the application questionnaire and uploading any supporting documents, videos, or URLs to support the application. The application questionnaire is usually made up of questions addressing different elements of the accelerator's acceptance criteria. For example, Table 4.1 shows the questions three different accelerators ask in relation to the founding team element of accelerator acceptance criteria. Startup founders may be able to answer some of the accelerator application questionnaire immediately, but others may take weeks to complete—perhaps because they may require the startup to undertake certain activities in order to meet the question's requirements. For example, a question asking for a demo video or company website may require a startup to create those prior to completing its application. Once applications are completed, accelerators will usually evaluate submitted applications and shortlist them for the next step of evaluation. This next step, step 3, is usually a 30- to 45-minute video or phone interview with one of the accelerator's program managers, venture partners or entrepreneurs-in-residence.[1] In the video or phone interview, the interviewer will dig into different parts of a startup's application, asking clarifying questions, asking for corroborating data, and asking validation questions about the information within the accelerator application. Typically, these questions will focus on the team, the product/service, product/market fit, and progress. Startups passing the video/phone interview will usually progress to step 4, the face-to-face interview or interviews. This may be a single face-to-face interview with the same or different program managers, venture partners, or entrepreneurs-in-residence. But it may also be organized as back-to-back interviews with different combinations of one or more program managers, venture partners, or entrepreneurs-in-residence. Where the latter is the case, they may all want to make their own independent assessment of your startup team and then triangulate their findings to arrive at a final decision. For many accelerators, step 4, the face-to-face interview, will be the final step. But some accelerators may include a fifth step that aims to enable the founding team and the accelerator staff to get to know each other better and to gauge whether the founding team is able to effectively work with the accelerator staff. For example, at 500 Startups, this is a two-day on-site workshop composed of host talks, founding team exercises, informal meetings, and pitch preparation sessions that culminate in the delivery of a final pitch.[2] 500 Startups then evaluates the founding team's coachability, ability to respond to feedback, and commitment to improvement. These evaluations are incorporated into the final decision to accept or not accept a startup into the accelerator. Finally, accelerators will notify applicants of the application outcome decision and may provide feedback on the strengths and improvement opportunities of the startup's application. (See Figure 4.1 for an example of the MassChallenge Accelerator's shortlisting funnel.)

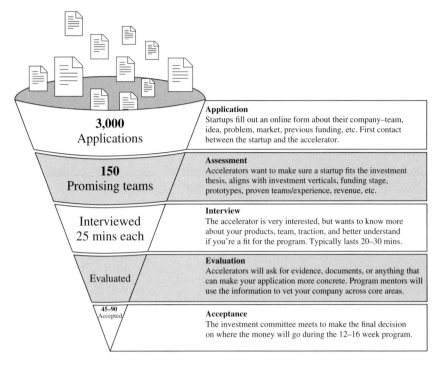

FIGURE 4.1 Example of an Accelerator Application Process and Shortlisting Funnel (MassChallenge accelerator)
Source: Adapted from Richards (2019).[3]

The Accelerator Application Questionnaire

Where to Find Accelerator Application Forms

Most accelerator application forms can be found on the F6S platform (www.f6s.com). This platform lists the majority of accelerator programs and enables users to search for accelerator programs by location, market focus, and whether the accelerator takes equity or not. The platform also functions as an application workflow platform, meaning it enables startups to apply for many accelerators from one website, rather than having to go through lots of different websites and forms (although some accelerators still prefer that you apply on their websites). F6S also enables users to search for other startup support programs and funding opportunities (e.g., government grants, angel investors, etc.). It is also a platform where accelerators and investors can search for startups. According to its website, the platform is home to over a million tech founders, more than 800,000 startups, and more than 10,000 startup programs globally.[4] AngelList (https://angel.co/accelerators/apply) is a similar platform that lists accelerators, although we found it to be more oriented towards investors. On f6s.com you can set up profiles for you and your startup just as you set up accounts at Facebook or LinkedIn. You can ask your co-founders to set up profiles too, and add them to your startup account. F6s enables users to follow others, chat, and send and receive messages like most social media platforms. Don't worry too much about these features, unless they support the main purpose—working on and submitting accelerator applications; or else accelerating your startup's progress.

Elements or Sections of the Accelerator Application Questionnaire

There are typically six to seven sections or elements of accelerator application questionnaires. Each of these sections or elements contains questions focusing on one or more accelerator acceptance criteria. In Table 4.1, column 2, we present the common sections or elements of accelerator acceptance criteria. These include information about the startup, the founders, the startup's product, product/market fit, progress, equity, and some accelerator-specific criterion. In columns 3 to 5 we show some of the different terminology used to describe these elements or sections. For example, section 1 (The Product or Idea) has been referred to as "The Idea" in Y Combinator applications. In contrast, The Farm Accelerator refers to it as the "Value Proposition" in its application. Similarly, section 5, "Progress," has been referred to as "Progress" in the Y Combinator application and in the Techstars application, but in The Farm Accelerator application it is separated into "Market Traction," "Product Progress," and "Revenue." Notwithstanding differences in terminology used to refer to these sections across accelerators, in the remainder of this chapter we unpack each of the common terminologies in more detail to clarify the types of questions asked and what accelerators are looking for in the answers to those questions.

TABLE 4.1 Common Sections or Elements of Accelerator Applications and Terminology Used to Refer to them by Different Accelerators[5,6,7,8]

No.	Common Element or Section	Y Combinator Terminology	Techstars Terminology	The Farm Accelerator Terminology
1	Company Overview	The Company	Company Information	Company Information
2	The Founders	The Founders	Team Information	Founder Information
3	The Product or Idea	The Idea	Idea	Value Proposition
4	Product/Market Fit		Market	Target Customer/ Market Opportunity
5	Progress	Progress	Progress	Market Traction Revenue Product Progress
6	Equity	Equity	Existing Shareholders and Equity	Existing and Planned Equity Allocation
			Capital Raises to Date and Terms	Outside Investment
7	Accelerator Specific Criterion	Others	Competition	Non-Founder Staff
			Domain Expertise	Founder Relocation and Attendance Capacity
			Novelty	
			Monetization	Vision
			User Acquisition Strategy	Competition
			Funding Needs, Burn Rate, and Runway	Company Structure and Location (e.g., LLC, C-Corp)
			Prior Accelerator Programs	Code (i.e., software code author)
			Anything Else Accelerator Should Know	Anything Else Accelerator should know
				Referral Source
8	Supporting Attachments	Company Website	About the Team Video	Company Website
		Demo URL or Video	Demo Video	Team Intro Video
		Example Projects Worked on	Pitch Deck	Company Intro/ Demo Video (Optional)
			Executive Summary	Executive Summary (Optional)
				Pitch Deck (Optional)

Company Overview

What Accelerators Are Looking for in This Section

This is often the simplest section of the accelerator application. In this section, accelerators are simply wanting to know basic introductory information about the startup, such as what the company name is, what the company does or makes, its industry and market. Additional questions in this section could include what the company form is (e.g., LLC, C-Corp, Pvt Ltd, Pty Ltd, not incorporated yet, etc.), and where the company was incorporated. Accelerators may also ask for supporting attachments to better understand your company. For example, they may ask for a company website or company introduction video.

Common Tips and Traps

The Elevator Pitch in Disguise

Communicating your startup's product/idea in a sentence or two is often referred to as the "elevator pitch."[9,10] Although accelerator applications don't directly ask, "Give us your elevator pitch," they are looking for it. Usually, it is disguised or implied in one of the early questions of the accelerator application questionnaire. For example, Y Combinator has asked, *"What is your company going to make?"* Techstars has asked, *"Please describe your company and the problem you're solving."* In contrast, The Farm Accelerator has been more direct, asking, *"What do you do? Keep it short and to the point—1 sentence."* Think of this sentence or two as your first impression, and what may be the most memorable part of your application. For many accelerator applications, the sentence may determine whether program managers seriously read the rest of your application. Even if some accelerator applications allow more than a few sentences, it is best to err on the side of conciseness and simplicity. Paul Graham puts this well in the opening quotation of this chapter. And he adds:

> *One good trick for describing a project concisely is to explain it as a variant of something the audience already knows. It's like Wikipedia, but within an organization. It's like an answering service, but for email. It's eBay for jobs. This form of description is wonderfully efficient.*

If your statement has to be longer than one or two sentences, you can still keep it concise and simple. And you can layer it to still get across the crucial information in the first sentence or two. For example, below is Dropbox's statement in its original Y Combinator application:[11]

> *Dropbox synchronizes files across your/your team's computers. It's much better than uploading or email, because it's automatic, integrated into Windows, and fits into the way you already work. There's also a web interface, and the files are securely backed up to Amazon S3. Dropbox is kind of like taking the best elements of subversion, trac, and rsync and making them "just work" for the average individual or team. Hackers have access to these tools, but normal people don't. It's currently in private beta and I add batches of people every few days. There are lots of interesting possible features. One is syncing Google Docs/Spreadsheets (or other office web apps) to local .doc and .xls files for offline access, which would be strategically important as few web apps deal with the offline problem.*

In Dropbox's application, the first sentence gets across concisely what Dropbox does. You could stop at that sentence and still get what they do. But each additional sentence explains a bit further. It can be challenging for first-time co-founders to be able to effectively communicate what their idea is in a sentence or two.[12] Often, founders get so deep into their product/service or technology that they can find it difficult to explain it in plain language to an outsider. Fortunately, there are ample high-quality elevator pitch guides that can be found via simple Google or YouTube searches. Accelerators often help program participants to supercharge their elevator pitches for maximum impact on customers, strategic partners, investors, and other stakeholders.

The Startup Website

Accelerators are interested in your startup's website, as it provides additional information about who your business is, what it does, how to contact it, and its credibility to potential customers and partners. Your company website can assist your accelerator application in many ways. Firstly, in an accelerator application, you are limited in the amount of information you can provide in the form response boxes (many responses are only 150–300 words, and some are only a few sentences). The website gives any accelerator program managers, who may be interested in accepting your startup into their program, somewhere to go to learn more about your startup, or for them to refer others who may be providing a second opinion on your startup. Second, your website can be a tool for public relations.[13] If you happen to get into an accelerator program, the program managers may do a press release which may refer to your company website. Even if they do not, journalists, potential customers, potential investors, and other stakeholders may look for information about your startup (e.g., to write articles about your startup, to partner with your startup, to acquire your startup, etc.). Your website becomes invaluable for this and any subsequent public interest in your company and your company's products and services. Finally, during an accelerator, the mentors and investors may introduce founders to potential investors, advisors, clients, and partners—the website becomes an important tool for selling your startup to that audience. Given these three benefits of your company website, we recommend paying attention to your startup's website.

The website does not have to be complex and costly. There are many website template builder sites that make building a website quick, cheap, and easy—no matter what your background or skill level is. Most of the hard work about branding, layout, text size, image size, and colors has already been done for you in the templates. The templates show you where to position your headings, images, punchy taglines, short paragraphs, and icons. Commonly used website template builder sites include strikingly.com, wordpress.com, wix.com, launchrock.com, and squarespace.com. Many template builder sites have freemium plans for the use of their services. Freemium plans mean you can get free use for the minimum services, but if you want extra services, such as hosting on your chosen domain name, you pay for them. If you sign up to a paid service, we suggest you pay monthly. During an accelerator, you'll probably update your website, and you may need to update your payment plan then, too. We suggest that one of the founders participating in the accelerator build the company website on a template builder site to enable your startup to update it at any time. This will save cost and communication challenges of having to get a contracted designer to make constant changes to the website. Before you start designing your website, we suggest you take the time to study and learn from popular product/service websites such as Apple, Amazon, Samsung, Microsoft, or Uber. Or you can study the websites of accelerator alumni or portfolio companies. You can also study the websites of competitors. Your website needs constant updates during the accelerator, so you don't need too much on it to begin with. The bare minimum you need is a few images of your product, a few paragraphs explaining how it works, some headlines, icons, and an inquiry form. Sometimes a pre-order form can be beneficial, as it enables people to leave their emails if they are interested in buying your product when it is ready. You definitely don't need to build e-commerce facilities, or to build your product and have it fully operational on your website. Further, it can be highly beneficial to find a domain name that is "hip" or "trendy" or "unique" and also easy to remember. This will help your startup get remembered and also get found on search engine sites.

The Founders/Team

What Accelerators Are Looking For in This Section

In this section of the accelerator application, accelerators want to understand how talented, committed, well-functioning, and adaptive the startup founding team is. But they don't want to just take your word for it; they want external validation or proof of it. Accelerators may differ in what they consider as talent, and in the order that they prioritize other team-related issues like commitment, team functioning, and team adaptability. For instance, a software-focused accelerator may look for different talent qualities than a media services–focused accelerator. As a result, the questions asked to assess founding team aptitude can vary from accelerator to accelerator. In Table 4.2, we provide examples of questions different accelerators have asked to assess whether applicants satisfy the founding team element of accelerator acceptance criteria.

Founding Team Talent

To understand the founding team talent (or knowledge, capabilities, and skills), accelerator applications will usually want to look into founders' educational backgrounds, working experience, and achievements. Regarding educational backgrounds, accelerators will usually ask for each founding team member's college or university, degrees, subject major, and year of graduation. Often, the majors

TABLE 4.2 Example of Questions Different Accelerators Have Asked in Relation to the Founding Team Part of Accelerator Acceptance Criteria

Acceptance Criteria Element	Y Combinator Questions	Techstars Questions	The Farm Accelerator Questions
The Founding Team	(1) For each founder, please list: Name, Age, Year of graduation, School, Degree (unfinished in parenthesis), and Subject for each degree; Email address; Personal URL, Github URL, LinkedIn U, Facebook ID, Twitter ID; Employer and Title for previous jobs. Put an asterisk before the name of anyone not able to move to the Bay Area. (2) Please tell us in one or two sentences about the most impressive thing other than this startup that each founder has built or achieved. (3) Please tell us about an interesting project, preferably outside of class or work, that two or more of you created together. Include URLs if possible. (4) How long have the founders known one another, and how did you meet? Have any of the founders not met in person? (5) If we fund you, which of the founders will commit to working exclusively (no school, no other jobs) on this project for the next year? (6) Do any founders have other commitments between now and the accelerator finish date inclusive?	(1) Please explain why your team is uniquely qualified to solve this problem. (2) How long have you been working together and how did the co-founders meet? (3) Is there someone on your team building your technology? (4) List if each founder is working on this full-time or part-time so we can better understand your resource allocation to this point. (5) If accepted into the program, can all founders attend the accelerator in person full-time?	(1) How many founders are in your company? (2) For each founder please provide or describe: – Their role in the company – Their educational background (School, degree, Major, Year of Graduation, relevant studies and projects, etc.) – A link to their personal LinkedIn profile – Describe previous startups they have worked on and anything else we should know about you. – Does the founder have any additional commitments (school, job, etc.) during the twelve-week program and beyond? If so, what are they? (3) Please describe any additional founders that aren't mentioned above. (4) Provide a one-minute video (max) introducing the founders, and what your company does. This video is informal; it can simply be a video recorded on your laptop, with your founders in the frame.

(continued)

TABLE 4.2 (continued)

Acceptance Criteria Element	Y Combinator Questions	Techstars Questions	The Farm Accelerator Questions
	(7) Do any founders have commitments in the future (e.g., finishing college, going to grad school), and if so what?		(5) How long have the founders known one another, and how did you meet? Have any of the founders not met in person?
			(6) Please list the percent of the company you have given to (or plan to give) each founder/employee, and anyone else you plan to give stock to. (It's important to discuss this early on).
			(7) Why do you think this is the right team to build this company? What do you understand about your business that other companies in your space don't?
			(8) If we fund you, how many founders will be able to move to Atlanta, GA, where The Farm operates, for the entire 12 weeks of the program?
			(9) If all the founders cannot physically attend for the 12 weeks, then please explain and list who specifically (including nonfounders) would be coming here in person for the duration of the program.
			(10) How many engineers/other nonfounder staff are on your team?
			(11) Please describe all nonfounder employees, roles, backgrounds, qualifications, and LinkedIn profiles, if possible.

indicate what domain knowledge, technical knowledge, or skills a founder might have. For example, education information may provide confidence to an accelerator that a founder with a recent double major in software engineering and petroleum engineering from Stanford has the relevant know-how to build a disruptive analytics platform for the petroleum industry. Examples of educational background questions include, from Y Combinator:

> For each founder, please list: Name, Age; Year of graduation, School, Degree (unfinished in parenthesis), and Subject for each degree.

And The Farm Accelerator has asked:

> For each founder please provide or describe: Their role in the company, their educational background (School, Degree, Major, Year of Graduation, relevant studies and projects, etc.), a link to their personal LinkedIn profile; describe previous startups they have worked on and anything else we should know about you.

Working experience serves a similar purpose but may better demonstrate or prove capabilities and skills a founder has acquired from practice, since there is external validation of these skills and capabilities. For example, if the Stanford petroleum engineering and software engineering graduate also spent three years working at ExxonMobil as technical lead for the most popular oil well and reservoir analysis software, the accelerator would be even more confident in the founder's talents. When evaluating working experience, accelerators may consider what types of organizations you have worked at, the state of practice of whatever you were doing at those organizations, how long you worked for the organizations, and what significant projects you worked on. For example, if a founder worked in advertising at Ogilvy & Mather, arguably the best advertising firm in the world, their advertising credentials would be considered top notch. How long you spent working at those organizations, what projects you worked on, and what promotions you received can also carry a lot of weight—as all these things may demonstrate deeper know-how. Both a founding team's educational background and work experience demonstrate whether the founders have deep knowledge of their products, customers, and industries; as well as whether they have the necessary technical expertise to build their product or service. Accelerators may ask more specific questions to flesh out founders' depth of technical, product, customer, and industry knowledge. For example, Y Combinator has asked:

> *What do you understand about your business that other companies in it just don't get?*

Most accelerators are usually interested in the founders' individual and team achievements as a proxy for individual founder and founding team determination and capability.[14] The more exceptional a founder or founding team's achievement, the greater their perceived capacity.[15] Some accelerators will ask a specific question related to individual founder and team achievements. For example, Y Combinator has asked:

> *Please tell us in one or two sentences about the most impressive thing other than this startup that each founder has built or achieved.*

If an accelerator does not directly ask, you would have an opportunity to mention any amazing founder or founding team achievements in questions about the founding team. For example, in Techstars' question *"Please explain why your team is uniquely qualified to solve this problem,"* founders could identify significant (and relevant) achievements that demonstrate that they are capable of succeeding with this startup. In earlier chapters, we noted Marc Andreessen's contention that three qualities are important in a lead entrepreneur—he or she should be a great product innovator, he or she should have great entrepreneurial skills, and he or she should have the capacity to be an effective CEO. Thus, accelerators may take a closer look at the lead founder's work experience and significant achievements for validating signals of capacity for product innovation, entrepreneurial skill, and strategic leadership skill.

Founding Team Functioning

As talented as individual members of the founding team may be, it may mean nothing if they are not able to work together as a team to get the job done.[16,17] Typically, issues like lack of trust, inability to delegate, poor communication, prioritization of ego over team and needs, jealousy, unhealthy conflict, and poor leadership cause team dysfunction.[18] Dysfunctional teams may undermine each other, engage in petty battles, work in isolation, politicize important product decisions, and take key stakeholders or the company hostage to individual founder personal needs. And team dysfunction often translates into derailed or significantly slowed execution, poor product quality, unkept customer promises, missed opportunity windows, and, ultimately, startup failure.[19] So, as good as a startup team's individual founder may be, accelerators want to know that, as good as a startup team's individual founders may be, they are actually capable of working together to execute effectively and efficiently. Accelerators will ask specific questions and look for evidence of effective team functioning. For example, Y Combinator has asked:

> *Please tell us about an interesting project, preferably outside of class or work, that two or more of you created together. Include URLs if possible.*
>
> *How long have the founders known one another and how did you meet? Have any of the founders not met in person?*

And Techstars and The Farm Accelerator have asked:

> *How long have you been working together and how did the co-founders meet?*

In many team-related questions, accelerators are looking for evidence that the founders can work together (e.g., maybe they have worked together on a challenging project in the past with great success or maybe they have made significant startup progress only possible through great teamwork). Accelerators are looking for evidence that the founders will remain together through the inevitable ups and downs of startup evolution (e.g., perhaps due to strong personal friendships,[20] having been through such ups and downs together in the past, etc.).

Founder Commitment

Accelerators are likely to be put off by founders who, while supposedly working on the startup, are going to be distracted by other projects such as study, a job, or another startup. They want to know that the founders are going to be working exclusively on the startup and are committed to doing what it takes for the startup to succeed. Early signals of this are the founders' commitment to attend and participate in the accelerator program full-time, over the typical three-month period. Examples of the types of questions asked to identify the level of founder commitment include the following from Y Combinator:

> *If we fund you, which of the founders will commit to working exclusively (no school, no other jobs) on this project for the next year?*
>
> *Do any founders have other commitments between now and the accelerator completion date inclusive?*
>
> *Do any founders have commitments in the future (e.g., finishing college, going to grad school), and if so what?*

And Techstars has asked:

> *List if each founder is working on this full-time or part-time so we can better understand your resource allocation to this point.*
>
> *If accepted into the program, can all founders attend the accelerator in person full-time?*

In contrast, The Farm Accelerator asks:

> *If we fund you, how many founders will be able to move to Atlanta, GA, where The Farm operates, for the entire 12 weeks of the program?*
>
> *If all the founders cannot physically attend for the 12 weeks, then please explain and list who specifically (including non-founders) would be coming here in person for the duration of the program.*

Samantha Strom, a Hazel Lane co-founder who participated in 500 Startups' thirteenth accelerator intake,[21] described how her accelerator application was initially rejected by 500 Startups because of her co-founder's lack of commitment.[22] Her co-founder's answers had signaled during the accelerator interview that the startup was not a priority for her. Of course, Samantha was disappointed at the loss of a great opportunity. But then she had an idea: she decided to negotiate with her uncommitted co-founder to see if she would step down. After a difficult negotiation, they were able to reach an amicable agreement for her to do so. Samantha then reached out to 500 Startups organizers to see if they would still consider her startup, now that the lack of co-founder commitment was no longer an issue. She subsequently got accepted into 500 Startups.

Flexibility/Adaptability

Finally, accelerators want startup teams that can learn quickly, make smart decisions, and adapt to the surprises and challenges of startup life.[23,24] Your founding team's experience, achievements to date, and interaction with the accelerator during the application process may signal whether your team has these qualities. And you may be asked questions or provided with challenges during the accelerator application process to test your teams' flexibility and adaptability.

Common Tips and Traps

Founders' Online Presence

Some accelerators will ask for and review each founder's social media accounts. For example, Y Combinator asks for each founder's personal webpage or blog, Github URL, LinkedIn URL, Facebook ID, and Twitter ID. Even if accelerators don't ask for these, we suggest founding teams take the time to search for online references to each founder, remove those that detract from the founding team's credibility, update the ones needing updating, and create those that do not exist. For example, this may involve creating professional LinkedIn profiles for each founder, removing unprofessional childhood blogs, or restricting trashy Facebook posts or photos. If the startup's and founding team's online presence is not aligned with what the founders are saying in accelerator applications, accelerator program managers may not trust the founders' answers. Or they may find contradictory or negative online information a risk to the accelerator's brand.

Accelerator-Specific Founder Characteristics

Different accelerators may look for different characteristics and values in founders. For example, Y Combinator prizes determination, flexibility, imagination, naughtiness, and friendship.[25] Whereas Techstars prizes a learning mindset, vulnerability, grit, obsession, respect, empathy, and humor.[26] To the extent that there are some generic characteristics successful founders share, you may find overlaps in the different characteristics sought—in spite of differences in terminology used to describe them. For instance, determination and naughtiness may overlap with obsession. It may be worth it for founding teams to look into the specific characteristics and values sought in founders by an accelerator prior to applying. This might better shape some of their accelerator application answers. For example, with regard to values, Y Combinator has some ethical expectations of founders that include treating co-founders and employees with fairness and respect, being honest with investors and partners, being honest in accelerator applications, treating money invested in the startup with respect, and generally behaving in a professional and upstanding way.[27] All else being equal, advance knowledge of the founder characteristics and values sought by an accelerator is likely to give a startup an edge over competing startups.

The Product/Idea

What Accelerators Are Looking for in This Section

In Chapter 3, Table 3.3, we discussed the key product criteria and best-case scenarios sought by accelerators. We noted that accelerators are interested in a startup's progress along the customer discovery and customer validation stages, as well as the startup's product risk and competitive barriers. Specifically, in relation to customer discovery, we noted that accelerators are interested in a startup's problem/solution fit, MVP, and product-line growth path. Also related to the product, we noted that accelerators are interested in the startup's product risks and the competitive barriers to copying or substitutes. Finally, in relation to customer validation, we noted that accelerators are interested in whether a startup has found product/market fit and a suitable business model. While most accelerators are interested in these criteria, each differs in what criteria are most important to them; and what the minimum requirements are for entry into the accelerator. Nevertheless, we address each product criterion here. Some accelerator applications have section headings, under which most of the questions relevant to that section are listed. For example, Y Combinator had a "Product/Idea" section, under which the questions assessing whether startups meet the product criteria were listed. But not all accelerators organize their questions into sections. Even where accelerators organize questions into sections or categories, it is common for some questions assessing product criteria to appear in different sections (e.g., the progress section). Still, what matters is that founders recognize which criteria or criterion a question is attempting to assess.

Problem/Solution Fit

Accelerators want to know if a startup has found problem/solution fit.[28] Specifically, accelerators want to know if the startup is solving a problem that is important enough and painful enough for a large enough group of people that they will pay a premium price for the proposed solution.[29] The more important and more painful the problem, and the larger the number of people with the problem, the better. The old adage from the 1800s, "build a better mousetrap, and the world will beat a path to your door," is often used as an example of the benefits of getting problem/solution fit right. Ash Maurya[30] frames finding problem/solution fit another way, by suggesting that it is found when founders are able to answer yes to these questions: *(1) Do I have a problem worth solving? (2) Is the problem solvable? (3) Is my solution something customers want to have and must have? (4) Will they pay for it?* In general, there is no shortage of founders thinking and asserting that the answer to all these questions is "yes" for their product. But the percentage of startups for which this is really the case is significantly smaller. As a result, accelerators need to be convinced that founders' assertions are true. That is, they want validated evidence to back up the assertions made.[31,32,33] What constitutes validated evidence can vary from accelerator to accelerator. But, in general, it can include founders demonstrating a clear understanding of target customers' needs (e.g., gained from extensive conversations with them about their problem), founders demonstrating the results of testing of the proposed solution with target customers, founders reporting on pre-orders of the proposed solution by the target customers, founders having target customers providing funding to build and trial the proposed product, founders reporting impressive search engine searches for their proposed product, and many other forms of potential evidence (only limited by founders' creativity). The evidence provided should back up assertions made by founders about how painful the problem is, assertions about the solvability of the problem by the startup, assertions about how many potential buyers are out there, assertions about how much they want the product, and assertions about their readiness to pay to have the product. Thus, as you answer accelerator application questions related to the product, we suggest focusing on ensuring you provide compelling answers to Ash Maurya's[34] questions and that you provide compelling evidence to back up your answers. Examples of problem/solution fit questions in accelerator applications have included Techstars':

> *Please describe your company and the problem you're solving.*
>
> *How is your solution uniquely addressing this problem?*

Similar to Techstars, Oracle Startup Cloud Accelerator has asked:

> *What is the problem that you are trying to solve?*

And The Farm Accelerator has asked:

> *What problem are you solving? Why is your solution better than your competition?*

If you are still unclear about what is required for problem/solution fit, Steve Blank, creator of the Customer Development model—of which Customer Discovery and Customer Validation are a part, recommends reading the following books to better understand problem/solution fit: *Talking to Humans—Success Starts with Understanding Your Customers* (by Giff Constable & Frank Rimalovsk), *The Four Steps to the Epiphany—Successful Strategies for Products that Win* (by Steve Blank), *The Lean Startup* (by Eric Ries), *Business Model Generation and Value Proposition Design* (by Alexander Osterwalder), *The Startup Owner's Manual* (by Steve Blank), and *The Founders Workbook* (by Steve Blank).

MVP

For the MVP (or minimum viable product), accelerators are first interested in whether the startup has built an MVP that customers are interacting with and providing feedback regarding how to improve the MVP. In the best-case scenario, they are looking for an MVP that truly solves the problem, and that has been tested on real-world customers in the target group who have provided valuable feedback to iterate the product to an acceptable level for that target group. But the MVPs of most accelerator applicants usually don't work as intended and will not be at this point.[35] Nevertheless, the better the MVP, the more likely it is that it will have been tested on real-world customers. And, therefore the closer it will be to being at an acceptable level for the target customer group. The closer it is to being at an acceptable level, the greater will be the startup's odds of being accepted into an accelerator. Questions relating to the MVP can be direct or indirect. For example, in Y Combinator's application they have directly asked:

> *What is your company going to make? If you have a demo, what's the URL? For non-software, demo can be a video.*

They follow up, in the Progress section, with:

> *How far along are you? Do you have a beta yet? If not, when will you? Are you launched? If so, how many users do you have? Do you have revenue? If so, how much? If you're launched, what is your monthly growth rate (in users or revenue or both).*

In contrast, Techstars has asked:

> *Please provide your revenue/customer/user growth KPIs or metrics. Include totals and month-over-month growth for the last six months. If your product is not yet in the market, how are you tracking progress – i.e., LOIs/MOUs, waitlist sign-ups, or other indicators of early market demand?*

Similarly, The Farm Accelerator has asked:

> *Do you have users/customers? How long will it take until you have your first paying customer? What roadblocks do you have to overcome to get*

there? How many users/customers do you have? What is your monthly growth rate (in terms of users/customers and/or revenue)?

In the absence of revenue/customer/preorder growth metrics, founders could describe their MVP tests, customer feedback, iterations to date, and closeness to getting the MVP to an acceptable level for that target group. If you don't have an MVP or a prototype, you can still apply for accelerators. Although your odds of acceptance will be lower, there are many accelerators you can still get into—particularly if you are solving a worthwhile problem, have found problem/solution fit, and have a great team. For example, Techstars' CEO David Cohen told the story of Everlater's founders Nate Abbott and Natty Zola's accelerator application. Nate and Natty were Wall Street types who loved to travel and wanted to build a platform for discovering and recording travel experiences. Having no knowledge of coding, they set out to teach themselves how to code so they could build the MVP. Cohen notes that although the MVP they built was crappy, they were accepted into Techstars because having something is better than having nothing and seeing their enthusiasm/commitment to learn code and overcome obstacles to developing the MVP impressed him.[36] Everlater had joined the Techstars accelerator in the summer of 2009 and gone on raise $750,000. It was acquired by AOL's MapQuest in late 2012 to become one of Techstars' most successful companies.

If you get into an accelerator without an MVP, be prepared to work on it as a high priority during the accelerator program. You will mostly likely need to have a prototype or MVP ready to demonstrate on demo day. You may also need to demonstrate your MVP to the accelerator program managers much earlier than demo day, such as in week 8. Often, the seed funding you get for participating in the accelerator is paid to your team in two or three installments (or tranches) over the course of the program, dependent on you achieving certain milestones or getting through particular performance hurdles or "gates." For example, you might get $50,000 at the end of the first week of the program, and $50,000 at week 10. So, after your first tranche, don't be surprised if you don't get any more funding until you have an acceptable MVP. It may be necessary to budget how and when your team spends the initial tranche of seed funding to ensure you have sufficient funds to get the MVP to an acceptable level.

For more information on how to build the MVP and get it to an acceptable level, we recommend visiting Steve Blank's website (https://steveblank.com/), which is full of great guides, tools, resources, and case studies related to customer discovery (e.g., finding problem/solution fit, building the MVP, testing, and iterating the MVP). We also recommend the following books: *The Four Steps to the Epiphany—Successful Strategies for Products That Win* (by Steve Blank), *The Lean Startup* (by Eric Ries), *Business Model Generation and Value Proposition Design* (by Alexander Osterwalder), *The Startup Owner's Manual* (by Steve Blank), and *The Founders Workbook* (by Steve Blank).

Product-Line Growth Path

Accelerators may not ask a question related to product-line growth path, but it is an issue that is important to many of them. Basically, they want to know whether you are a single-product company (e.g., you have made a once-off product such as an MP3 player design) or whether your product has related services and spin-offs that can sustain having an organization built around it (e.g., search engine technology or the iPhone platform). When you discuss your idea, solution, or product, we suggest discussing possible services and spin-offs related to your product. For example, in Dropbox's Y Combinator accelerator application, co-founder Drew Houston added the following sentence to his response to the question about what his company made or what his product was:

> . . . *There are lots of interesting possible features. One is syncing Google Docs/Spreadsheets (or other office web apps) to local .doc and .xls files for offline access, which would be strategically important as few web apps deal with the offline problem.*

Later, when answering a question about how the startup will make money and how much, he added at the end of his answer:

> *I've already been approached by potential partners/customers asking for a web services API to programmatically create Dropboxes (e.g., to handle file sharing for Assembla.com, a website for managing global dev teams). There's a natural synergy between project mgmt/groupware web apps (which do to-do lists, calendaring, etc. well but not files) and Dropbox for*

file sharing. I've also had requests for an enterprise version that would sit on a company's network (as opposed to my S3 store) for which I could probably charge a lot.

Together, his responses demonstrate to accelerator application reviewers that the startup has a versatile product with lots of related services and spin-offs for different customer groups (e.g., consumer, enterprise, online, offline, dev teams/webapp makers, etc.). Thus, accelerators could be confident that this was a product worth building a business around and that it could be a valuable and a sustainable business.

Product Risks

In Chapter 3, we noted that accelerators want to ensure that a startup's product has no significant limitations or safety and liability issues. If such limitations or issues exist and are insurmountable or costly to resolve, the risk to the startup is escalated dramatically. We provided the example of St. Joseph's® Children's Aspirin which, when first introduced, had studies come out suggesting it could cause Reye's Syndrome and thus could be dangerous to children—the product immediately lost its main market share.[37] Accelerators may not directly ask a question related to product risks in the accelerator application, but as you discuss the product we suggest you consider what limitations or safety/liability issues may come to application reviewers' minds and allay them. Although a startup may get away with not addressing such issues that may arise in application reviewers' minds, especially where an application does not ask, founders will likely reduce their odds of acceptance by not addressing such issues. If not addressed in the online application, we suggest preparing some responses to possible questions that may come up in the interview. Examples of products that may have such limitations or safety issues include healthcare products and services, products requiring complex or expensive manufacturing, and products in regulation intensive settings. Types of limitations and safety/liability issues can include requirements for key decision-maker sign-offs, which can only be obtained with significant difficulty (e.g., doctors in healthcare), highly error-prone manufacturing arrangements (e.g., outsourcing complex manufacturing to low-cost, low-standards regions when consumers are in high-standards regions), and having products that require complex and lengthy government-approval processes, etc. Founders could address accelerators' potential concerns by demonstrating an awareness of the issues, and by offering well thought through strategies to overcome them.

Competition and Competitive Barriers

If your product is a runaway success that customers are clamoring to get their hands on, other entrepreneurs may be enticed to seize the opportunity from your startup (e.g., through better and faster execution). Existing businesses may also be enticed to capture the opportunity by adding your product to their existing product lines or incorporating the features of your product into their existing products. Alternatively, they may invest heavily in promoting a substitute product that can deliver your startup's market the same benefits that customers are clamoring for. Either way, the presence of one or more of these competitors can jeopardize a startup's chances of success—particularly where competitors have more money, more talented/proven teams, and established processes (e.g., for making, marketing, selling, distributing, and selling product). Such competitors are likely to have better odds of success than a startup that may still have to raise money, undertake strategy/operational/financial validation, and successfully scale to fully seize the opportunity. So, accelerators want to understand who your current and potential competitors are, your understanding of their true threat, and the barriers your startup may have to future competition. For instance, barriers may include intellectual property being owned by the startup, requirements for unique technical knowledge to be able to compete, exclusive access to manufacturing/distribution channels, or the startup's product innovation being so far ahead that it will take prospective competitors years to catch up. Most accelerator application questionnaires will have a direct question related to competitive barriers. For example, Techstars (Colorado) and H-Farm Accelerator (Italy) have asked the following question:

> *Please list names and websites of three to five of your competitors.*

In contrast, Y Combinator (California), Climate-KIC DACH Accelerator (Berlin, Munich, Zurich, and Vienna), and 10X Accelerator (Ohio) have asked the following questions:

> *Who are your competitors, and who might become competitors? Who do you fear most?*

As we noted earlier, your response should demonstrate how well you understand who your current and potential competitors are, how well you understand their true threat, and existing barriers to competition your startup has or intends to erect.

Product/Market Fit

Accelerators would be very excited if they came across a startup that was in a monster market and had found product/market fit. That is, where the customers in that market had tried its product, trusted it, and wanted more of it. But this is the exception rather than the norm for accelerator applicants. Most accelerator applicants are BPMFT (before product/market fit), and most accelerator program managers expect them to be. However, program managers want to know which market your startup is pursuing, the potential of that market, and how close you are to finding product/market fit (i.e., how close target customers are to accepting/trusting/wanting more of your startup's product). This section of the application can be thought of as needing to make two arguments: the first about the startup's market potential and the second about what evidence of market traction there is. In the first argument, the focus is on convincing accelerator program managers of your market's size and potential (e.g., how big is it now, how big can it be, how profitable could it be, what credible evidence is there of all these assertions?). In the second argument, the focus is on providing compelling quantitative evidence of the market demand for your product. As we noted in Chapters 2 and 3, DuckDuckGo founder Gabriel Weinberg achieved this by showing venture capitalists strong evidence of the number of monthly searches for his search engine and the visits to his website. On seeing it, Union Square Ventures invested in DuckDuckGo, saying that they became convinced that it was both possible to change the basis of competition in search (i.e., search engines) and also time to do so.[38] Accelerator applications vary in where they put product/market-fit related questions. Some will have these questions in the "Progress" section, some will have it in a "Market" or "Market Traction" section, and others will have them in the "Product" section. A good argument can be made for the questions belonging in each of those sections. Examples of accelerator product/market fit questions have included, for Techstars:

*Please provide your revenue/customer/user growth KPIs or metrics.
Include totals and month-over-month growth for the last six months. If
your product is not yet in the market, how are you tracking progress –
i.e., LOIs/MOUs, waitlist sign-ups, or other indicators of early market
demand? (1000 characters)*

The Farm Accelerator separates the questions into a "Market
Opportunity" question:

*How big is the market opportunity for your product/service? Please pro-
vide supporting data.*

And "Market Traction" question:

*Do you have users/customers? How long will it take until you have your
first paying customer? What roadblocks do you have to overcome to get
there? How many users/customers do you have? What is your monthly
growth rate (in terms of users/customers and/or revenue)?*

Y Combinator has had their product/market fit questions in
their Progress section:

*How far along are you? Do you have a beta yet? If not, when will you?
Are you launched? If so, how many users do you have? Do you have revenue? If so, how much? If you're launched, what is your monthly growth
rate (in users or revenue or both)?*

Business Model

Similar to product/market fit, accelerators are interested in
understanding a startup's business model and how far a startup
is from finding business model/market fit. That is, from finding
a profitable, scalable, and sustainable way to serve customers in
the startup's market. If a startup has found business model/mar-
ket fit, the lifetime of a customer exceeds the cost of serving that
customer. So if a startup adds up all the monetized benefits of
serving the customer (e.g., for Facebook this might include advertising revenue, in-app purchase fees, payment fees, etc.) and these

exceed the direct and indirect costs of serving the customer (e.g., software development, infrastructure, support services, legal, insurance costs, etc.) it may be onto a good business model—depending on the extent to which current and likely future revenue exceed current and likely future costs. Examples of the types of questions asked in relation to business models have included, from Y Combinator:

> *How do or will you make money? How much could you make?*

Techstars has asked:

> *How do you plan to acquire customers/users?*

The Farm Accelerator has asked:

> *Are you generating revenue? How? How much? If not, how do you plan on generating revenue?*

Common Tips and Traps

Not Shooting Yourself in the Foot When Describing the Market Opportunity

Accelerator decision makers sometimes might not know anything about your industry or market, so you may have to give them a crash course and highlight the opportunities that exist. The more you can blow decision makers away with your knowledge of the industry and market, the better your odds of acceptance. Typically, this is best done with intimate knowledge of the data on market size, market growth rate, key competitors and innovators, market segments, buyer behavior, purchase prices, approaches to distribution, customer frustrations, etc. Although sometimes accelerator decision makers may know nothing about your industry, often they will know that industry/market much better than you. They may not show it, perhaps because they want to see how well you know the industry and market. While you want to demonstrate intimate knowledge of the market and of how great the market opportunity is, avoid making statements like "... *it's a $50 billion market, if we capture just 2% of* *that we could be a billion-dollar company!.* "Such statements can instead show that you lack thoughtfulness, real understanding, and experience in that market.

Getting Your First Piece of Traction

The accelerator application question about traction is probably going to be the question that is the biggest determinant of whether you get invited to the accelerator interview or not. It is the closest thing to objective proof that your market (or some other unexpected users) want your product. Ideally, it should communicate growing momentum in users adopting your product.[39,40] Although there are many different ways to demonstrate traction, it is most convincing in the following order: profitability; revenues; active users; registered users; engagement; partnerships/clients; and traffic. Below are some examples of ideas you could consider pursuing to capture your first quantifiable piece of traction. For more ideas, you could search online for startup traction ideas and examples. There are also some great books on traction, such as *Traction: How Any Startup Can Achieve Explosive Customer Growth* (by Gabriel Weinberg and Justin Mares). (See Table 4.3.)

Progress

In Chapter 3, we explained that accelerators are usually very interested in a startup's progress to date, as a gauge of how likely it is that a startup has the right product, for the right market, and with the right team to execute in that market.[41] So, accelerator applications usually contain at least a few questions about the type and extent of progress made by the team. Progress questions may be in a section referred to as Progress—which makes it easier to identify them. But sometimes progress-related questions are separated out and included in the product, or product/market fit, or traction sections. The aim of answers to progress-related questions is to demonstrate the rate at which the startup is improving the product, progressing towards finding product/market fit, and executing in other important areas. The faster a startup's progress, the more likely it is that it has the right product, for the right market, and has the right team

TABLE 4.3 Examples of Different Types of Traction and Approaches to Demonstrating That Traction in an Accelerator Application Response

Type of Traction	Example
Profitability	"We have five small customers using our oil well optimization software at one or more of their sites. They currently each pay an annual subscription fee of $249,900. Our annual cost to develop, host, and support the software is currently $350,000."
Revenue	"Our revenue YTD is $250,000. It has been growing 50% month-on-month since we introduced the latest version of our MVP six months ago."
Customers	"We recently signed Amazon as our first customer. We have signed an agreement to have our smart stock take solution in three of their warehouses."
Pre-orders	"We launched our product online and began taking pre-orders two months ago; we have already taken 10,000 pre-orders."
Active or registered users	"Our user registrations were growing at 10,000 users per month until three months ago when we introduced a feature to allow registrants to upload their contacts list and see who they knew that was also using the service. Since then, our registrations have been growing at 50,000 users per month."
Web/search traffic	"We're getting 400–500 visitors to our website daily, and each visit results in around 15 pageviews." or "There are 150,000 Google searches per month for our solution, and 25,000 google searches for our company."
Engagement	"We shared a demo of our product on a Facebook post, which has received 180,000 likes in the past three months."
Partnerships	"We have signed an agreement with the leading lock manufacturer to manufacture and distribute our product."
Media	"We have had our story featured in our country's national newspaper and have received 1,729 email enquiries about our product."

to execute and seize the market opportunity before some unknown competitor. Also, the rate of progress is the rate at which the startup is being de-risked. That is, a startup with a rapid rate of progress is becoming a safer and safer bet each month—which is attractive to existing and future stakeholders. One way to illustrate how accelerators may see progress is to imagine that the startup journey involved climbing Mount Everest (the world's highest mountain). All else being constant, someone who climbs halfway within four weeks is more likely to make it to the top at all, and to make it there first, than someone who is still fidgeting around at the base after four weeks. Similarly, all else being constant, someone who makes it to the halfway point in four weeks is also much more likely to make it to the top at all, and to make it there first, than someone who has taken eight weeks to make it halfway. In both situations, the first climber demonstrates that they can execute better and that there is less risk of loss if you bet on them over the other climber. As outlined in Table 4.4, accelerator application progress questions for Y Combinator have included:

> *How long have each of you been working on this? Have you been part-time or full-time? Please explain.*

TABLE 4.4 Example Questions Y Combinator Has Used in the Progress Section of Its Accelerator Application and Two Example Startups' Responses

Y Combinator Progress Question	Paystack (Lagos, Nigeria)	Task Pigeon (Sydney, Australia)
How far along are you?	Private beta. We are piloting with a dozen merchants, and we have hundreds of merchants on our waiting list.	Task Pigeon is a live, revenue-generating startup that has been growing monthly active users by an average of 17% for the last eight months.
		We have proven that individuals and teams are willing to pay for our application with 65 paying users added during Startup School. We have also successfully started to grow Monthly Recurring Revenue with our largest team comprising 15 users from a $1 billion publicly listed company in the UK.
		In addition, we have started to prove demand for our marketplace offering that augments the underlying task management application. In the past week we have had two users sign up to utilize this service, tapping into our ability to provide Virtual Assistants on demand (just one of the offerings we have) to assist with tasks they needed to complete.

(*Continued*)

TABLE 4.4 (continued)

Y Combinator Progress Question	Paystack (Lagos, Nigeria)	Task Pigeon (Sydney, Australia)
If you've already started working on it, how long have you been working and how many lines of code (if applicable) have you written?	Since November 2014	I have been working on Task Pigeon for over 18 months now. During this time I have worked full-time hours on Task Pigeon each and every week but do still hold down another job (with the view to go full-time on Task Pigeon ASAP).
		I understand that this is often not viewed favorably, but I would argue that I put in just as much if not more effort than the majority of founders out there. I have sacrificed a lot to ensure I have the time to dedicate to Task Pigeon with early mornings, late nights, and letting go of a number of hobbies/sports I previously pursued.
		Furthermore, deciding to retain my job for the time being was a conscious decision I made. Having that income has allowed me to invest more in Task Pigeon and ultimately provides an endless runway of funding so that I can continue to test and iterate where required in order to achieve our ultimate goal of empowering individuals and teams to get more done each day/week.
Which of the following best describes your progress?	Private beta	Launched
How many users do you have?	12 Pilot merchants and up to 400 on the waiting list	In September 2018 we had 418 Monthly Active Users. Our Monthly Active User base has been growing at 17% MoM for the past eight months.
		What has surprised me the most is our ability to attract some large companies to Task Pigeon, even though we are an early stage startup. Our largest paying customer is a 15-user team from a $1 billion UK-listed company.
		Engagement is also increasing month on month. For example between August and September the number of new tasks created by our users increased by 32%.

Y Combinator Progress Question	Paystack (Lagos, Nigeria)	Task Pigeon (Sydney, Australia)
Do you have revenue?	Yes	Yes
How much revenue?	$1,300	$1,520
What is your monthly growth rate?	We are currently growing our waiting list at 10x, and transaction volume at 15x.	17%
If you've applied PREVIOUSLY with the same idea, how much progress have you made since the last time you applied? Anything change?	By the last application, it was just a prototype. Now we're already running live transactions, and we've released additional libraries.	No, I have never previously applied to YC.

How far along are you? Do you have a beta yet? If not, when will you? Are you launched? If so, how many users do you have? Do you have revenue? If so, how much? If you're launched, what is your monthly growth rate (in users or revenue or both)?

And for Techstars:

Please provide your revenue/customer/user growth KPIs or metrics. Include totals and month-over-month growth for the last six months. If your product is not yet in the market, how are you tracking progress – i.e., LOIs/MOUs, waitlist sign-ups, or other indicators of early market demand? (1000 characters)

Prior to answering the progress-related questions in the accelerator application, it may be worth considering what breakthrough product and product/market fit achievements your team has made. As we noted in Chapter 3, other types of progress breakthroughs could include securing industry leading hires, securing enviable clients and strategic partners, securing funding, securing critical intellectual property protection, and achieving critical marketing or publicity wins. There are a variety of example responses to progress-related questions. Table 4.4 provides an example of two startups' responses to Y Combinator's progress questions at the time. Paystack was accepted into Y Combinator and Task Pigeon missed out.

Equity

As we noted in Chapter 3, accelerators want to know who has control of the startup, what they will contribute or have contributed, and what restrictions or risks existing company ownership might have on the existing and future investors.[42,43] We discussed the ideal criteria most accelerators are looking for: a simple cap table, founders who have sufficient equity to have control and a long-term incentive to build the company (especially after fundraising and stock options for future hires), minimal restrictions on being able to have simple future fundraising negotiations, and minimal risk of equity-related disputes that may disrupt the startup (e.g., due to lengthy legal battles and cost, effects on founder morale, effects on decision making, and introduction of negative political dynamics).[44,45,46,47] Each of these criteria can have a significant impact on future company valuation and risk to an investor's invested capital. Table 4.5 provides an example of two startups' responses to Y Combinator's application equity section questions. Paystack was admitted into Y Combinator and Task Pigeon missed out.

TABLE 4.5 Example Questions Y Combinator Has Used in the Equity Section of Its Accelerator Application and Two Example Startup Responses

Y Combinator Equity Questions	Paystack (Lagos, Nigeria)	Task Pigeon (Sydney, Australia)
Have you incorporated, or formed any legal entity (like an LLC) yet?	Yes	Yes
What kind of entity and in what state or country was the entity formed?	Trading entity created in Lagos, Nigeria	Pty. Ltd. company in Australia
Please describe the breakdown of the equity ownership in percentages among the founders, employees, and any other stockholders.	Shola—80% Employee Pool—10% Advisory Pool—10%	Paul Towers – founder and CEO = 100%
List any investments your company has received. Include the name of the investor, the amount invested, the premoney valuation/valuation cap, and the type of security sold (convertible notes, safes, or stock).	None, still funded by founder	N/A
Please provide any other relevant information about the structure or formation of the company.		

Other Common Accelerator-Specific Criteria

In addition to the sections we have discussed, many accelerator applications will contain some questions unique to them. Often these questions may be found at the end of the application; but they can also sometimes be found earlier in the application. Sometimes these questions will have their own sections. For example, more and more applications are having a "Legal" section. In this section, accelerators usually want to make sure that none of the founders are under non-compete or intellectual property agreements that may actually make the product the property of, for example, a past organization they have been associated with.[48] They also want to make sure that the product (e.g., code) has not been made by someone who might actually have a legal claim to the intellectual property. If there are legal issues with your startup, it does not necessarily mean the accelerator will not accept you. Instead, they may be able to help your startup resolve them early—before it is too late.

Accelerators may also have some questions related to your funding ask. That is, how much money you need and what you plan to do with it. Your response to such questions can signal a lot about the founding team (e.g., how ambitious you are, how realistic you are, how well you understand your business, how safe investors' money will be in your hands, etc.). Related to this, some accelerators may ask for financial projections. This is usually not common but if asked, it can also provide a lot of insight into how well you understand your market, business, and revenue model.

Other types of questions can be quirkier; though, rest assured the accelerator probably takes that seemingly quirky question quite seriously. For example, Y has had questions such as the one below:

> *Please tell us something surprising or amusing that one of you has discovered.*
>
> *What is the most impressive thing, other than this start-up, that you have built or achieved?*

Table 4.6 provides an example of three startups' responses to these Y Combinator application questions. Dropbox and Paystack were admitted into Y Combinator and Task Pigeon missed out.

TABLE 4.6 Example Questions Y Combinator Has Used in the "Other" or Accelerator-Specific Questions Sections Application and Three Example Startup Responses

Y Combinator Question	Dropbox (San Francisco, US)	Paystack (Lagos, Nigeria)	Task Pigeon (Sydney, Australia)
Please tell us something surprising or amusing that one of you has discovered.	The ridiculous things people name their documents to do versioning, like "proposal v2 good revised NEW 11-15-06. doc," continue to crack me up.	N/A	The limit of human potential is something we all underestimate. Six years ago I read the story of Pheidippides who ran from Athens to Sparta (a distance of 153 miles) to seek aid in fighting the invading Persians. He is said to have run the distance in a day and a half or 36 hours. This run had never been replicated until 1982 when five Royal Air Force officers attempted the course. Three of them completed it, proving it could be done and the following year a competition was born. Today the course record stands at 20 hours and 25 minutes, but it was the original story that propelled me to take up the sport of ultrarunning myself (since put on hold to focus on my startup). While I haven't completed a 153-mile race I have competed in numerous 24-hour endurance events and 100km trail runs. Each and every time I believe I have learned something new about myself, as well as the power of perseverance and commitment to a goal or cause.

With regard to the second Y Combinator question about the most impressive achievement, Y Combinator co-founder Paul Graham had this to say:

> To me, this is the most important question on the application. It's deliberately open-ended; there's no one type of answer we're looking for. It could be that you did really well in school, or that you wrote a highly-regarded piece of software, or that you paid your own way through college after leaving home at 16. It's not the type of achievement that matters so much as the magnitude. Succeeding in a startup is, in the

most literal sense, extraordinary, so we're looking for people able to do extraordinary things.

How Accelerator Applications Are Evaluated

Elizabeth Yin, a general partner at Hustle Fund and former partner who ran 500 Startups' Mountain View accelerator, proposes that the accelerator application evaluation process is typically made up of seven to eight stages. At stage 1, all accelerator applications are triaged to a common area such as an online application management platform. This is usually irrespective of whether the applications have come through referral or via the online application form. At stage 2, a quick review of all the applications is undertaken to check what the company does and whether it fits with the particular accelerator's focus. For example, a software focused accelerator might divide applicants into super high-tech companies, high-infrastructure companies, free consumer apps, and everything else. Those in the "everything else" category that are non-software may be notified at that point that they are not a good fit for the accelerator.[49] Based on the category a startup is in, the team may be evaluated for capacity to make it in that category. At stage 3, the accelerator checks what stage of startup evolution the startups are (e.g., idea, customer validation, product/market fit). Those not at the accelerator's preferred stage are notified and provided with feedback. At stage 4, the startup's idea and market opportunity are usually evaluated. Startups that are seen to be in a good market and that could be big are usually invited for stage 5, the first interview. This is a 20- to 40-minute informal chat over Skype for accelerator reviewers to meet the team and ask clarifying questions about the application (e.g., tell us more about the team, why/how did you decide to do this, how is what you're doing really different from xyz etc.). If, after stage 5, the accelerator reviewers are impressed with the team and the market opportunity, they will advance the startup to stage 6, the second interview. This will usually be a face-to-face deep dive into customer acquisition (e.g., who are the customers, why/how do they buy, what is the revenue model, how well is it working, etc.). After the interview, the

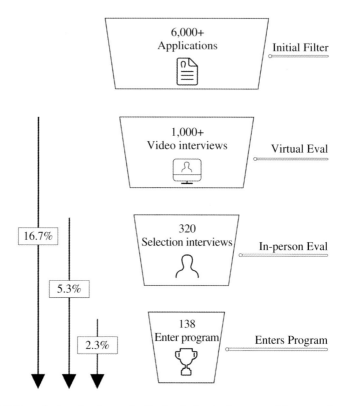

FIGURE 4.2 Example of an Accelerator Application Evaluation Process and Corresponding Conversion Rates (for Startup Bootcamp in 2016—16.7% of Applicants Got to Video Interview, 5.3% Made It to In-Person Interview, 2.3% Were Accepted into the Program)
Source: Adapted from Startup Bootcamp (2016).[50]

reviewers may have enough information for stage 7, making a "yes" or "no" decision. If they don't, there may be a follow-up stage, stage 8, where any remaining questions are clarified via email or via a third interview. Elizabeth warns that early reviews usually last less than a minute on each application, so it's important for founders to be concise as possible. She also advises that, while awaiting an accelerator decision, startups should get in touch with the accelerator to communicate any new progress made, as it may be the difference maker. She notes that accelerators see the application process as a continuous rather than fixed decision point. See Figure 4.2 for an overview of an accelerator application evaluation process and the corresponding conversion rates.

Case Study 3: LEAPIN Digital Keys' Journey through Three Different Accelerator Applications (Italy, United States, and Germany)

The Startup

Our startup offers a complete end-to-end Narrowband Internet of Things (NB IoT) smart access control solution that includes NB IoT smartlocks, smart access control systems/platforms, digital keys apps, APIs, and smartlock Software Development Kits (SDK). We were looking for fit with the right accelerator to accelerate our development. We had previously been through state, national, and international business planning competitions (usually coming second). We had also been through some national and international university incubators, an Australian government startup grant program, a European Union startup program, and an international startup program. Each of these provided a small amount of seed funding ($10,000–$50,000), and advice with a different spin. Although we had done well in these competitive grants and startup programs, in hindsight, we were just very early with our product. Even now it is still a bit early. But each of these competitions, grants, and incubators helped us better refine problem/solution fit. And it provided necessary funds to work on our MVP and pay for patents, etc. Given that our product was both hardware (involving traditional lock manufacturers and electronics manufacturers) as well as software (cloud and mobile software platforms), we found it challenging to identify which accelerators would be the right fit for us. Some accelerators saw us as being in the hospitality and leisure market, some saw us as being in the lock manufacturing market, some saw us as a software company, and others saw us as being in the emerging IoT market. How they saw us and their focus mattered to us, as we anticipated it would impact whether they had the right types of advisors, investors, and potential partners to help our startup. We were leaning towards accelerators interested in IoT startups as well as hospitality and leisure startups, since we had done some successful trials of our product in the hospitality and leisure industry in Australia.

The 10x Accelerator Application (Columbus, Ohio, USA)

Finding the Accelerator

After our challenges raising VC funding locally, we started to consider whether our type of startup (Hardware and Software), at our stage of evolution (finding product/market fit), might actually have to change location. We considered the United States as a location that might better suit our startup. We believed that the combination of easier access to funding, larger funding sizes, and greater access to software and hardware partners and employees could work in our favor. With this thinking, we decided to search for and apply for U.S. accelerators on www.f6s.com. This is how we came across the 10xelerator in

(Continued)

Columbus, Ohio, United States. The timing of the 10x accelerator intake suited us (fall 2013). And when we looked into it, we found it was in its third year of operation at the time. It had already had some successes with alumni such as Launchgram (an entertainment app startup that had recently had an early exit) and Acceptd (an education app that had just closed a $3 million investment round). 10x did not seem to have a focus on any particular types of startups but marketed itself as being *"for energetic and game-changing entrepreneurs"* and targeting early-stage startups in a variety of industries. The 10x accelerator was sponsored/funded by a new state government fund, private venture capital funds, and was in partnership with the Ohio State University.

The Decision to Apply

The biggest challenge we faced was the challenge of relocating from Australia to the United States for the duration of the program. In addition, we would have to consider relocating permanently to the United States after the program was finished to be able to take full advantage of the local networks, including raising investment capital from Columbus Angels and VCs. Eventually, we were able to settle on two to three founders agreeing to go if our application was successful.

The Application

Since we had already completed an Australian accelerator a year earlier, we had a good idea on how to fill out the application form—although we weren't sure how much more challenging it was going to be to get into the U.S. one. We expected that there ought to be more competition at least. Steve only needed to spend around 15 minutes on the application form, filled out via www.f6s.com. Our accelerator application questions and responses are included below. We have taken out any commercially sensitive information. (See Table 4.7.)

Acceptance

We were invited for a Skype interview about two weeks after the submission deadline for the accelerator. We received an email about one week later notifying us that we were successful in getting into the program. The program managers advised us that we should consider relocating to Columbus, Ohio, permanently after the program had finished. The program managers also went to great trouble and care to help us prepare for U.S. visas, as well as to help us settle in to their new town. For example, they took us on tours, visits to local bars and restaurants, invites to football games, etc. Our cohort mostly included fashion startups, big data startups, IoT startups, gaming startups, and business intelligence startups. All of them were early-stage startups, with only one having income at all.

TABLE 4.7 LEAPIN Digital Keys' Responses to the 10x Accelerator

Accelerator Application Section	Accelerator Application Questions	LDK's Responses/Answers
Company overview	In your three-minute video submission, which will be evaluated by our pool of judges, please make sure to address the following: Convince us that the problem you are solving (or the opportunity that you are exploiting) is big and needs to be solved immediately. Convince us that your solution is THE answer to the problem and how you will create real value for your customers. What specific hurdles do you see ahead for your project, and how do you intend to overcome them? What is so unique about your team that makes you think you can solve this big problem, and why should we believe you? (experience, interests, talents, etc.)	Video provided.
Team	How many founders are there?	2
	Can all team members attend the 10x program in person?	Yes
	How long have the founders worked together as a team?	2 1/2 years
	Briefly describe the roles and experience for each team member.	Steve Dunn - CEO
		Responsible for Business Development, Marketing, Sales, Accounting, Strategy, Capital raising
		MBA, former Manager Local Government
		******* CTO
		Responsible for IT, Programming, Design
		BA Comp. Sc.
		Seven years' experience as Developer

(Continued)

TABLE 4.7 (continued)

Accelerator Application Section	Accelerator Application Questions	LDK's Responses/Answers
	Where does the team plan for the startup to be physically after the program?	Where the opportunities take us.
	Briefly describe each team members' time commitment during and after the program.	Full-time commitment
	Briefly describe all prior startup experience for each team member.	Steve Dunn
		Exclusive supplier in Cairns, North Queensland, of dairy products.
		CEO of company that delivered Education Programs to schools.
		********
		IT company CEO
	What category sector is your business? (e.g., Consumer Internet, Cybersecurity, Big Data, etc.)	Consumer Internet, e-commerce, hospitality retail, and logistics
Product	Briefly describe your stage of customer discovery and/or market research. (e.g., the idea is still being formulated, you've spoken with customers about the problem, you've received feedback on your solution from users, etc.)	Our market has been validated by the success of similar product offerings such as Lockitron (14,000 orders in a crowd-funding campaign for $2.2 Million in 30 days) August 26,000 orders in four weeks, One Fine Stay Sherlock $13 million capital raise, Unikey/Kevo secured a partnership with one of the global leaders in lock manufacturing and raised over $2 million in capital. Relayrides acquiring Wheelz for their smartphone unlocking technology. Getaround raising $13 million including from CEO of Yahoo. GM, Ford, and Hyundai announcing new cars to incorporate smartphone unlocking technology.
		All of these companies have patents after LEAPIN's priority date, none at all, or if they do have a patent it is for tech that is more complex and more expensive than LEAPIN's patent-pending technology.

Accelerator Application Section	Accelerator Application Questions	LDK's Responses/Answers
	Briefly describe why and how you chose this particular idea.	My love affair with Digital Keys began with a loathing for keycard locks. Like most people I'd never really stopped to think about locks and keys before in my life. That was until I started renting a permanent apartment inside an Australian hotel, where I was constantly being locked out by the failing keycards.
		This was in 2007. Like many hotels in Australia, a lot of the apartments are owned by independent parties, often retired couples or families. The owner rents their apartment out for a permanent rental or a holiday rental. If it's a holiday rental, then there is usually some on-site management such as a hotel chain. If it's a permanent rental, then it's common that an off-site real estate agency managers the property on the owners' behalf.
		So at least once or twice a week, I found myself being locked out of my apartment, as the keycard would simply stop working. That little red light on the top of the lock soon began to drive me mad. Perhaps you've experienced it before? Now this wouldn't have been too much of a problem if my apartment was, say, on the same floor as the reception desk. But my apartment was on the fourth floor, and the reception desk was on the bottom floor of the apartment building on the other side of the car park, and up the long driveway. There was no reception desk in the building I lived in. There used to be one. Someday someone realized they didn't need a reception desk on our side, and so they closed it.
		Well there were actually two separate car parks that I had to walk across, one for my building and one for the other building. This car park was always busy. There were no walkways. In the wet season it was like a lake. By the time I got to the reception desk, there always seemed to be a line-up. My keycard seemed to somehow decide to conk itself out every time a bus load of Chinese tourists had arrived to check in.
		One other thing I noticed with my keycard, was that it also seemed to conk out every time I came back from shopping. And, yes, it also liked to conk out every time I had ice cream or margarine in the shopping bags.

(Continued)

TABLE 4.7 (continued)

Accelerator Application Section	Accelerator Application Questions	LDK's Responses/Answers
		Now this wouldn't have been too much of a problem either, if we weren't living in the tropics—or if there was air-conditioning in the hallway. I guess most of the rooms on our floor were permanent rentals, and nobody wanted to pay for the common area air conditioning.
		Now, once again this wouldn't have been much of a problem—but my wife is from a cold climate. My wife is from some mountain ranges in central Japan. And our little girl was only two at the time (tantrums!). So by the time I had to wait in the queue at the reception desk, to get to speak to the front desk reception staff to ask them to re-magnetize my card, I was pretty pissed off. The reception staff never seemed happy either. Perhaps there were plenty of other people like me coming down all the time to visit them to get our keycard working again—and they hardly ever got a break from it all?
		So it wasn't that I was simply being locked out of my apartment that caused me to look for an alternative. It was the combination of melting ice cream, un-air-conditioned hallways, stifling humidity, restless child, frustrated wife (who also knew how long it took each time to go back to the reception desk to get the keycard re-magnetised), busloads of Chinese tourists, long queues, snotty reception desk staff, and dangerous wet car parks, that lead me on my digital keys journey.
		Like any journey these days, it began on the internet. I began looking for alternatives to keycards. We had the mag-stripe type of lock in our apartment. I learned these types of locks became prevalent in hotels around thirty years ago. The snotty reception staff told me that these mag-stripe locks were the ones prone to being demagnetized when held next to a mobile phone or car key fob. That didn't help, as I always carried my phone and car key fob in my pocket everywhere I went. In time I built the core root of the problem into the solution.

Accelerator Application Section	Accelerator Application Questions	LDK's Responses/Answers
	What is the addressable market size for your idea?	300,000 Airbnb properties
		47 million shipping containers
		Top 10 hotel chains have between 600,000 and 700,000 rooms
		Approx 170,000 new commercial buildings under construction each year in United States
		124,000 schools and universities in United States
		Approx 70 million school lockers in United States
	What's the most recent milestone you've achieved?	PCT patent application lodged priority date Feb. 2011. US Patent published Jan. 2013. International Search Report says all 18 claims novel, inventive, and industrially applicable.
		Completed Australian Federal Government Commercialisation Australia Program (Skills and Knowledge)—at the time one of only 250 companies in two years in Australia to have completed program.
		Concept proven in an Australian resort and a Sydney Hotel.
		Graduated from a Global Accelerator Network Program (ANZ Innovyz), and from a University Incubator (Gold Coast Innovation Centre—Griffith University Queensland).
		Assembled a team of industry experts and professionals including John Hossli, the former president/CEO of Hafele North America (Hafele is the largest architectural supply company in the world with a lock manufacturing arm). Other team members include Greg Siegele, who has taken a tech startup to a seven-figure sale within four years, and several award-winning IT developers.
		Currently in licensing discussions with three "lower-tier" lock manufacturers in the United States and Europe, including SAG Schlagbaum, Tellcard Systems, and Codelocks (there are only around 10 other companies of similar size in Europe and United States). It is also in discussion with the world's leading meta-search engine for vacation rental properties (tripping.com), and other local Australian companies in the hospitality industry.

(Continued)

TABLE 4.7 (continued)

Accelerator Application Section	Accelerator Application Questions	LDK's Responses/Answers
		June 2013, received an unsolicited approach from a well known U.S.-based Non-Practicing Entity to monetize LEAPIN patent.
	What's the next most important milestone for the business, and what is your time/cost estimate to achieve it?	LEAPIN's strategy is to engage an experienced licensing executive to carry out a licensing campaign in the USA and Europe over an eighteen-month period, targeting competitors, startups, and manufacturers discussed above. The executive will be supported by the Inventor/co-founder and its established team including IP attorneys, legal team, and experienced advisors in the applicable industries. LEAPIN seeks to raise $500,000 on a company valuation of $1.5 million to carry out its licensing strategy. Considering the growth in this industry, and the wide-ranging applications of its product offering, LEAPIN is looking to finalize a sale out of companies it licenses to within three years for in excess of $10 million.
Business information	When did the company start?	February 2011
	Are you legally formed, and if so where?	Yes as a Pty. Ltd. in South Australia, Australia
	Has there been any money invested to date, and if so how much?	$50,000
	Do you plan on raising money in the future, and if so how much and when?	Yes—$500,000 as soon as possible to embark on the aforementioned licensing campaign.
	Upload Google analytics for the past year.	Uploaded
	Please upload any additional slide decks, information, files, etc. to help us better understand your business.	investor pitch deck.pptx

Reflections on the Accelerator Application

Knowing what we know now, two of the questions in the application could have been answered much better. Firstly, we misunderstood the question *"Briefly describe your stage of customer discovery and/or market research."* Instead of using this response to highlight traction and demonstrate how far advanced our startup was, we provided market validation data. Steve knew that it was important to validate the market somewhere in his responses, but this was not the right question to do this. During the Australian accelerator (Innovyz), Steve saw firsthand how most mentors and investors had never heard of smartlocks and IoT (as we said earlier, back in 2012 our product was just far too early). So, his intention was to get the points down early in the application, about the early success stories for startups in this space. Fortunately, there was a second question specifically asking about milestones. If this question was not specifically asked, we most likely would have received an immediate rejection. Another question we answered poorly was *"What is the addressable market size for your idea?"* We were attempting to show the many different market opportunities for our product. But it came across as a lot of unrelated random numbers that would have confused most reviewers, who may have wondered whether we understood our market. We should have simply answered with the size of our market in billions, and then the CAGR (compound annual growth rate). Then we could have identified an initial target segment we were hoping to capture and the strategic reasons for doing so. Also, credible supporting statistics would have been good to include here.

The H-Farm Accelerator Application (Ca' Tron, Italy)[51]

Finding the Accelerator

We found the H-Farm Deutsche Bank IoT Accelerator Program while searching for accelerators programs on www.f6s.com. It struck us as being a potentially good fit since it was IoT focused and, being in Europe, it presented an opportunity to link up with a different type of client in Europe (where we noticed smartlocks were more embraced by hotels than in Australia). Some leading lock and electronics manufacturers were also located in Europe. We anticipated there would also be benefit from having a number of countries in close proximity, whereas in Australia we found ourselves needing to take 24-hour flights to Europe, the Americas, and Asia—which were costly also. Often these flights related to forming partnerships, doing trials, or raising funding. We had concluded that our type of startup was probably not a good fit for the venture capital community in Australia at the time; although this community has now developed.

The Decision to Apply

One of the immediate challenges for the team was the relocation decision. We (the founders) had met while studying at university, when we were all much

(Continued)

more flexible and could travel around the world easily, especially with competition grant money taking care of the cost of travel, except maybe for Steve (as he had a young family). But by the time the team discovered the H-Farm Accelerator program, Steve's young family had expanded, and the others had gotten married and started working. The startup was not generating any revenue, and it was unclear how far off such revenue might be. The H-Farm Accelerator provided some funding for founders to live in Italy for four months. Steve (the lead entrepreneur) decided he would relocate for the four months and potentially look into staying in Italy if LEAPIN was accepted, although the latter idea was something he had yet to discuss with his wife and young kids. Another member of the team, a non-founder, decided to go with him if the application was successful.

The Application

We had some experience with accelerator applications and so did not find the application process too challenging. We were able to reuse many of the same answers and had achieved significant progress since our last application. Our accelerator application questions and responses are included in Table 4.8. We have taken out any commercially sensitive information.

Acceptance

Two weeks after the submission deadline, we were invited for a Skype interview. The interview mostly involved introductions and discussion of elements of the application. A week after the Skype interview, we received an email notifying us that we were successful in getting into the program. The LEAPIN team quickly scrambled to organize to leave for Italy.

We thought we would be the most advanced startup in the accelerator. But when the accelerator started, we were shocked to find that all the other startups were very advanced relative to us. All of them had fully developed products, had achieved product/market fit, had well established teams, had previously raised capital, and had significant revenue. Notwithstanding that, from the very first day of the accelerator, LEAPIN, and one other international team, were constantly told by the program managers, mentors, and associated investors that we should start planning and preparing to live in Venice, Italy, permanently after the program had finished. The program managers also went to great trouble and care to help the two international teams prepare Italian visa applications, and they also went to great lengths to help the international teams settle in to their new town (e.g., taking them on tours, visits to local bars and restaurants, etc.).

Reflections on the Accelerator Application

In hindsight, we answered the market question well this time around (as compared to the 10xcelerator application). But we probably should have had references for the statistics provided. This response was cut straight from a past

TABLE 4.8 LEAPIN Digital Keys' Responses to H-Farm Deutsche Bank IoT Accelerator

Accelerator Application Section	Accelerator Application Questions	LEAPIN's Responses/Answers
General Info	Website	www.leapin.biz/
	Email address / mobile number	Retracted for confidentiality
	Where is your team located?	Australia
	Have you already raised funds?	Yes, government grants
	How did you hear about the Deutsche Bank Accelerator?	F6s.com
Idea	Please provide a short, concise description of your business	We offer a smartlock solution including a software development kit (SDK) and Application Programming Interfaces that benefit manufacturers through reduced costs and minimal infrastructure changes and provide greater sales opportunities. For property owners and managers, LEAPIN streamlines property management efficiencies, improves services with smartphone apps, removes the risk of security breaches, attracts new clientele (e.g., tech savvy millennials), and returns money to SME hotels.
	What problem/s are you solving for your customers?	We offer a smartlock solution including a software development kit (SDK), and Application Programming Interfaces that benefit manufacturers through reduced costs and minimal infrastructure changes and provide greater sales opportunities. For property owners and managers, LEAPIN streamlines property management efficiencies, improves services with smartphone apps, removes the risk of security breaches, attracts new clientele (e.g., tech savvy millennials), and returns money to SME hotels.
	What is interesting/new about your business?	We've been selected as the only smartlock partner in the NB IoT forum for the new NB IoT rollout.

(Continued)

TABLE 4.8 (continued)

Accelerator Application Section	Accelerator Application Questions	LEAPIN's Responses/Answers
Team	How many people are there in the team?	Four
	How many developers/ engineers are there in the team?	One
	Please list each founder name, position, and quick background	Steve Dunn CEO, MBA, Uni of SA Sam Faukner, CTO, BA Comp Science Richard Busulwa, CFO, BA Accounting, PhD (cand) Ben Luks, CMO, BA Marketing.
Market	Please tell us about your market including size, growth, customers	The smartlock market is part of the global Internet of Things market, which has been predicted to grow to €12.6 trillion in 2022, as more devices come online, and a bevy of platforms and services grow up around them. The Internet of Things is expected to be the largest device market in the world, estimating that by 2019 it will be more than double the size of the smartphone, PC, tablet, connected car, and the wearable market combined. According to market analysts, one of the product categories that will no doubt be reinvented over the coming decade is security and access control. The smartlock market is expected to see explosive growth in the coming decade with a predicted CAGR of more than 75% by 2020. Established security and home hardware companies increasingly face competition from upstarts introducing a new breed of smart and connected locks into the market. The lock market will be significantly disrupted in the coming decade, as a new league of connected locks come available.

Accelerator Application Section	Accelerator Application Questions	LEAPIN's Responses/Answers
	Who are your competitors? What differentiates you? Include URLs.	Basis of competition: Product/solution Website Type of smartlock Sale price Battery power life Hospitality/ consumer sector Integrations Method of entry/technology
		Competitors: August www.august.com Deadbolt attachment € 162 6 months Consumer HostAssist with Airbnb Apple Homekit Smartphone/Bluetooth, Wi-Fi
		Kevo by Kwikset www.kwikset.com/kevo Deadbolt € 184 12 months Consumer HostAssist with Airbnb Smartlock/Bluetooth, metal key, Wi-Fi
		RemoteLock www.remotelock.com Lever € 221 12 months Consumer HostAssist with Airbnb, PMS, WBE PIN/number pad, OTP (time-sensitive PIN)
		Differentiation: LEAPIN Digital Keys SmartLocks www.digitalkeys.com.au

(Continued)

TABLE 4.8 (continued)

Accelerator Application Section	Accelerator Application Questions	LEAPIN's Responses/Answers
		All locks—e.g., Lever, Knobset, deadbolt attachment, deadbolt, locker locks, rimset locks, furniture locks, combo locks, mortise locks €60–€300 (depending on lock type, order size, existing product, and partner)
		1–2 years (approx 30,000 activations, currently). Up to ten years with NB IoT chips and modules Hospitality and Consumer PMS, WBE, CM, Hotel Loyalty Apps (current) soon to be HostAs
Product	Define the stage of your product	Live
	What have you built so far? What do you plan to build in the next six months?	In early 2016, the LEAPIN SDK was implemented by Schulte Schlagbaum AG (hereby referred to as SAG), a German lock manufacturer who released on the market the basic a product called SAFE-O-TRONIC Access (May 2016). The launched SmartLock currently only utilizes the Digital Keys as a time-sensitive PIN, see Figure ***, and staff must still distribute the digital key to guests with supporting software. With LEAPIN's specifications, SAG have achieved 1200 sales of the new smartlocks to 4 hotels in Germany in the first month of launch, and sales every month since have been between 1500 and 2000. LEAPIN and SAG have an ongoing licensing agreement. SAG anticipates sales to increase 10–20% per month. However, LEAPIN and SAG are aware that further development, including the guest loyalty apps and smartphone unlocking, is required to attract the interest of more hotels and chains including Logis Group and Hotusa Group, both of which have expressed interest in a large-scale beta trial.

Accelerator Application Section	Accelerator Application Questions	LEAPIN's Responses/Answers
Execution	What are some possible ways of monetizing your solution?	Royalties from licensing Sharing in a % of the online transaction fee from bookings on the Guest Loyalty App with digital keys Monthly fees
	Have you reached any outstanding Milestone?	M1 Smartphone app prototype completed. Field trials of smartphone app with interfacing number pad smartlocks carried out in a Gold Coast Australian Resort (two rooms) for six months. Discovered the need for interfaces to Property Management System (PMS). July 2011–Dec. 2011. M2 Web check-in software prototype completed with PMS interfaces. Field trials in Sydney Hotel (32 rooms) for eight months with interfacing number pad smartlocks provided by Kaba Ilco. Discovered need for interfaces to Online Travel Agencies (via Channel Managers) and to a more sophisticated PMS. Feb. 2012–Nov. 2012 M3 Web check-in software and interfaces prototype completed with a new PMS and Channel Manager and interfacing number pad smartlocks provided by Resortlock. Paying customers in Marrysville, Victoria (nine bed and breakfasts), and a student boarding house in Adelaide. Discovered need for more functions for complete self-management automation; different hardware design and for additional functions for hotels (e.g., adding Near Field Communication technology to the smartphone apps)

(Continued)

TABLE 4.8 (continued)

Accelerator Application Section	Accelerator Application Questions	LEAPIN's Responses/Answers
Extra	What do you expect to achieve during the 4-month program?	Large-scale beta trials in hotels in Europe with existing partners and committed hotels and hotel chains.
	How many total team members can locate in H-Farm for the full 4-month program?	Two
	Upload a presentation about your startup (.key, .pdf, .ppt)	LEAPIN Digital Keys investor slide deck Aug. 2016.pptx

European Union (EU) grant application, which LDK worked on with a grant auspicing company with years of experience in preparing successful grant applications. Many of the sections in that grant application were similar to the questions in this accelerator application form (and many other accelerator application forms). This response was done well, as we firstly highlighted the larger overall market of IoT (which is what the accelerator was about), then we showed the role that smartlocks and smart access control played in the market, and then discussed the predicted growth rates. We also gave a commentary on the market evolution, mentioning it was ready for disruption. We offered some comparisons to other markets to highlight the enormous size of the market.

The answer to question 2 about LEAPIN's competitors was also directly cut from the EU grant application. The grant auspicing company had offered us a helpful tip. That was, when doing a product comparison, try to include as many features of the competitors' product offering in there—but at the same time these features should also be contrasting to the startup's features. So, we chose to include information about pricing, battery life, integration, and technology standard, as we knew our product offered significant differences in these fields. The third thing we did well in this application was the response to the progress/milestones question. Once again this was copied from the successful EU grant application and was worked out with the support of the grant auspicing company who had done thousands of successful EU grant applications over many years. Instead of just writing a sentence in general language about the milestone such as "launched product," we provided significant details regarding the size of the trials, the customers' names and locations, the exact length of the trials, the partners' names, and even what needs were discovered in the milestones (we could provide such detail because of the accelerators' confidentiality policy). One question we did not answer well was the question about monetization. If this was an application to a general "non-themed" accelerator, then the answer might have been fine. However, as this was an IoT accelerator, we should have highlighted some typical IoT monetization business models such as making money from big data analytics, or API call fees, or even well-known SaaS models.

The Techstars Powered Metro Accelerator (Berlin, Germany)
Finding the Accelerator

Through the H-Farm Accelerator, we were linked with some powerful traditional and electronic lock manufacturers in Germany. After the accelerator, we continued to develop these relationships and to co-develop and trial smartlocks together. Through this experience, we came to realize the limitations of working remotely with these strategic partners (e.g., different time zones plus differences in language and business practices, etc.). So, we started to consider whether it would be beneficial for us to have a physical presence in Germany. We searched for German accelerators on www.f6s.com, and were surprised to find the Techstars powered METRO Accelerator for Hospitality located in Berlin, Germany. The sponsor of the accelerator was "Metro." Metro, as of 2010, was the fourth-largest retailer in the world measured by revenues (after Wal-Mart, Carrefour, and Tesco). We were excited by this accelerator since Techstars' record of success was first-rate. On top of this, it was a tech accelerator focused on the hospitality industry. And it was located in Germany. So we could develop our relationships with strategic partners located in Germany and connect with potential new hospitality customers/investors and advisors.

The Decision to Apply

As with other accelerators, the biggest challenge in the decision to apply was relocating for the fourth time, this time to Germany. Steve had relocated from Brisbane (a city in Australia) while his family remained. The founding team had then relocated to Columbus, Ohio. Then to Italy. And now the issue was whether our families would accept departing again for at least another half year to go to Germany—especially Steve's wife and kids—since he had moved every single time. Nevertheless, the team found a way to get two founders to go.

The Application

Every time that we applied for an accelerator, we did so after achieving new significant milestones or breakthroughs. In the successful application to the Australian accelerator in 2011 (Innovyz), we had just completed trials of our digital keys apps. Apps were still relatively new to consumers then. We had also just won our university's business planning competition (the University of South Australia Pank Prize). When we next applied for the 10x accelerator in the United States (fall of 2013), we had just signed a licensing deal with a leading European lock manufacturer and were finishing building our C++-based

(Continued)

Software Development Kit. When LDK successfully applied to H-Farm (in 2017), we had just received the European Commission grant. We had also signed a partnership deal with Vodafone and Huawei. The reason that on this occasion we were applying for Techstars (in mid-2018), was because we had just launched our new complete end-to-end NB IoT smart access control solution, completed trials of this solution, and received a 1000 unit paid purchase order. We reasoned we had proved our product in the marketplace and had started generating revenue—a significant milestone for us. We hoped the accelerator would help us move to the next stage. Our application responses were as shown in Table 4.9.

TABLE 4.9 LEAPIN Digital Keys' Responses to Techstars Powered Metro Accelerator

Accelerator Application Section	Accelerator Application Questions	LEAPIN's Responses/Answers
General info	Website	www.leapin.biz/
	Email address/mobile number	Redacted for confidentiality
	Where is your team located?	Australia
	Have you already raised funds?	Yes, government grants
	How did you hear about the Deutsche Bank accelerator?	F6s.com
Idea	Please provide a short, concise description of your business	We offer a smartlock solution including a Software Development Kit (SDK), and Application Programming Interfaces that benefit manufacturers through reduced costs and minimal infrastructure changes and provide greater sales opportunities. For property owners and managers, LEAPIN streamlines property management efficiencies, improves services with smartphone apps, removes the risk of security breaches, attracts new clientele (e.g., tech savvy millennials), and returns money to SME hotels.

Accelerator Application Section	Accelerator Application Questions	LEAPIN's Responses/Answers
	What problem/s are you solving for your customers?	We offer a smartlock solution including a Software Development Kit (SDK), and Application Programming Interfaces that benefit manufacturers through reduced costs and minimal infrastructure changes and provide greater sales opportunities. For property owners and managers, LEAPIN streamlines property management efficiencies, improves services with smartphone apps, removes the risk of security breaches, attracts new clientele (e.g, tech savvy millennials), and returns money to SME hotels.
	What is interesting/new about your business?	We've been selected as the only smartlock partner in the NB IoT forum for the new NB IoT rollout.
Team	How many people are there in the team?	Four
	How many developers/ engineers are there in the team?	One
	Please list each founder name, position and quick background	Steve Dunn CEO, MBA, Uni. of SA Sam Faukner, CTO, BA Comp Science Richard Busulwa CFO, BA Accounting, PhD (cand) Ben Luks, CMO, BA Marketing
Market	Please tell us about your market including size, growth, customers	The smartlock market is part of the global Internet of Things market, which has been predicted to grow to €12.6T in 2022, as more devices come online and a bevy of platforms and services grow up around them.

(Continued)

TABLE 4.9 (continued)

Accelerator Application Section	Accelerator Application Questions	LEAPIN's Responses/Answers
		The Internet of Things is expected to be the largest device market in the world, estimating that by 2019 it will be more than double the size of the smartphone, PC, tablet, connected car, and the wearable market combined. According to Market Analysts, one of the product categories that will no doubt be reinvented over the coming decade is security and access control. The smartlock market is expected to see explosive growth in the coming decade with a predicted CAGR of more than 75% by 2020. Established security and home hardware companies increasingly face competition from upstarts introducing a new breed of smart and connected locks into the market. The lock market will be significantly disrupted in the coming decade, as a new league of connected locks come available.
	Who are your competitors? What differentiates you? Include URLs	Basis of competition:
		Product/solution
		Website
		Type of smartlock
		Sale Price
		Battery Power Life
		Hospitality/Consumer Sector
		Integrations
		Method of entry/technology
		Competitors:
		August www.august.com
		Deadbolt attachment € 162

Accelerator Application Section	Accelerator Application Questions	LEAPIN's Responses/Answers
		6 months Consumer HostAssist with Airbnb, Apple Homekit Smartphone/Bluetooth, Wi-Fi
		Kevo by Kwikset www.kwikset.com/kevo Deadbolt € 184
		12 months Consumer HostAssist with Airbnb Smartlock/Bluetooth, metal key, Wi-Fi
		RemoteLock www.remotelock.com
		Lever € 221 12 months Consumer HostAssist with Airbnb, PMS, WBE PIN/number pad, OTP (time-sensitive PIN)
		Differentiation:
		LEAPIN Digital Keys SmartLocks www.digitalkeys.com.au
		All locks: e.g. Lever, Knobset, deadbolt attachment, deadbolt, locker locks, rimset locks, furniture locks, combo locks, mortise locks €60–€300 (depending on lock type, order size, existing product, and partner)
		1–2 years (approx 30,000 activations—currently. Up to 10 years with NB IoT chips and modules Hospitality and Consumer PMS, WBE, CM, Hotel Loyalty Apps (current) soon to be HostAs
Product	Define the stage of your product	Live

(Continued)

TABLE 4.9 (continued)

Accelerator Application Section	Accelerator Application Questions	LEAPIN's Responses/Answers
	What have you built so far? What do you plan to build in the next six months?	In early 2016, the LEAPIN SDK was implemented by Schulte Schlagbaum AG (hereby referred to as SAG), a German lock manufacturer, who released on the market the basic product called SAFE-O-TRONIC Access (May 2016). The launched SmartLock currently only utilizes the Digital Keys as a time-sensitive PIN, see Figure ***, and staff must still distribute the digital key to guests with supporting software. With LEAPIN's specifications, SAG have achieved 1200 sales of the new smartlocks to four hotels in Germany in the first month of launch, and sales every month since have been between 1500 and 2000. LEAPIN and SAG have an ongoing licensing agreement. SAG anticipate sales to increase 10–20% per month; however, LEAPIN and SAG are aware that further development, including the guest loyalty apps and smartphone unlocking, is required to attract the interest of more hotels and chains including Logis Group and Hotusa Group, both of which have expressed interest in a large-scale beta trial.
Execution	What are some possible ways of monetizing your solution?	Royalties from licensing Sharing in a percentage of the online transaction fee from bookings on the Guest Loyalty App with digital keys Monthly fees

Accelerator Application Section	Accelerator Application Questions	LEAPIN's Responses/Answers
	Have you reached any outstanding Milestone?	**M1** Smartphone app prototype completed. Field trials of smartphone app with interfacing number pad smartlocks carried out in a Gold Coast Australian Resort (two rooms) for six months. Discovered the need for interfaces to Property Management System (PMS). July 2011–Dec. 2011. **M2** Web check-in software prototype completed with PMS interfaces. Field trials in Sydney Hotel (32 rooms) for eight months with interfacing number pad smartlocks provided by Kaba Ilco. Discovered need for interfaces to Online Travel Agencies (via Channel Managers) and to a more sophisticated PMS. Feb. 2012–Nov. 2012. **M3** Web check-in software and interfaces prototype completed with a new PMS and Channel Manager and interfacing number pad smartlocks provided by Resortlock. Paying customers in Marysville, Victoria (nine Bed and Breakfasts) and a student boarding house in Adelaide. Discovered need for more functions for complete self-management automation; different hardware design and for additional functions for hotels (e.g adding Near Field Communication technology to the smartphone apps)

(Continued)

TABLE 4.9 (continued)

Accelerator Application Section	Accelerator Application Questions	LEAPIN's Responses/Answers
Extra	What do you expect to achieve during the four-month program?	Large-scale beta trials in hotels in Europe with existing partners and committed hotels and hotel chains
	How many total team members can locate in H-FARM for the full four-month program?	Two
	Upload a presentation about your startup (.key, .pdf, .ppt)	LEAPIN Digital Keys investor slide deck Aug 2016.pptx

Acceptance

We were invited for a Skype interview about two weeks after the submission deadline for the accelerator. We felt we did badly in this interview. We had so much going on with the manufacturers that our preparation suffered. But, three weeks later, we were invited to another interview, then another, then another—all over a three-week period. These were with a program manager one on one. Each was unexpected, and so our preparation was limited. Despite the four interviews, we were not offered a place. The main feedback we received was that we were "too early," having only just launched our product onto the market. We were shocked! It was a hard pill to swallow, considering what it had taken to get to this point, the partnerships we had, and that we had real revenue. Interestingly, no hardware startups were selected in this cohort.

Reflections

Thinking back, our traction section answer could have been more detailed, like it was in the previous two applications. Instead, the answer was left deliberately focused only on the traction regarding getting our product in the marketplace. We were so excited about having revenue that we thought there was no need to highlight any other milestones. This was a big mistake as we had lots of other progress milestones. The response to the competition question could also have been more like the response provided in the previous application to H-Farm, with extra facts or features about the competitors' products. We could then have contrasted this with the facts and features of the startup's product and business. However, once again, this was kept to an absolute minimum to try and allow the message about having product working and selling in the marketplace to dominate the application. The milestones achieved around the time of each accelerator application were very different, and so in turn, each application was quite different with a bias on each of the milestones. The biggest learnings from the applications were the ability and need to be able to synthesize so much information, with so much detail, specifics, and directness in each sentence. This not only provided credibility, but also gave the opportunity for the program managers to carry out detailed research or due diligence on the application if they wanted to.

Notes

1. P. Vijayashanker, "Startup Accelerator Interview: How to Ace Your Interview with 500 Startups," 500 Startups, March 4, 2019, accessed August 1, 2019, https://500.co/startup-accelerator-interview/.
2. Ibid.
3. R. Richards, "Accelerators vs. Incubators: How to Choose the Right One," MassChallenge, March 19, 2019, accessed August 1, 2019, https://masschallenge.org/article/accelerators-vs-incubators.
4. "F6S," accessed August 1, 2019, https://www.f6s.com/f6s.
5. D. Houston, "Dropbox's Original YC application," 2007, accessed August 1, 2019, https://www.YCombinator.com/apply/dropbox/.
6. "TechStars. Application Preview," TechStars, accessed August 1, 2019, https://www.TechStars.com/application-preview/.
7. Ibid.
8. The Farm. "The Farm Accelerator Application Questions," April 2018, accessed August 1, 2019, https://thefarmatl.com/app/uploads/2018/04/AcceleratorApplication_TheFarm.pdf/.
9. S. Wise, "I've Heard 20,000 Elevator Pitches: Here's What They've Taught Me About Getting Funded," *Inc.*, February 13, 2018, accessed August 1, 2019, https://www.inc.com/sean-wise/what-10000-hours-of-investor-pitches-can-tell-you-about-landing-perfect-pitch-in-21st-century.html.
10. H. Gafni, D. Marom, and O. Sade, "Are the Life and Death of an Early-Stage Venture Indeed in the Power of the Tongue?

Lessons from Online Crowdfunding Pitches," *Strategic Entrepreneurship Journal* 13, no. 3 (2018): 3–23.

11. Houston, "Dropbox's Original YC Application."

12. Wise, "I've Heard 20,000 Elevator Pitches."

13. J. Nieto, R. M. Hernandez-Maestro, and P.A. Munoz-Gallego, "The Influence of Entrepreneurial Talent and Website Type on Business Performance by Rural Tourism Establishments in Spain," *International Journal of Tourism Research* 13, no. 1 (2011): 17–31.

14. D. Harper, "Towards a Theory of Entrepreneurial Teams," *Journal of Business Venturing* 23, no. 6 (2008): 613–626.

15. T. Cooney, "What Is an Entrepreneurial Team?" (Editorial), *International Small Business Journal* 23, no. 3 (2005): 226–235.

16. M. Zwilling, "Five Warning Signs Your Startup Team Is Going To Kill Each Other," accessed August 1, 2019, *Business Insider Australia,* January 11, 2011, https://www.businessinsider.com.au/investors-deal-harshly-with-dysfunctional-teams-2011-1.

17. M. Zwilling, "7 Must-Have Attributes of a Member of a Super Startup Team," *Entrepreneur,* July 17, 2015, accessed August 1, 2019, https://www.entrepreneur.com/article/248318.

18. M. Swyers, "7 Reasons Good Teams Become Dysfunctional," *Inc.,* September 27, 2012, accessed August 1, 2019, https://www.inc.com/matthew-swyers/7-reasons-good-teams-become-dysfunctional.html.

19. Zwilling, "Five Warning Signs."

20. D. Chen, "The No BS Approach to Getting into Y Combinator," *Medium,* March 17, 2016, accessed August 1, 2019, https://medium.com/swlh/how-to-get-into-y-combinator-the-no-bs-approach-820cbedbc904.

21. J. Erickson, "500 Startups Announces Batch 13 in Mountain View," 500 Startups, April 27, 2015, accessed August 1, 2019, https://500.co/mountain-view-batch-13/.

22. S. Strom, "How I Got into 500 Startups (Batch 13)," 2015, accessed August 1, 2019, https://www.startupgrind.com/blog/how-i-got-into-500-startups-batch-13/.

23. B. Clark, "5 Crippling Characteristics Entrepreneurs Need to Get Over," *Forbes,* June 6, 2012, accessed August 1, 2019, https://www.forbes.com/sites/brianclark/2012/06/06/characteristics-entrepreneurs/#c1d805922c91.

24. P. Graham, "What We Look for in Founders," October 2010, accessed August 1, 2019, http://paulgraham.com/founders.html.
25. Ibid.
26. A. Barber, "Building a Startup: 7 Qualities of Great Teams," Techstars, January 10, 218, accessed August 1, 2019, https://www.TechStars.com/content/accelerators/the-seven-qualities-of-a-great-founding-team/.
27. "Founder Ethics," Y Combinator, June 2018, accessed August 1, 2019, https://www.Y Combinator.com/ethics/.
28. S. Blank, *The Four Steps to the Epiphany: Successful Strategies for Products That Win* (BookBaby, 2013).
29. Ibid.
30. A. Maurya, *Running Lean: Iterate from Plan A to a Plan That Works* (Sebastopol, CA: O'Reilly Media, Inc., 2012).
31. Blank, *The Four Steps to the Epiphany*.
32. T. R. Eisenmann, E. Ries, and S. Dillard, "Hypothesis-Driven Entrepreneurship: The Lean Startup." Harvard Business School Entrepreneurial Management Case (812-095) (2012).
33. E. Ries, *The Lean Startup: How Today's Entrepreneurs Use Continuous Innovation to Create Radically Successful Businesses* (Crown Books, 2011).
34. Maurya, *Running Lean*.
35. B. Scordato, "Your Startup's MVP Isn't Working, But Here's What Might," *Fast Company*, February 10, 2018, accessed August 1, 2019, https://www.fastcompany.com/40528348/your-startups-mvp-isnt-working-but-heres-what-might.
36. D. Cohen, "The Perfect email," March 6, 2011, accessed August 1, 2019, http://davidgcohen.com/2011/03/06/the-perfect-email/.
37. Kauffman Foundation, "Address Your Limitations and Reduce Your Liabilities," January 17, 2007, accessed August 1, 2019, https://www.entrepreneurship.org/articles/2007/01/address-your-limitations-and-reduce-your-liabilities.
38. B. Burnham, "Duck Duck Go." Union Square Ventures blog, 2011, accessed October 2, 2018, https://www.usv.com/writing/2011/10/duck-duck-go/.
39. G. Weinberg, "What Taking On Google Taught Me About Startup Traction," *Fast Company*, September 29, 2015, accessed August 1, 2019, https://www.fastcompany.com/3051613/what-taking-on-google-taught-me-about-startup-traction.

40. H. Greenstein, "How to Show Market Traction," *Inc.*, June 22, 2011, accessed August 1, 2019, https://www.inc.com/howard-greenstein/how-to-show-market-traction.html.

41. D. Cohen, "What Investors Look For in Startup Projects—with TechStars Founder David Cohen," Codementor, May 26, 2015, accessed August 1, 2019, https://www.codementor.io/startups/tutorial/investors-look-startup-projects-open-qa-TechStars-founder-david-cohen.

42. C. Pauwels, B. Clarysse, M. Wright, and J. Van Hove, "Understanding a New Generation Incubation Model: The Accelerator," *Technovation* 50–51 (2016): 13–24.

43. D. L. Hoffman and N. Radojevich-Kelley, "Analysis of Accelerator Companies: An Exploratory Case Study of Their Programs, Processes, and Early Results," *Small Business Institute* 8, no. 2 (2012): 54–70.

44. J. Maher, "4 Things Investors Secretly Look For in Your Cap Table," *Startup Grind*, 2016, accessed August 1, 2019, https://www.startupgrind.com/blog/4-things-investors-secretly-look-for-in-your-cap-table/.

45. Ibid.

46. A. Johansson, "5 Cap Table Management Issues Every Business Owner Faces," *Inc.*, May 1, 2017, accessed August 1, 2019, https://www.inc.com/anna-johansson/the-5-biggest-problems-with-cap-table-management.html.

47. W. Thompson, "Why Your Accelerator Rejected You," 500 Startups, July 15, 2016, accessed August 1, 2019, https://500.co/why-accelerator-rejection/.

48. S. Ford and D. Probert, "Trial by Market: The Brightstar Incubation Experiment," *International Journal of Entrepreneurial Venturing* 2, no. 2 (2010), doi:10.1504/IJEV.2010.034821.

49. E. Yin, "How Do Seed Investors Benchmark Startups?," October 16, 2016, accessed August 1, 2019, https://elizabethyin.com/2016/10/16/how-do-seed-investors-benchmark-startups/.

50. Adapted from StartupBootcamp, Startup System Analysis, 2016, accessed August 1, 2019, https://relayto.com/startupbootcamp/startup-ecosystem-analysis-smxqytkt.

51. In Chapter 1, we included a case study of what happened with LDK during the H-Farm accelerator they participated in. We have included below the steps leading up to the startups acceptance into that program.

CHAPTER

5

How to Handle the Accelerator Interview

*Confronted with a tough question or interviewer, many peo-
ple become visibly stressed, nervous, verbose, even angry or
hostile—their postures change, their voices speed up, and they over-
talk and under-listen.*

Andrea Barrica, YC alumnus; co-founder, inDinero;
past venture partner, 500 Startups

What Is an Accelerator Interview and Why Is It Important?

As we have discussed in previous chapters, out of the many applications they receive, accelerators want to select those with the
best product/idea, the most compelling progress towards finding
product/market fit with a great market, and those with the best
teams. The challenge for accelerators is determining the extent
to which each of these criteria is true for each startup. This challenge is more pronounced given the limited time accelerators have
to get through applications—especially those accelerators receiving hundreds or thousands of applications. Given this, each stage
of an accelerator application is essentially an opportunity to collect, validate, triangulate, and tease out information from a range
of perspectives, so as to arrive at the most accurate assessment of
each applicant. Thus, the purpose of an accelerator interview is to
provide accelerators with an opportunity to dig deeper, and better
understand startups and founders who made it through review of
the written/electronic applications. An accelerator interview is not
a job interview or an investor interview. Although it may share some
common success factors with job interviews and investor pitches, it

169

requires preparation that is unique to it. And different accelerators approach the accelerator interview differently. For example, Y Combinator has done short 10-minute interviews focused on the founders and their ideas.[1] Whereas 500 Startups has done more in-depth 20- to 30-minute discussions focused on people and growth.[2] Irrespective of the interview approach taken and the particular focus of the accelerator, succeeding in the accelerator interview is usually crucial to making it into the accelerator. And, depending on the accelerator, making it into the accelerator is usually crucial to accelerating access to funding, accelerating startup evolution, and ultimate exit value for founders.

The Interview Process and Interview Questions

The accelerator interview stage is usually made up of two or more interviews. The first interview is often a virtual interview done over video conferencing software such as Skype, Google Hangouts, Zoom, or FaceTime (on Apple Devices). This interview is usually followed by a face-to-face interview at the accelerator premises. Accelerators may then hold a third or fourth interview, if they are still not certain or still have questions to clarify for a particular startup. In addition to these interviews, some accelerators will also include an on-site trial or workshop to assess the ability of the founding team to work effectively with accelerator staff. For example, we noted in Chapter 4, that 500 Startups has a two-day on-site workshop composed of host talks, founding team exercises, informal meetings, and pitch preparation sessions that culminate in the delivery of a final pitch.[3] 500 Startups has used this workshop participation to further evaluate the founding team's coachability, ability to respond to feedback, and commitment to improvement. Along with interview information, 500 Startups has used the workshop participation evaluations, which are incorporated into the final decision, to accept or not accept a startup into the accelerator.

The Virtual Interview

Prior to a face-to-face interview, or in place of a face-to-face interview, you may have to do a virtual interview. For many accelerators, virtual interviews fall into two categories. They are either a screening vehicle for the face-to-face interview or a replacement for the face-to-face interview, especially for remote startups. Where a virtual interview is used to shortlist accelerator applicants for the face-to-face interview, it will usually be much shorter (e.g., between 10 and 20 minutes). Often it may be conducted by accelerator operational staff who ask two to five questions to determine if the founders are real, what their story is, their level of commitment/maturity, and their startup's stage of evolution or development. Interviewers may also ask indirect questions checking for the presence of any red flags (e.g., see example of turnoffs identified in Chapter 3). For some accelerators you may have two short virtual interviews (e.g., each with a different team or each having a different focus). Either way, at the end, the interviewer(s) will usually make an on-the-spot decision and let you know whether you are advancing to the next interview stage—although sometimes this decision may come a short period after the interview (e.g., between a few days and up to a week or two after the virtual interview). The first virtual interview could go longer and be held by a more senior and final decision maker (e.g., a partner or program manager). Whether this happens or not usually depends on how your startup came to submit the accelerator application. For example, if you were targeted and invited by the accelerator to submit an application, you may be deemed to have already passed the first stages of screening. Not all startups do a virtual interview (e.g., if founders live locally, then a short face-to-face interview can replace the virtual interview). Founders living locally may still be offered a virtual interview, but those who choose a virtual interview may signal a lesser level of commitment to those who choose a face-to face interview. For startups doing a virtual interview, a few weeks after you submit the online application or after the accelerator application deadline, you may receive an email advising you that you have made it to the first interview stage. This email will usually provide you with the interview details (e.g., what video conference software platform to use, what the ground rules are, how many interviewees will be there, the format of the interviews, etc.). Commonly, the email will also provide an overview of the remaining stages of the selection process, when you are likely to receive funds if you are successful, what the key dates are in relation to finalizing acceptance, and where to find answers to frequently asked questions.

On the day of the interview, you may have to use a pre-forwarded link to log into the meeting software platform, or you may be called via Skype/FaceTime, or you may be provided with a number to call. Make sure that your whole team is there, that you prepare for any technical difficulties/surprises that may occur (e.g., weak internet connection, misplaced login details, team members being late to the call, etc.). If these challenges arise on your end, this can reflect negatively on your team (e.g., if you can't prepare properly for an accelerator interview, how are you going to prepare for meetings with potential investors, potential clients, etc.). Once you log into the meeting software platform and connect with the interviewer(s), don't be surprised if they skip pleasantries and jump straight into the questions. Also, don't be surprised if they interrupt you or cut you off part way through your responses. And don't be surprised if they are so direct, it seems as though they are attacking you. For example, you may be confronted for avoiding questions, or not answering the questions directly, making you feel like you are back in high school at the principal's office. Skipping pleasantries and being direct may actually be good for your startup, as pleasantries may rob your startup of the opportunity to be asked important questions on the interviewers' minds. In what will likely seem like no time, the virtual interview will come to an end. Interviewers will let you know, either in the meeting or via email afterwards, whether you are advancing to the next stage or not. They may also provide you with some feedback.

The Face-to-Face Interview

If you pass the virtual interview, you will receive an invitation to the face-to-face interview. This invitation will identify the time and location of your interview, as well as what to do once you arrive. On arrival, you may find you are one of many teams that are there for the interview. If it is not obvious, you may need to find out the specific room for your interview. You may also benefit from working out who is on your interview panel, if this was not specified in the original interview invitation. Since you may be asked to demo your product/idea, you need to have a way to demo it and be sure that it will actually work when the time comes. The earlier you arrive, the more time you will have to find all the information you need, do some research on the people in your interview panel, and get comfortable in the interview or presentation setting.[4] Some accelerators even provide the opportunity for some mock interviews prior to the real thing for those who arrive early. You may suddenly find the nerves growing in the presence of other teams, which may seem better prepared and more of a sure bet than your team.[5] Some teams are very competitive and may attempt to undermine your confidence or give you misleading information. Once you are called into the interview, interviewers may skip pleasantries and jump straight into questions (similar to the virtual interview), or they may engage in some pleasantries and give you an opportunity to get into your elevator pitch and demo. You could be asked up to 80 questions within a very short period, in rapid-fire style, with the expectation that you will answer each question directly and succinctly in less than 15 seconds. Although you might have prepared for every question, you will likely be asked questions you never expected. Midway through your responses, interviewers may interrupt your or cut you off and move on to another question (similar to the virtual interview). There may be questions that seem to dig and dig and dig into a particular issue, as well as others that ask only a single question about an issue. Some accelerators may organize for you to be interviewed by different groups of interviewers, and others may have all the interviewers in the one interview. Some accelerators may split your team up and interview each team member separately in parallel. Although it may seem like your interview is going for an eternity, your interview will be over in around five to fifteen minutes. After the interview, you will find out if you will be making it to the next stage or if that was the end of your application journey for that particular program. Although we have called it typical, in reality, how interview day occurs can vary significantly from accelerator to accelerator. Differences can be driven by location and physical space constraints, the volume of applicants reviewed, the number of reviewers involved, the number of international teams the accelerator is targeting, the focus of the accelerator interview, and many other issues.

Accelerator Interview Questions

Accelerator interview questions will vary from one accelerator to the next. This is as it should be, since accelerators have different focus and different acceptance criteria. Also, accelerators have different ideas about when a startup is deemed to meet each acceptance criterion. Nevertheless, in Table 5.1, we provide some examples of the types of questions that can be asked. We have grouped these into the common accelerator application acceptance criteria sections or elements. Ultimately, as we have previously noted, accelerators are attempting to understand and validate the extent to which your startup meets these criteria. The interview, similar to the accelerator application questionnaire, is a vehicle for collecting additional information or validating previously collected information about your startup. Some interview questions may be a repeat

TABLE 5.1 Example Accelerator Interview Questions

Section or Common Element	Example Questions
The product/idea	1. What does your company do? 2. So, what are you working on? 3. What makes new users try you? 4. Where is the rocket science here? 5. Are you open to changing your idea?
The founders	1. Will you reincorporate as a U.S. company? 2. What's an impressive thing you have done? 3. Who is "the boss"? 4. Six months from now, what's going to be your biggest problem? 5. What domain expertise do you have? 6. How do we know your team will stick together? 7. Why do all the founders have equal equity?
Traction or product/market fit	1. Why do the reluctant users hold back? 2. Where do new users come from? 3. What are the top things users want? How do you know? 4. How are you understanding customer needs? 5. How do you know people want this? 6. What do they use to solve that problem right now? No, what do they really use to solve that problem right now? 7. Why are these users good users to try to solve problems for? 8. What other kinds of users could you go after once you get all these users using your software?
Progress/execution	1. Have you raised funding? 2. What's the worst thing that has happened? 3. What is your burn rate? 4. What's the biggest mistake you have made?
Other	1. What do you understand that others don't? 2. How much does customer acquisition cost? 3. What do you plan to do if you don't get accepted? 4. Why did you choose this accelerator program?

of the written accelerator application questions (interviewers may be validating what you have already said in the application), and some may be new (these may be seeking new information that can only be gathered via the interview medium). The list of questions we have provided is not an exhaustive list. That is, it simply provides an example of the types of questions you can get. You may be able to find more online or by contacting accelerator alumni to discuss what additional or unexpected questions they faced. However, this does not mean you will not still face some unexpected questions in your interview. As accelerators and accelerator programs evolve, so too do acceptance criteria, and thus application questionnaires and interview questions.

What Can Go Wrong in the Accelerator Interview

Serial startup founder Andrea Barrica, a former 500 Startups venture partner and Y Combinator alumnus, advises startups to undertake solid preparation for the accelerator interview. She points out that founders can underestimate the interview and then, faced with tough interviewers or tough interview questions, they can engage in self-defeating behaviors driven by nerves (e.g., overtaking, lying, not really listening, becoming defensive, or getting hostile, etc.). Drawing on her experiences and the reflections of a range of AngelPad, 500 Startups, and Y Combinator alumni, she identifies several things that commonly go wrong in accelerator interviews.[6] These range from founders not understanding the questions being asked (therefore providing irrelevant answers), founders talking too much (e.g., going off on a tangent, overexplaining things, or relentlessly overselling), founders saying one thing but their body language saying another (e.g., defensive posture, attack-style answers, being too clinical in answering), founders getting defensive/providing defensive answers, founders not telling any stories or telling the wrong stories, founders having deflating or negative energy, and the founding team having a strange team dynamic (e.g., disagreeing with each other, interrupting each other, signaling power struggles, having founders there who don't say anything). These types of behaviors create uncertainty in the minds of interviewers. For example, it can signal turnoffs such as lack of preparation (and thus lack of seriousness/commitment). Or it can signal more troublesome issues beneath the surface (e.g., immaturity, not being honest, lacking sufficient confidence, being overconfident, not being authentic, etc.). Since there is a validation element to the interview (similar to a job interview), too much incongruence between what you write in the accelerator application and what you say in the interview can also be detrimental (e.g., you make out in the accelerator application that customers love your product and it is about to explode in the market, but in the interview your present contradicting traction data and unconvincing customer discovery data).

Common Tips and Traps

In addition to Andrea Barrica's advice, a range of accelerator program managers and accelerator alumni offer advice on common tips and traps of accelerator interviews. We briefly summarize some of the standout advice below.

Do Your Research

Gabriela Matic, Techstars alumnus and program director of the UK-based Ignite Accelerator, advises that founders should do their research prior to the accelerator interview. As a part of this research, they should know what types of startups the accelerator looks for, how it works, and what is unique about it. She notes that while interviewers are aware that founders may have several applications out there at once, they still need to be clear about why they are wanting to get into interviewers' particular accelerator over others.[7,8] We noted in Chapters 3 and 4 that some accelerators' values may be an implicit part of their acceptance criteria. For example, founders who signal in an interview that their values contradict Y Combinator's founders' ethics[9] too much may reduce their attractiveness significantly, in spite of meeting most of the other accelerator acceptance criteria. The StartupYard Accelerator staff had this to say:[10]

> Research us . . . Understanding what we know, what our experience is, and what kinds of teams we have accelerated in the past will give you a natural advantage when talking to us about your future at StartupYard.

Overprepare

Several accelerator alumni advise prospective interviewees to prepare to the point of overdoing it[11]—even though this can be difficult, given everything else a startup demands of founders. Atrium CEO, Twitch co-founder and former Y Combinator partner Justin Kan[12] had three suggestions on how founders should prepare. He suggests that first founders should find people who have done the interview and talk to them about the experience, ask what questions they were asked, and ask them to do mock interviews. Alumni may be more honest than alternate avenues of acquiring this information. Second, founders should think through answers to common questions, write those answers down, and rehearse their responses. This way, they won't have to think or make up responses on the fly. And they won't have to worry about saying the wrong thing. Third, they should practice their interview under extreme or stressful circumstances, as these are the circumstances they may face in the real interview. Other alumni have added other preparation activities such as ensuring founders understand common accelerator terminology (e.g., traction, customer discovery, sales funnels, etc.). For example, Kwindla Kramer, Daily.co co-founder and Y Combinator alumni, had this to say[13]:

> . . . one last piece of advice. Know the definitions of basic accounting terms that are relevant to your startup: revenue, recurring revenue, gross merchandise volume, contract, LOI, margin, and profit."

Finally, Y Combinator partner Michael Seibel advises that there are plenty of websites with sample interview questions; so, founders should seek these out and practice.[14]

Plan the Interview

Earlier in this chapter, we outlined all the things that can go wrong in the interview and, in particular, the risks of signaling strange team dynamics that are a turnoff for many accelerators. Given these risks, founders ought to plan how they will approach and answer accelerator interview questions to contain things that commonly go wrong, and to ensure that they do not signal strange team dynamics. For example, they can consider who will answer what questions and how, who will memorize what metrics and other data (e.g., who will answer product-related questions, who will answer related questions, who will answer traction questions, who will answer questions about the startup's metrics, what key metrics they will cite, what should happen if one founder starts answering a question that another founder is better equipped to answer, what happens if someone freezes up during the interview, who will demo the product if needed and how, what the team will do if things start to go wrong, how the team will convey a pleasing personality, how the team will be energizing, etc.). Founders can also plan what stories to tell, the best way to tell these stories, what critical points to emphasize about their product/market, how to deal with red flags during the interview, how they will ensure they come across as a cohesive/well-functioning team, and how they plan to avoid signaling the common accelerator turnoffs we outlined in Chapter 3. Founders should also understand and plan how they will deal with their interview jitters (e.g., nervous tics, talking too fast, swaying from side to side, becoming a deer in headlights, etc.).[15] But founders shouldn't get so fixed on their plan that they become inflexible in the face of unanticipated questions or unexpected interviewer approaches to the interview. Also, they should ensure that they remain authentic rather than coming across as formulaic or fake.

Start Off on the Right Footing

The first question about what your company does is the most impactful and yet most difficult to get right. This question is usually a *"what does your company do/for what market/what makes you so great"* question and, essentially, an invitation to give your elevator pitch in 20–30 seconds or less.[16,17] Andrew Norris, Taplytics co-founder and Y Combinator alumnus, warns:

> *Nail your elevator pitch. If I have to spend 10 minutes figuring out what you are doing—you're not getting in.*

Andrea Barrica suggests a response something like:[18]

> *We are Paid, Autopilot for Accounts Receivable. We help companies invoice their customers and get paid with 200% return on their ROI.*

Michael Seibel adds that when answering the first question, founders should avoid jargon—so much so that their mom or dad should be able to understand what their startup does from the answer to the first question. He also adds that when introducing themselves at the start, founders should make it clear which founder does business and which founder does tech.[19]

Smile, Be Energizing and Show Personality [20]

The StartupYard Seed Accelerator staff advise founders to make sure they smile during the interview.[21] Although it may seem cheesy, smiling can change the whole mood of the interview. And many accelerators are actually assessing not only your team's IQ, but also its emotional intelligence (EQ). Andrea Barrica notes that it can be deflating and downright unenjoyable to interview companies who don't bring any "aliveness, energy or personality."[22] The need for aliveness, energy, and personality can be amplified more if your startup is interviewed after one that sets the bar very high in that area. To better understand the significance of accelerators' interest in your team's EQ, consider what a lack of aliveness, energy, or personality says about your team's ability to attract and retain star employees as well as key customers and partners. Another way to look at it is to imagine that you are evenly matched with another startup competing for the same spot in the accelerator, but their team shows more aliveness, energy, and personality in their interview. Which team is likely to be more memorable and therefore have the edge? Andrea had this to add:[23]

> *Pump yourself up with music, go to a morning rave, read the journal entries from the day you quit your job to become an entrepreneur—do whatever it takes to bring your most authentic, alive self to your interview. Your only job in an interview is to make someone in that room excited about you and your company.*

Tell a Story/Know the Power of Story

When talking about your product/market, team, or customers in the interview, stories can be potently powerful for you to be understood, empathized with, and be remembered.[24] Andrea Barrica suggests finding and telling interesting and memorable stories about each of these areas.[25] For example, you can come up with a story explaining what makes your product so great for its market, a story indicating why you are such a great team, and a great customer or user story (e.g., that shows the great pain they were experiencing and how their life is so much better because of your product). Being able to tell a great story, and to tell it succinctly, will not only be invaluable in the interview but also with customers, investors, strategic partners, and the media. Andrea Barrica had this to say about the team story:

> *I always ask "How did you all meet?" Most investors want to bet on strong co-founder relationships that can withstand the tough times. A few of the teams we interviewed laughed, looked at each other, waited for the other to speak, started talking at once, then sentimentally reported the "story of how they met." I call this the "newlywed effect," and it's something that I appreciate very much.*

Be Concise

Founders should ensure that they are able to answer all questions in 15 to 20 seconds. Andrea Barrica advises that this means answering each question as briefly as possible and avoiding going off on a tangent at all times.[26] This can be difficult to do if founders are making up each answer on the spot. Thus, preparation is essential to being able to be concise. As we have noted earlier, such preparation can involve finding the different types of accelerator interview questions, writing responses that succinctly answer the questions, and rehearsing the delivery of these responses to the point where the responses are clear, concise, and impactful. Fortunately, there is an app for that. That is, there are websites and apps that simulate the accelerator interview with countdown times for each type of question (e.g., see https://jamescun.github.io/iPG/).

Be Authentic[27]

Accelerators want to understand and be comfortable with the founders they are betting on, and who they are going to spend a lot of time with, under challenging conditions. This is difficult if the founders are pretending to be who they are not. They may do this through the use of buzzwords, being too pitchy or scripted, putting up an opaque exterior or poker face, or attempting to be too formal. If founders are afraid to show who they really are, accelerators may worry just how bad their real selves may be. But surely there are aspects of their authentic selves that may help founders get into an accelerator and aspects that may prevent them from getting in—should founders show aspects of their authentic selves that will compromise their odds of acceptance into the accelerator? In relation to this question, Andrea suggests that founders bring their best selves to the interview.[28]

Be Willing to Say You Don't Know

At some point in one of the interviews, founders will most likely find themselves confronted with a question they don't understand or don't know the answer to. Founders shouldn't be afraid to admit that they don't know, but perhaps explain some ways they might go about finding out the answer (e.g., seeking the advice of accelerator mentors or accelerator alumni, creating experiments, or undertaking online research, etc.).[29] Admitting you don't know can demonstrate intellectual honesty, humility, and courage. And identifying ways you can seek help to find out can signal your coachability. In fact, some interviewers may deliberately ask questions that founders have no way of knowing the answers to, so they can gauge how founders approach such challenges.[30]

Don't Get Defensive

Justin Kan, a former Y Combinator partner, as well as Atrium and Twitch founder, advises founders to keep in mind that they are being interviewed by people who have likely evaluated and interviewed thousands of startups. As a result, they are most likely hypersensitive to founders getting defensive about a question and will interpret it as an inability to process constructive criticism—and thus not being ready for the accelerator.[31] Based on his advice, founders should consider what might trigger them in the interview and plan how they will deal with it, so they don't come across as defensive. Justin suggests that instead of being defensive about a question, founders want to show that they have considered the question and that they will do the homework to better answer it.[32] But defensiveness is not only visible through what you say; it can also be visible through your body language (e.g., crossed arms, facial expressions, etc.).

In relation to this, Andrea warns:[33]

> *Be aware of the story you are telling with your body, not just your words.*

Know Your Data and Metrics

Come prepared with traction data, results of customer discovery experiments, and market data. We noted earlier that traction often trumps all as the single best evidence that your startup has found or is on the verge of finding product/market fit. But your choice of data and metrics needs to be relevant. Interviewers will want to dig into what data/metrics you have, why you selected that data and those particular metrics, and how the data and metrics have changed or grown over time. Your team may choose to split up memorization, provision, and discussion of these metrics to maximize how intimately you know and succinctly explain each one. Kwindla Kramer, a Y Combinator alumnus, proposes that traction is its own story that can trump everything else that happens in the interview:

> *If you're applying to YC with, say, $150k/month of recurring revenue and revenue is growing 30% each month, your interview is probably going to go pretty well.*

Know Your Direct and Indirect Competition

Through experience reviewing thousands of accelerator applications and having a diverse portfolio of startup alumni, interviewers will likely know your direct and indirect competitors better than you. But they want to know how well you understand your competition, and whether you have clear and credible "secret sauce" or differentiation. Andrea Barrica advises that you should avoid describing your company's advantage in terms of features and incremental differences—that startups need to demonstrate that they are much more than marginally better.[34] Upcounsel co-founder Mason Blake puts it this way:

> *Being marginally better than your competitors is not enough—you really need to have a key differentiator, a reason to switch, something you do MUCH better.*

Be Prepared to Discuss Your Weaknesses

For all the great things they have going for them, most startups will have one or more weaknesses, accelerator turnoffs, or red flags (e.g., solo founder, prohibitive location, prohibitive cap table, glaring poor past decisions, a founder with a criminal record, etc.). Some founders will pretend these don't exist or attempt to cover them up. Others will become deer in headlights when these come up in interviews. Michael Seibel advises founders to expect questions digging into their red flags and, rather than dwelling on the negatives, should be ready with clear and concise answers about their implications and what the startup is prepared to do about them.[35] For example, in Chapter 5 we outlined how 500 Startups alumna Samantha Strom dealt with her uncommitted-founder red flag.[36] In her case and with her particular red flag, she took action immediately after the interview ended and retrospectively contacted interviewers to update them of her action.

Know Your Big Three and Make Sure They Are Understood and Remembered

A lot of ground may need to be covered during the interview. And different people on the interview panel may have different motivations and agendas for the interview. Some may even try to dominate and intimidate founders. As each interviewer pursues their own line of questioning, time can run out before you have had a chance to convey the magic in your startup. As a result, Andrea Barrica advises that,[37] along with delivering a great elevator pitch, startups should identify the top three things they want to convey and the three things they don't want to bring up. That way, they can look for opportunities to maneuver the interview to focus on their top three things (e.g., great traction, great team, great execution), and away from the three things they want to avoid (e.g., very early stage, no MVP, bad cap table, etc.). But she warns:

> *If you get derailed, you can maneuver back to your Top Three. We also suggest knowing the Top Three things that you DON'T want to bring up, but we also warn that these things might actually belong on your Top Three list.*

So, founders can have strong answers prepared and rehearsed for the things they don't want to bring up. Or, founders may choose to bring up such issues in the interview and deal with them, rather than let them get discovered and judged without founders having had a chance to address them.

Be Congruent

We noted earlier that each stage of an accelerator application is essentially an opportunity to collect, validate, triangulate, and tease out information from a range of perspectives, so as to arrive at the most accurate assessment of each applicant. And that where information gathered from different sources is in conflict, more risk may be attributed to your application (e.g., risk that you are lying, risk that you don't understand your business, or risk that the accelerator misunderstands your business). Thus, it is important that what you say in the interview is not at odds with what is in your original electronic application—unless you have executed so well since your application, that your startup is an advanced state relative to the state it was in at the time of the application. Nevertheless, make sure you know what you said in the application well, and can explain why what you are saying now differs from what you said in the application. Andrea Barrica had this to say about the importance of being congruent:[38]

> *We'll be digging into your application. Remember to revisit the application you submitted before your phone screen, or better yet have it in front of you!*

Rehearse, Rehearse, Rehearse

We have outlined the short, fire gun, almost uncontrollable nature of accelerator interviews, as well as the wide ground and depth they often need to cover. Given this nature of accelerator interviews, founders need to anticipate the interview questions, prepare great responses to them, and rehearse, rehearse, and re-rehearse the effective delivery of their responses.[39] Such rehearsal will help founders eliminate technical jargon, marketing speak, ambiguous terms, opaque acronyms, and stress-driven behaviors.[40] In doing so, it maximizes the succinctness and impact of founders' answer delivery. Succinct and impactful answers also enable interviewers to cover greater ground and to dig deeper, ensuring that they don't leave the interview with unanswered questions about the startup. Interviewers who leave with unanswered questions may make negative assumptions that significantly reduce a startup's chances of getting accepted. For example, if an accelerator does not get an opportunity to ask you about a red flag that is on their mind, they may assume the worst.

A number of accelerator alumni have spoken about approaches to interview preparation that have prepared them well for the accelerator interview. For example, Kwindla Kramer, Daily.co co-founder and Y Combinator alumna, discusses[41] how his team searched for and prepared a list of about 100 common accelerator interview questions. They then wrote down the answer to each question. After this, they rewrote and refined each answer over and over until it was only a few sentences in length and said something impactful about their key strengths (strong team, great market size, and great execution). At that stage, they were pre-launch, with no traction—a likely red flag. They wrote the final agreed answer to each question on flash cards, and then practiced, practiced, and practiced again, until each question could be answered conversationally yet succinctly and with maximum impact—irrespective of the combination of questions used. They had a hardware demo and practiced giving their demo over and over to different people until they could give it on demand, while distracted, with different types of users/different devices/different prototype interactions/different obstacles and while answering different questions. Eventually, they were more than satisfied that they could deliver an impactful demo irrespective of the challenge that came up. They went into their interview relaxed, knowing they had done everything they could for their interview to go well. Justin Kan suggests that founders practice answering their interview questions under extreme circumstances that mimic the intensity of being grilled by interviewers. He reasons that by being prepared for the worst, founders should find the interview is a breeze. He had this to say about such preparation[42]:

> *A friend of mine whose wife recently got accepted into YC shared a hilarious but clever tip: practice under manufactured duress. He told me that he would literally throw socks at her, dance in the background, or yell at her while she was reviewing answers—anything to try and throw off her focus.*

Plan for the Unexpected[43]

Don't expect the interview to go according to plan. As we have previously discussed, the questions are often rapid fire, so that controlling the direction of the interview is often a challenge, and interviewers are likely to interrupt your scripted answers.[44] All this can throw you off balance and make sticking to your plan a real challenge. Tak Lo, partner at the Hong Kong office of the Zeroth.ai accelerator, advises interview applicants to not be surprised if some accelerator interviewers do one or more wild things to throw interviewees off balance[45] (e.g., starting interviews 15 minutes earlier or later than planned, making the interview schedule deliberately confusing/unpredictable, making sure something goes wrong during the interview, deliberately making positive but incorrect assumptions about a startup to see if founders correct them, asking founders to solve specific problems on the spot, continuously shifting the format or location of the interview, asking the same questions over and over, doing a good cop/bad cop routine, asking questions and then starting to type very loudly, etc.).[46]

Case Study 4: Listen Notes' Y Combinator Interview[*47] (USA)

I had put in several applications to Y Combinator (YC) while still working but had been rejected. I think I had put in seven applications in total. I don't know why I continued to apply after so many rejections. I guess I'm naturally a very optimistic person. Anyhow, in late November I thought I would try again. Unbeknownst to me, the application deadline had already passed. I thought maybe I could put in a late application—but I was surprised to discover that YC is biased against late applications. I decided to fill in and submit the application form anyway, what was the worst that could happen? I was shocked when, within a few days of submitting my application, I received an invitation to an YC interview at YC headquarters in Mountain View, California. I almost couldn't contain my excitement. The day before the interview, I received an email from YC which had the following paragraph:

> The partners may interrupt you, be abrupt, ask multiple questions at once, or ask questions you've already answered in your application. Please don't think that they're being purposefully rude. They're trying to maximize the short amount of time they have with you to make a big, life-changing decision (for all of us).

*Listen Notes' founder reflects on his Y Combinator Interview.

I braced myself. My wife drove me on interview day, and we arrived at YC headquarters nearly three hours early. We got some photos taken of us in front of the YC sign outside of the building. Then I went to the front desk, typed in my username, and got an YC sticker with my name, my startup name, my interview batch, and my interview day. From talking to other people there, I heard that about 9,000 startups had applied, 500 were invited to interviews that occurred over eight days and, out of these 500, up to 150 would be accepted. On my interview day, the interviews were organized into three tracks. Each track was allocated its own interview room and three to four interviewers. Each startup team had 10 minutes to answer questions from the interviewers.

Once I worked out my track and where my interview was, I realized I had a lot of time to kill before my interview. But I was not the only one who arrived that early. Most of the other founders were in the common area reading their phone or tablet screens, talking among themselves, and practicing interview questions. Some of the founders there were clearly nervous. And others looked more relaxed. I went to strike up conversation with the founders who looked relaxed and not busy. I was surprised to find that most of them had been working on their ideas for between one and two years. The startups were at different stages and had different things going for them. Some had great revenue, some had big teams, some had great hardware prototypes (e.g., Virtual Reality and IoT hardware), and some had amazing founders. Clearly YC was going to take each of them over my startup. I suddenly started to feel doubt creeping in. My prototype was nowhere near as good as theirs, I wasn't as qualified, I hadn't been working on my startup as long . . . I tried telling myself to stop thinking like this—this wasn't going to help me in the interview. But I couldn't stop. I shouldn't have spoken to the other teams.

Finally, I was saved from my ruminations when someone called for me, and summoned me to follow them to the room for my startup's track. I picked up my laptop and lots of printouts I had brought along with graphs of web traffic, podcast growth, etc. As I entered, I felt like I was entering the Jedi Council. There were four YC interviewers seated in a row on the same side of a long table. I was surprised to recognize two of them as YC partners, whose published online content I followed. Once in the room, I greeted and shook each of their hands and then sat down. I noticed a 10-minute countdown clock on the table. Three of the interviewers got straight into it and started bombarding me with question after question. Luckily I had advance notice of what the interview would be like and how direct they might be. Although the interview was only 10 minutes, you would be surprised how many questions

(Continued)

can be asked during that time. Some of the questions I was asked included: What are you building? Who will use your product? Why do people want to use your product? How big is the podcast industry? What's your roadmap? How do you make money? How much money will you make per year? How many searches do you get per day? And many more I can't remember now. The interview was nearly up and I had still not been asked to do my demo. But I felt happy with how I was actually doing. I remained calm and was controlling the pace of my answers. With 30 seconds still on the clock, the interviewers stopped asking questions and ended my interview. This wasn't good. In my gut I knew it meant they had already lost interest in me and my startup. They thanked me for my application, and I walked out of the interview certain I was a 100% rejection. I didn't want to leave in case I made it to the next interview. So, I hung around the common area for another 45 minutes or so until an assistant walked over and advised me there wouldn't be any more interviews for me. I walked out of the YC building to meet my wife, and we decided to go for dinner in Cupertino.

While at dinner, I received the following email:

"Hi ****

Unfortunately, we've decided not to fund Listen Notes. You're a smart, technical founder, and your traffic—40k monthly uniques—is impressive, especially for how long you've been working on this. It sounds like you're expecting podcasts to grow into what websites are today, but we'd like to hear how that happens. How can podcasts generate the same/ more revenue? Also—this is an extremely crowded space. We left the interview not fully understanding how you win it. The insight to use meta tags for search doesn't seem like a lasting competitive advantage that would allow you to build a huge standalone company. Best of luck as you build the business.

I wasn't upset. It was good enough validation that I had received an interview invitation. After seeing the other startups, I could see why I hadn't been accepted. I was a solo founder, whereas most of them had strong teams. Many founders there had Ivy League educations whereas I did not. Most founders had been working on their startups much longer than me and were much more advanced. Their startups had a lot of other advantages over mine.

Notes

1. A. Barrica, "7 Lessons from 500, YC, Angelpad Alum—How to Prepare for Any Accelerator Interview," 500 Startups, July 2, 2015, accessed August 1, 2019, https://500.co/7-lessons-from-500-yc-angelpad-alum%E2%80%8A-%E2%80%8Ahow-to-prepare-for-any-accelerator-interview/.
2. Ibid.
3. P. Vijayashanker, "Startup Accelerator Interview: How to Ace Your Interview with 500 Startups," 500 Startups, March 4, 2019, accessed August 1, 2019, https://500.co/startup-accelerator-interview/.
4. R. Sherman, "10 Presentation Skills Top Executives Live By," *Business Credit* (June 2002): 46–47.
5. C. Anderson, "How to Give a Killer Presentation," *Harvard Business Review* (June 2013): 121–125.
6. J. Stillman, "3 Ways to Screw Up Your Accelerator Interview," *Inc.*, July 8, 2015, accessed August 1, 2019, https://www.inc.com/jessica-stillman/3-ways-to-screw-up-your-accelerator-interview.html.
7. G. Matic, "What We Are Thinking during Your Accelerator Interview," *Ignite*, June 8, 2017, accessed August 1, 2019, https://blog.ignite.io/what-we-are-thinking-during-your-accelerator-interview-57a0f408a235.
8. "Interviewing with an Accelerator: A Few Do's and Don'ts," *StartupYard*, 2017, accessed August 1, 2019, https://startupyard.com/interviewing-with-an-accelerator-a-few-dos-and-donts/.
9. Y Combinator, "Founder Ethics," accessed August 1, 2019, https://www.ycombinator.com/ethics/.
10. "Interviewing With an Accelerator."
11. Ibid.
12. J. Kan, "YC Interview: Founder's Guide to Acing Your Y Combinator Interview," *Atrium*, October, 29, 2018, accessed August 1, 2019, https://www.atrium.co/blog/yc-interview-guide/.
13. K. Kramer, "Y Combinator Interview Advice + Live Practice Sessions," accessed August 1, 2019, https://hackernoon.com/y-combinator-interview-advice-live-practice-sessions-87886a3cbf8a.
14. M. Seibel, "My Top Ten Pieces of Advice for Preparing for a YC Interview," October 31, 2015, accessed August 1, 2019, https://twitter.com/mwseibel/status/660557656927563776.

15. Barrica, "7 Lessons from 500, YC, Angelpad Alum."

16. Ibid.

17. Seibel, "My Top Ten Pieces of Advice."

18. Barrica, "7 Lessons from 500, YC, Angelpad Alum."

19. Seibel, "My Top Ten Pieces of Advice."

20. "Interviewing With an Accelerator: A Few Do's and Don'ts."

21. Ibid.

22. Barrica, "7 Lessons from 500, YC, Angelpad Alum."

23. Ibid.

24. E. O'Connor, "Storytelling to Be Real: Narrative, Legitimacy Building and Venturing," in *Narrative and Discursive Approaches in Entrepreneurship: A Second Movements in Entrepreneurship* , edited by D. Hjorth and C. Steyaert (University of Illinois at Urbana–Champaign's Academy for Entrepreneurial Leadership Historical Research Reference in Entrepreneurship, 2004), available at SSRN: https://ssrn.com/abstract=1497283

25. Barrica, "7 Lessons from 500, YC, Angelpad Alum."

26. Ibid.

27. J. Livingston, "Tips for YC Interviews," *YC News,* November 15, 2015, accessed August 1, 2019, https://blog.ycombinator.com/tips-for-yc-interviews/.

28. Barrica, "7 Lessons from 500, YC, Angelpad Alum."

29. "Interviewing With an Accelerator: A Few Do's and Don'ts."

30. Ibid.

31. Kan, "YC Interview: Founder's Guide."

32. Ibid.

33. Barrica, "7 Lessons from 500, YC, Angelpad Alum."

34. Ibid.

35. M. Seibel, "How to Pitch Your Company," July 19, 2016, accessed August 1, 2019, http://www.michaelseibel.com/blog/how-to-pitch-your-company.

36. J. Erickson, "500 Startups Announces Batch 13 in Mountain View," 500 Startups, April 27, 2015, accessed August 1, 2019, https://500.co/mountain-view-batch-13/.

37. Barrica, "7 Lessons from 500, YC, Angelpad Alum."

38. Ibid.

39. C. Anderson, "How to Give a Killer Presentation," *Harvard Business Review* (June 2013): 121–125.

40. Seibel, "How to Pitch Your Company."

41. K. Kramer, "Y Combinator Interview Advice + Live Practice Sessions," 2016, accessed August 1, 2019, https://hackernoon.com/y-combinator-interview-advice-live-practice-sessions-87886a3cbf8a.
42. Kan, "YC Interview: Founder's Guide."
43. Livingston, "Tips for YC Interviews."
44. Seibel, "My Top Ten Pieces of Advice."
45. T. Lo, "What You Should Get Out of Your Accelerator Interview," LinkedIn, April 12, 2016, accessed August 1, 2019, https://www.linkedin.com/pulse/what-you-should-get-out-your-accelerator-interview-tak-lo/.
46. S. Cooper, "Here Are the Top Tech Companies' Secrets to Hiring the Best People," *Medium*, March 22, 2016, accessed August 1, 2019, https://medium.com/conquering-corporate-america/here-are-the-top-tech-companies-secrets-to-hiring-the-best-people-33f432c39db2#.l92dq60wk.
47. Adapted from W. Fang, "My Y Combinator Interview Experience (W18)," Broadcast, January 12, 2018, accessed August 1, 2019, https://Broadcast.Listennotes.com/my-y-combinator-interview-experience-w18-c12e6d98c1d0.

CHAPTER

6

Should You Give Up Equity to Get into an Accelerator?

A first-time founder team or set of early employees do not have years of experience seeing the ins and outs of board governance, or how subtle deal terms and decisions play out in terms of economics and power. The preferred (VCs, seed funds, accelerators), however, are usually repeat players. They know the game, and how to play it. This means that the set of core advisors that common stockholders hire to leverage their own experience and skill set in "leveling the playing field" is monumentally important.

José Ancer, partner in Startup and
Emerging Technology Group, Egan Nelson LLP

Equity as a Prerequisite to Getting into an Accelerator

Accelerators usually make a seed investment of between $10,000 and $250,000 in cohort companies participating in their programs.[1] For this seed investment, they typically take 3 to 10% equity (or ownership stake) in each cohort company. In particular accelerator locations or regions, the seed investment can be as high as $2.5 million for equity of 50% or more. This, of course, would require that startups have this type of valuation. In Chapter 3, we noted that the costs of operating an accelerator can range from $300,000 to several million—depending on the cohort size, quality of the accelerator companies, quality of the accelerator facilitators, quality of the accelerator network, quality of professional services offered, quality of the accelerator space, and more. Accelerators usually charge each cohort company a fee to cover some of these costs.[2,3] For example, at the time of publication of this book, 500 Startups charged a $37,500 fee to participate in its program[4]—although this came out of the $150,000 investment the accelerator made in each cohort companies.

Not all accelerators require equity in cohort companies. Some accelerators provide a stipend payment (e.g., $10,000) to all cohort companies but don't take equity. Others make cohort companies compete for a chance to receive a single stipend payment. Yet others provide no stipend and take no equity, but instead charge a fee for cohort companies to participate in the program. Where a particular accelerator fits largely depends on how the accelerator is funded and the objectives of the program. All accelerators incur program operating costs, and these costs can be funded privately, through strategic partnerships (e.g., with investors or corporate sponsors), through government grants (e.g., economic development grants), through philanthropic grants, or through other means.[5] The accelerator program's purpose also has an impact, since some programs are run for public contribution or other purposes. For example, Y Combinator's not-for-profit cohort companies are provided with a $100k donation.[6] Figure 6.1 provides some data on the proportion of for-profit versus not-for-profit accelerators.

Giving Up Equity to an Accelerator

The majority of accelerators requiring equity as a prerequisite for entry often invest money for that equity. For example, top-tier

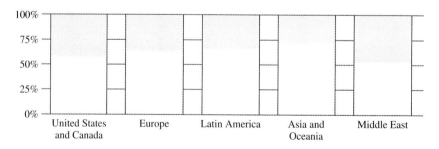

FIGURE 6.1 Proportion of Accelerators across Continents That Are for-Profit (White) versus Those That Are Not-for-Profit (Gray) (Not-for-Profit Accelerators Typically Do Not Take Equity)
Source: Adapted from Gust (2016).[7]*
*It was unclear in the study if Africa and the Middle East were bundled together or if there were no not-for-profit accelerators in Africa.

accelerators typically invest between $100,000 and $250,000 for approximately 7% equity. So, if a startup is seeking investors or investment in the first place, this question is really more about whether the accelerator is right for the startup as an investor and whether the investment amount is right for the startup—since the startup would typically have to give up equity for the investment. For example, an accelerator with a standard investment of $100,000 for 7% equity may place a $1.4 million valuation on all cohort companies participating in the accelerator. Some startups may see themselves as having higher valuations, but find that the accelerator investment amount and equity requirement are nonnegotiable. The issue, then, is whether the benefits of the particular accelerator outweigh the costs of a perceived lower valuation, although some founders have expressed concern that low accelerator valuations can negatively impact valuations that can be accepted by future investors, Startup-Yard staff have argued that accelerators are not typical investors. And therefore the equity they take does not define startup valuations. They point out that investors should know this or be told if they do not.[8] Some accelerators have devised agreements that avoid the need to price shares and put a valuation on the company at the time of entering the accelerator. For example, Y Combinator's Simple Agreement for Future Equity (SAFE) gives the accelerator, in return for the money it invests in cohort companies, rights to equity in the future, once specific (contractually agreed) fundraising or liquidation events occur (e.g., venture capital funding, acquisition, etc.).

If a startup is not seeking investment and is not willing to give up equity, there are zero equity accelerators. Zero equity accelerator programs aim to provide the same or similar benefits to accelerators without equity as a prerequisite for participation.[9] In place of equity, such programs may charge a participation fee or other form of compensation. But they may also charge nothing and expect nothing in return. Such programs provide founders with the option of having the accelerator experience without needing to give up equity.[10] However, for some startups, equity accelerators are still preferred since these startups may need the equity investment money provided by equity accelerators (e.g., such funds can pay for relocation costs, fund MVP development, fund finding of investable traction, or fund necessary legal costs such as intellectual property protection). Also, some of the better zero equity accelerators are exclusive to people in particular locations (e.g., countries or regions), or who are affiliated with particular institutions (e.g., universities), or who are serving particular constituents (e.g., people living below the poverty line). Usually, the particular institution providing funding to cover accelerator costs is seeking to use an accelerator program to serve those constituents or provide them with venture creation opportunities. So, depending on your location and institutional affiliation, zero equity accelerators may or may not be a genuine option for your startup. Finally, equity and zero equity accelerators typically have a different set of incentives and will go to different lengths to support their cohort companies. For example, equity accelerators may have a stronger incentive to ramp up hands-on support to help a startup with a challenging issue like navigating an acquisition process. But then they may be much more hands-off if they see minimal possibility of an exit event or a pay day. In contrast, zero equity accelerators may have a stable level of support service that does not change with the odds of an exit event occurring, but lack the ability to ramp up hands-on resources on an ad hoc basis (to facilitate an acquisition, for example).

Founders should carefully weigh the benefits offered by an accelerator against what they give up for those benefits (i.e., both equity costs and any related opportunity cost). Time spent going through an accelerator is an obvious opportunity cost (i.e., consider the other potential uses of that time and the benefits that might have come from that use of the time). There are also other opportunity costs besides time. For example, an accelerator taking a startup on the wrong path may cause that startup more harm than if it had not "helped" it in the first place. Or an accelerator that takes too much equity at too low a valuation may actually make the startup unattractive to particular investors for a certain timeframe. This timeframe may be enough for the startup to miss an opportunity window (e.g., if an accelerator invests at a valuation of $300,000, it may be difficult for an investor to be willing to invest at a valuation of $1 million only three months later—unless the investor can clearly see $700,000 worth of value during the three-month program. In contrast, the investor might have invested at a $1 million valuation if the initial investment at a lower valuation had not occurred (assuming the company had a justifiable valuation close to $1 million at the time the accelerator invested).

Giving Up Equity to Multiple Accelerators

We came across plenty of founders who had been through multiple accelerators, giving up equity each time (for example, we came across a founder who had taken the same startup through eight accelerators). We wondered how much of the company he still retained, since many of these accelerators had anti-dilution clauses. Having so many accelerators on his cap table might also turn off some investors (e.g., it may complicate funding negotiations, investors may wonder why the startup has not made it after so many programs and so much advice, or investors may think there isn't adequate equity left to appropriately incentivize the founder after subtracting investment equity and equity required to compensate future employees with stock options).

What Else Do Founders Give Up in Accelerator Term Sheets?

A term sheet sets out the basic terms and conditions pertaining to the equity being given up to the accelerator. The terms and conditions usually relate to issues such as what percentage of equity (or how many shares) is the accelerator buying, at what company valuation and therefore at what price per share the accelerator is getting these shares, what protective and control rights the investor gets with their equity, what the investor can do and not do when certain future events eventuate (e.g., future fundraising, company acquisition, insolvency, etc.). Typically, the term sheet sets out what is being agreed to in plain language, and it is later used as the basis for lawyers to draw up the binding legal agreement.[11,12,13,14,15,16] Although term sheets are not usually binding, often founders are bound to nondisclosure agreements (i.e., not to disclose term sheet discussions), and to exclusivity (not to enter into term sheets with other accelerators or investors at the same time). Depending on the nature of the rights given to accelerators, these rights are extra things founders give up in addition to the equity. We briefly outline the key types of rights commonly found in term sheets as well as other elements of accelerator term sheets. Our purpose in outlining and briefly explaining the different elements here is to touch on some potential issues and implications related to them so founders have a simple starting point from which to investigate further or seek out professional advice.

Key Elements of Accelerator Term Sheets

Term Sheets can differ from accelerator to accelerator. But in general, since all term sheets are attempting to achieve similar objectives, there are many common elements—even if the clauses within these elements may differ slightly.[17] The most common elements or sections of term sheets include types of securities, valuation, anti-dilution provisions, founder vesting, liquidation preference, voting rights, dividends, and veto rights or protective provisions.[18,19] It can be invaluable for founders intending to enter accelerators to understand these different elements, to understand what accelerators (and investors) are aiming to achieve through each term sheet element, and to understand the implications of accepting them. See Figure 6.2 for common elements of accelerator term sheets.

Types of Securities (or Types of Shares)

Type of equity (or type of stock) issued to accelerators can differ. For example, a startup may issue preferred equity or common equity.[20,21,22] In the event of liquidation (e.g., closing the company, bankruptcy, merger, acquisition), preferred stock holders have a priority payout over common stockholders.[23,24,25] Startup founders typically have common stock. Some accelerators will want preferred

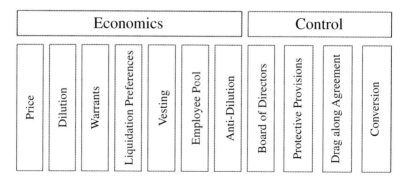

FIGURE 6.2 Common Elements of the Accelerator Term Sheet and Their Focus on Economics (Cost of Equity and Exit Value) or Control (Decision Making)
Source: Adapted from Feld (2011).[26]

stock (so that in the event of liquidation, they have priority payout), some will accept a mixture of preferred and common stock, and others will take common stock.[27]

Valuation

The valuation (or value) of a company determines the price at which equity is bought and, therefore, how much investment money is received for a particular percentage of equity being given up.[28,29,30,31,32,33,34] If accelerator investment amounts and percentage equity requirements are fixed, then these may set the default value of your company in the eyes of some investors (although some may not see the accelerator investment as a true investment, and may ignore the value at which the accelerator invested). Still, it is worth considering what valuation the accelerator investment places on your startup, and what the opportunity cost of this might be. Accelerators may want to include a clause in the term sheet that defers the valuation at which they purchase equity until a future event (e.g., formal fundraising round or acquisition), or they may want to pre-set any future investments they make at a particular valuation. Accelerators may refer to a pre-money valuation (the value of the company before they put in their money) or a post-money valuation (the value of a company after they put in their money). Some accelerators may want to include an option pool[35] (e.g., to be able to issue options to future employees) in the valuation. This can mean further dilution (beyond the dilution incurred to issue the accelerator its equity). Founders need to be aware of whether the valuation (and any included employee options percentage) is pre- or post-money and what the impact on founder's ownership percentage will be.

Anti-Dilution Provisions

Each time a company issues new shares, existing shareholders' ownership percentage of that company gets reduced.[36] For example, a shareholder with 10% of the company may find that, after the company issues new shares (e.g., to accelerators, investors, key employees etc.), their shareholding is suddenly reduced to 7%.

Accelerators may want to include anti-dilution clauses that prevent their equity from being diluted at all, or at least until certain conditions are met.[37,38] For example, an accelerator may want to include a clause that prevents their equity from being diluted until a startup raises funding of $500,000. This would mean that the accelerator's percentage ownership could not be diluted if new shares are issued to an investor for $250,000 or if new shares are issued to a key employee as a performance incentive. Anti-dilution clauses have been reported to be in almost 95% of venture capital (VC) financings, protecting VCs from future financings taking place at low valuations (e.g., if a founder chooses to give away free equity to family/friends, the VC is protected from the dilutive effect). Accelerators seek the same protections for their investment equity. The downside of anti-dilution clauses for founders is that issuing equity for an investment amount lower than what is stipulated in the anti-dilution clause dilutes their own percentage ownership of the company.[39,40,41] Founders may find themselves in a difficult tradeoff where, on the one hand, they have to take the $250,000 offered by an investor, or the company goes insolvent; but, on the other hand, taking it means diluting their percentage ownership in the company.

Founder Vesting

Vesting refers to shareholders earning their ownership percentage based on achieving particular performance hurdles or working for the startup for a particular period of time.[42,43] For example, a new cofounder may be allocated 9% equity that vests monthly over three years—meaning they will earn 0.25% of the equity each month that they work. If they resign or are terminated after one year, then they only keep 3% of that equity and lose the rest. Although vesting is usually attached to employee stock options or to new cofounders being added to a startup who have not earned their equity yet, some accelerators may want to include a vesting clause for a proportion of the original co-founders' equity (the last thing accelerators want is to invest $250,000 and have the majority equity holders walk away but still hold onto their equity). A founder vesting clause would essentially mean that once the accelerator puts in their money, a proportion of founders' percentage ownership would have to be earned over a certain period of time (e.g., four years). If one of the founders leaves the startup or is fired from the startup before that period has expired, then they lose whatever portion of the equity they have not yet earned.

Liquidation Preference

This part of the term sheet discusses how much of the company's net assets accelerators get if the company is liquidated (e.g., shut down, goes bankrupt, or is sold/acquired) and what priority the accelerator has over other shareholders with a claim to those net assets.[44,45] Often, all of a company's creditors and shareholders are ranked by the order in which they will be paid until the company's assets run out. Creditors will usually be paid first, but accelerators may want to make it a condition that they have a preference over any other shareholders once creditors are paid.[46,47,48] This ensures that they have a chance of getting all or some of their initial investment back, before other shareholders start to get paid. Some accelerators may want participating rights.[49,50,51,52,53] These allow them, as a "preferred" stockholder, to get back their money first and then receive their percentage ownership of what remains. For example, an accelerator may invest $250,000 for 20% equity with a $250,000 liquidation preference. In this case, if the company is acquired for $1 million, the accelerator will get its $250,000 back first and then 20% of the remaining $1.75 million (for a total of $600,000).

Voting Rights

In this section, accelerators may want to set out who can vote, and what proportion of the voters is required to approve changes to the rights, privileges, or status relating to different types of shares (e.g., preferred shares).[54,55,56] They may also want to set out who can approve the creation and issuing of new shares, to whom shares can be issued, who can approve the declaration and payment of dividends, who can approve changes to board composition, and who can approve a liquidation event.[57,58] If accelerators don't set out voting rights and procedures, founders may act in ways that compromise the accelerator's interest once they have the accelerator's money or once they no longer need the accelerator. But if the voting rights and procedures are too onerous or too restrictive, they may create significant opportunity costs for founders.

Dividends

A startup may get to a point where it is earning sufficient profits to justify paying out dividends to stockholders. Accelerators may want to specify whether they are entitled to a dividend and what percentage of the dividend they are entitled to.[59,60,61,62,63] They may also want to specify whether dividends will be cumulative (i.e., guaranteed), and whether they will be paid in cash, ordinary stock, or additional preferred stock. Paying dividends as additional preferred stock further dilutes founders over time.

Board of Directors

The board is the main governing body of a company.[64] So in this section of accelerator term sheets, accelerators will want to set out who will be on the board and what board votes are required for board decisions.[65,66,67,68,69] For example, the accelerator may want to have their own representative on the board, as well as an independent director. And they may want board decisions to be unanimous, or at least to have the agreement of their director or of the independent director.

Veto Rights or Protective Provisions

Accelerators may want to set out the situations in which they can reject a particular decision or action from being taken by the founders. For example, they may want to include a clause like "no modification to the incorporation documents or company constitution without our approval." These veto rights often protect accelerators' interests from poor founder decisions. But they can also create challenges for founders where the decision is not necessarily a poor one—just one not in the accelerator's best interest.[70,71,72,73,74] For example, founders may want to sell the company at a certain point for $13 million to have a sure exit, but the accelerator may have the right to veto the decision and do so—wanting to take a change on an exit valuation of at least $100 million.

Negotiating Accelerator Term Sheets

For many accelerators, the equity investment amount, the required amount of equity, and the equity investment terms are fixed. It is essentially a take-it-or-leave-it situation for startups. Where this is the case, founders who may have fought hard to get accepted into an accelerator will be faced with a challenging trade off. Fortunately, most of these accelerators publicize their accelerator agreements, so that prospective startups can review these in advance of applying, and decide if the terms are acceptable to the founders. Where an accelerator's terms are negotiable, founders will need to consider what to negotiate, why, and how.[75] In such a negotiation, it is rare that a startup will get its way on all aspects of the term sheet it wants changed. But it is likely to get its way on some of the desired changes. We have outlined the key term sheet elements so founders can think about how clauses in these areas are likely to impact their ownership, control, and operation of the company. Although it is rare for founders to be able to afford it, getting good legal advice is likely to be invaluable in the long term.[76] Thinking through which elements of the term sheet and what particular clauses within these elements matter most to them can be beneficial to ensuring they get concessions on the most important issues to the founders (for example, this might include no vesting, no veto rights, no anti-dilution, and no preferred stock; or it could include no inclusion of stock option pool in pre-money valuation, and no participation rights). Further, thinking through an effective negotiation approach,[77] and getting support with negotiations (e.g., from an appropriate advisor) can be invaluable. Irrespective of the approach taken to accelerator term sheets, it is critical for founders to enter accelerator term sheet negotiations fully understanding and accepting the potential operating constraints, potential legal costs, potential opportunity costs, potential company valuation, and potential exit issues that are embedded within the term sheets.[78] This can often be much more important than concern over the amount of equity given up to get into the accelerator.

Case Study 5: Impact of Signing Multiple Accelerator Agreements on a Startup's Capital-Raising Rounds[*]

Our Journey through Multiple Accelerators

We are in the smart devices market. Our product is part hardware, part software, and part software support. What we do is very new and also very challenging from a quality and security point of view. Even if our product ticks all the quality and security boxes, the appearance or perception of them is just as important. Our approach to both actual and perceived quality/security of our product offering has been to focus on forming strategic partnerships with trusted brands and to distribute through these brands. We sought out accelerators as a vehicle for establishing such partnerships. We had developed some partnerships in Europe and the United States early on in the development of our startup. Even though we were not based in Europe or the United States, we wanted to strengthen these partnerships and develop new ones. Of course, Europe and the United States are big markets, too. Considering all of the above, and also considering the benefits we got out of participating in an accelerator in our home town, we sought out accelerators in Europe and the United States.

From Acceptance Letter to the Accelerator Term Sheet

For each accelerator, we have had to sign an investor agreement or a binding term sheet, which outlined all the conditions of the accelerator's investment in our startup.

Generally, after being notified of acceptance into each of the accelerators, we received an email with a list of documents and a checklist of those documents. This usually included things such as an acceptance letter, a program participation agreement, and the accelerator's investor agreement or term sheet. In this email, or in follow-up emails before we started day 1 of the program, we also received things such as a calendar of events (sometimes it was only for the first couple of weeks or the first month), a needs-assessment document, and other housekeeping details (such as accommodation details and visa arrangements). Each of the accelerators advised us that we would discuss the term sheet/investment agreement in detail one-on-one, or in a meeting between the whole startup team and the accelerator's program management team. A follow-up discussion in a group session during the first week of the program would also occur. Therefore, we were advised, there was no need to race into signing the agreement before turning up on day 1. We were told by the accelerator program managers that the most important document initially to sign, as soon as possible, was the program acceptance letter.

[*]Reflections from the startup's CEO—startup and accelerator names changed for anonymity.

We were generally advised by the program managers to get our own legal advice before signing the term sheet/investment agreement. Of course, we generally lacked the money to get such advice. We had exhausted most of the goodwill we could draw on for free legal advice in our contacts (mostly using it for IP protection, preparing strategic partnership agreements, and solving contractual issues that cropped up from time to time). But we were told that if we didn't have our own lawyers, or could not afford one, then we could speak to the lawyer mentors associated with the program. Some accelerators provided a number of hours of free legal advice for startups who needed the advice. We were given introductions to those lawyers in an email before the program began, or we were introduced to the lawyers in the first week or two.

Getting Legal Advice

We took advantage of the free legal advice in the first accelerator program by contacting and meeting our free lawyer. He advised us to seek further clarification on a couple of terms in the term sheet. In particular, he advised us to negotiate the anti-dilution clause in the contract, which prevented us from diluting the accelerator's equity until we had raised at least $500,000 in a single round. The free lawyer advice time was limited to 10 hours, and we had used some of that time to sort out an intellectual property issue that had arisen (we couldn't ask our existing commercial lawyers to help with the IP issue because we already owed them a lot of money). Since there was not enough free legal time to attempt to iron out the clause, and since we were really desperate for the cash from the accelerator's investment, we didn't want the negotiations to drag on. It could have meant someone taking us to court for unpaid bills, or ceasing to provide us a service we needed at a critical time (for example, cloud hosting for our tech trials, statutory tax filing that was overdue, and patent filings still outstanding for some countries). Plus, we were confident the accelerator was going to help us raise a seed round. So we signed.

The Term Sheet Negotiations Grape Vine

From the first week, it was common for cohort companies to chat about the investor agreements during lunch breaks or at the pub. And all teams were eager to hear if the other teams had signed off yet. We found out that we were the first to sign. I recall there were a couple of teams who were over two months into the program, and they were still negotiating. It's not like we didn't think about our agreement before signing it. I discussed the agreements each time with my startup team, and we had further discussions after the legal advice. But with growing negative cash flow and constant pressure to find the next source of cash to pay off escalating bills, we generally saw it as a sign

(Continued)

now and get cash as fast as possible or delay and start another distracting bill payment escalation issue (we had already been through a couple of these, and they were so time consuming and distracting). We wanted to keep our focus, energy, and attention on other things while we were in the program. At first, we were also overwhelmed by all the investor and legal jargon in the agreements. In subsequent accelerators we learned more about the language in the agreements and the implications of different terms from the accelerator training sessions. In addition, we started doing more online research and taking advantage of the free legal advice each program offered to refine our understanding.

Although we had already signed the term sheet, it was interesting hearing how other teams in the accelerators were going with their negotiations—some teams got very worked up or passionate when they discussed where other teams' negotiations were at. Some teams even talked about how they were advised that some of the terms were *"ridiculous,"* and they can never sign the agreement as it was. Some said they thought there were terms in there designed to take advantage of cohort companies. Others said the accelerators are *"trying to rip us off."* However, we never felt this way about any of the accelerators we went through. Perhaps we received good legal advice, and the other team's legal advice was not so good. Or perhaps we had trust in the accelerator that they would not rip us off. Or perhaps we were too trusting and not cautious enough. Anyway, we quickly built trust in the accelerators we went through. We believed that they existed to support us, not to rip us off. Our startup often dealt with a number of commercial lawyers, often on a weekly basis—usually for intellectual property–related issues and contract issues related to trials and partnership agreements (hence some of our bills pressure!). From this experience, we found that commercial lawyers' advice often focused on "the worst case scenario." Sometimes it scared us out of doing deals altogether when, in hindsight, we should have done them. Based on this, it didn't alarm us that other teams were still negotiating a couple of months after the accelerator started—we thought they were likely overreacting to the legal advice. Surprisingly, the negotiations continued into the third month. And, as demo day approached, we noticed things were starting to become tense and awkward between those startups that were still negotiating and the accelerator program managers. For example, those teams still negotiating often turned down invites to attend social evenings at bars and pubs with the other teams, complaining they had no money, as they had not yet signed the investor agreement and been paid. We would have been in trouble if we didn't get our money in the first few weeks.

Pressure to Sign the Term Sheet

There was never any pressure to sign the term sheets from the program managers. After our first accelerator, we started asking for some changes in the term sheets. When we submitted our suggested changes, the program managers would advise us immediately that the document would go up to their legal teams, and that we just had to wait until we heard back from them. There was never a straight answer to when the lawyers would get back to us about an issue. We learned never to hold our breath or expect responses regarding written documents for at least a week or two when dealing with lawyers. We found lawyers were always busy. There were never any bad feelings between our team and the program managers during the first couple of weeks when we were waiting to hear back about the term sheet changes. If we brought it up, the program managers quickly replied, "*We'll have to follow up with the legal team and get back to you on that one.*" The program managers always seemed to wash their hands of all responsibility very quickly. I guess that seems logical considering it was a legal document and the program managers weren't lawyers. The fact that the negotiations about the term sheet were pushed to the side, out of the program managers' control, was probably a good thing. It removed most of the awkwardness or uncomfortable feelings coming from the negotiations.

Term Sheet Concerns

As I said earlier, in our first accelerator there was a non-dilution clause, which meant that the accelerator's equity stake could not dilute even if we got new investors on board. Subsequently, we were advised by many investors that this was not a fair clause for any investment agreement. And we were advised that the general rule of thumb is that these types of clauses should not exist, as all investors dilute equally each time a new investor comes on board. That this is just how the game is played, so we were told. In another accelerator, we were a little concerned by an *options clause*, which meant that the accelerator would not immediately take the equity in our startup, and would only *"exercise"* their option to take equity in our company during an investment round, such as a series A or B. Further, this option stated that if we had a high valuation, then they would get a higher percentage of equity. But if the valuation was low, then they would get a lower percentage equity stake. At the time of receiving the investment agreement with this clause, our startup was on a bootstrapping strategy, so we paid little attention to it.

In yet another accelerator, we were concerned with the accelerator request that all IP that the company developed, forever and a day, would reside in the new company we had formed specifically for the accelerator. We had to register a new company in the foreign country where the accelerator was held. We were

(Continued)

advised that our operating company, which we had set up before the accelerator and which had been receiving revenue from government grants, business plan competition prize monies, accelerator investments, and even some families/ friends, could not hold the company's IP. At first, this clause concerned us and our commercial lawyers. But, after receiving advice from an IP lawyer, we became comfortable with this term. Our IP lawyer advised us that it's common for startups and other companies to hold IP in a "holding company," which is separate from the "operating company." So that if the operating company gets sued, or simply goes bankrupt, the IP doesn't go with it and remains safe in the holding company.

Impacts of Signed Term Sheets on the Startup after the Accelerator

We received some legal advice early on in our startup that any agreement can be renegotiated at a future date. With this advice in mind, we pushed on confidently, knowing that if there were major issues in the accelerator investment agreement that became a problem in the future (for example, affecting our ability to raise a series A investment round), we could renegotiate. We were convinced the accelerators were interested in supporting us in any way to help us grow and become a success. So we were confident that there would not be any reason why, at a future date, an accelerator would not be willing to cooperate with us and renegotiate. We couldn't imagine the accelerator refusing to renegotiate and to be willing to make changes if it was necessary for our company to grow and scale.

Incidentally, we recently found ourselves in just such a situation, as we were through a capital-raising round. When things progressed to the due diligence stage, with the investors in the funding round, we found ourselves needing to renegotiate all the accelerator investment term sheets, as there were a number of clauses and conditions in there that were unattractive to the prospective investors. For example, the aforementioned option clause introduced uncertainty that the investors did not like, as they did not want their shares to be significantly diluted later or at any time. We learned that these investors really don't like potential surprises like that. Also, the types of shares stipulated in the accelerator agreement became an issue with some investors, as these were not appropriate types of shares to have in our country for raising investment. Then, we had to issue shares to key employees, and, of course, the non-dilute clause became a problem here too. It had now been a few years since we did the accelerators, and for some of them, let's just say their term sheets have changed over time to become more founder friendly. But we are still under the old, more restrictive terms. So far, the renegotiations have been difficult, and we've found some of the accelerators taking very rigid stances on the terms. We keep going back and forth, but it is challenging to come to agreement on term changes. Each time we hit a brick wall regarding an issue in the term sheets, we go back to our lawyers for more advice and to strategize new ideas or ways to get around the issue, rather than having endless dialogue that gets us nowhere. It's been an emotional rollercoaster ride negotiating with the accelerators and the investors. We're not sure how it will end. But we just want to make sure we get the foundation right for future fundraising rounds.

Lessons Learned and Final Thoughts

I've learned that if you want to negotiate the investment agreement during the accelerator program, or at any future date, then the process will be slow and dragged out. This is no different from any legal negotiation our startup has been through. Generally it takes time for legal departments/lawyers to respond and to provide advice. And the advice provided, when it finally does come back, can often highlight the worst-case scenario. Therefore, you have to think about finding some compromise between your startup's pressing needs, what's required to act on the advice received, and the possibility of stubbornness from the accelerators in the negotiation. The glacial negotiation speed from the accelerator's end can become a problem if your startup has no money (especially if you are spending money to fly overseas and also have to pay for accommodation while abroad). So make sure you budget for the first month or two of the program, without needing to rely on the accelerator seed investment.

The advice I would give founders about signing term sheets is this: generally the accelerator presents the idea that the term sheet is negotiable. This is indeed true, but the negotiations can drag on for a very long time if you want to make genuine term changes. We have also found that even after the dragged-out negotiations, a compromise must be reached; you won't just get your way. We've found it hard to predict what term sheet elements and clauses were going to be attractive or unattractive to particular investors. My advice is that if you are going to sell equity in your company to any investor, whether that's an accelerator, an Angel Investor, or a VC, you have to accept there will be a lot of terms and conditions and things that you don't like, and there will be other things in there that commercial lawyers don't like, and future investors might not like. But in the end, I think the startup should place some trust and faith in the accelerator. That's if startups have done their research about the accelerator, and validated that it is a successful and founder-friendly accelerator. If there are many alumni that have gone on to raise significant rounds of capital, and they have been going a long time, and they speak well of the founder-friendliness of the accelerator—then you should be able to trust that the accelerator knows what they are doing.

Notes

1. Y.V. Hochberg, "Accelerating Entrepreneurs and Ecosystems: The Seed Accelerator Model," in *Innovation Policy and the Economy*, ed. J. Lerner and S. Stern, Vol. 16, National Bureau of Economic Research (Chicago: University of Chicago Press, 2016), 25–51.
2. AngelPad, "Common Accelerator Terms You Need to Understand before Signing (Accelerator Terms Sheet)," AngelPad, accessed August 1, 2019, https://angelpad.com/b/accelerator-terms-sheet/.
3. P. Smith, "Startup Accelerators Need to Change," accessed August 1, 2019, https://thenextweb.com/insider/2015/07/01/startup-accelerators-need-to-change/.
4. 500 Startups, "FAQs," 500 Startups, accessed August 1, 2019, https://500.co/faqs/.
5. M. Leatherbee and J. Gonzalez-Ubribe, "Key Performance Indicators," in *Accelerators: Successful Venture Creation and Growth*, ed. M. Wright and I. Drori (Edward Elgar, 2018), doi: https://doi.org/10.4337/9781786434098.
6. K. Nathoo, "The Y Combinator Deal," accessed August 1, 2019, https://www.ycombinator.com/deal/.
7. Adapted from Gust, "Global Accelerator Report 2016," accessed August 1, 2019, http://gust.com/accelerator_reports/2016/global/.
8. "Accelerators and Valuation: Stay Grounded," StartupYard, 2015, accessed August 19, 2019, https://startupyard.com/accelerators-valuation-stay-grounded/.
9. T. Levasseur, "This is the Biggest Benefit Accelerators Offer Startups," accessed July 13, 2019, https://medium.com/@cambridgetricia/the-biggest-benefit-accelerators-offer-startups-3e246ac4ef03.
10. K. Thayer, "Zero Rent, Zero Equity: Why This Accelerator Has a Different Agenda," *Forbes*, July 17, 2015, accessed July 13, 2019, https://www.forbes.com/sites/katherynthayer/2015/07/17/zero-rent-zero-equity-why-this-accelerator-has-a-different-agenda/#5f7964c27b3d.
11. B. Feld and J. Mendelson, *Venture Deals* (Hoboken, NJ: John Wiley & Sons, 2011).

12. T. Miller, "Term Sheets: The Definitive Guide for Entrepreneurs," accessed August 1, 2019, https://www.capshare.com/blog/term-sheets-guide/.

13. B. Feld, "Venture Deals: Chapter 4: Economic Terms of the Term Sheet," *Venture Deals,* July 30, 2011, accessed August 1, 2019, https://www.venturedeals.com/archives/2011/07/venture-deals-chapter-4-economic-terms-of-the-term-sheet.html.

14. J. Ancer, "Relationships and Power in Startup Ecosystems," *Silicon Hills Lawyer,* February 18, 2019, accessed August 1, 2019, https://siliconhillslawyer.com/2019/02/18/relationships-and-power-startup-ecosystems/.

15. Miller, "Term Sheets."

16. Ibid.

17. S. W. Smith and T. J. Hannigan, "Swinging for the Fences: How Do Top Accelerators Impact the Trajectories of New Ventures," paper presented at the DRUID15 conference, Rome, June 15–17, 2015.

18. "Y Combinator Term Sheet," accessed August 1, 2019, https://blog.ycombinator.com/wp-content/uploads/2019/01/Series-A-1.png.

19. AngelPad, "Common Accelerator Terms."

20. Founders Club, "Understanding Startup Investments."

21. Miller, "Term Sheets."

22. Feld, "Venture Deals: Chapter 4."

23. Ancer, "Relationships and Power in Startup Ecosystems."

24. Miller, "Term Sheets."

25. Ibid.

26. Adapted from B. Feld, "Venture Deals," accessed August 1, 2019, https://www.venturedeals.com/.

27. Founders Club, "Understanding Startup Investments."

28. Miller, "Term Sheets."

29. Feld, "Venture Deals: Chapter 4."

30. Ancer, "Relationships and Power in Startup Ecosystems."

31. Miller, "Term Sheets."

32. Ibid.

33. T. Miloud, A. Aspelund, and M. Cabrol, "Startup Valuation by Venture Capitalists: An Empirical Study," *Venture Capital* 14, nos. 2–3 (2012): 151–174.

34. Leatherbee and Gonzaelz-Uribe, "Key Performance Indicators."
35. B. Nivi, "The Option Pool Shuffle," accessed August 1, 2019, https://venturehacks.com/option-pool-shuffle.
36. D. J. Denis, "Entrepreneurial Finance: An Overview of the Issues and Evidence," *Journal of Corporate Finance* 10 (2004): 301–326.
37. Miller, "Term Sheets."
38. Feld, "Venture Deals: Chapter 4."
39. Ancer, "Relationships and Power in Startup Ecosystems."
40. Miller, "Term Sheets."
41. Ibid.
42. B. Nivi, "Accelerate Your Vesting upon Termination," accessed August 1, 2019, https://venturehacks.com/accelcration-termination.
43. T. F. Hellman and N. Wasserman, "The First Deal: The Division of Founder Equity In New Ventures" (working paper 16922, National Bureau of Economic Research), http://www.nber.org/papers/w16922.
44. Miller, "Term Sheets."
45. Feld, "Venture Deals: Chapter 4."
46. Ancer, "Relationships and Power in Startup Ecosystems."
47. Miller, "Term Sheets."
48. Ibid.
49. Ibid.
50. Feld, "Venture Deals: Chapter 4."
51. Ancer, "Relationships and Power in Startup Ecosystems."
52. Miller, "Term Sheets."
53. Ibid.
54. Ibid.
55. Feld, "Venture Deals: Chapter 4."
56. Ancer, "Relationships and Power in Startup Ecosystems."
57. Miller, "Term Sheets."
58. Ibid.
59. Ibid.
60. Feld, "Venture Deals: Chapter 4."
61. Ancer, "Relationships and Power in Startup Ecosystems."
62. Miller, "Term Sheets."
63. Ibid.

64. J. M. Fried and M. Ganor, "Agency Costs of Venture Capitalist Control in Startups," *New York University Law Review* 81, no. 3 (2006): 967.
65. Miller, "Term Sheets."
66. Feld, "Venture Deals: Chapter 4."
67. Ancer, "Relationships and Power in Startup Ecosystems."
68. Miller, "Term Sheets."
69. Ibid.
70. Ibid.
71. Feld, "Venture Deals: Chapter 4."
72. Ancer, "Relationships and Power in Startup Ecosystems."
73. Miller, "Term Sheets."
74. Ibid.
75. M. Bartus, "Negotiating Term Sheets," Cooley GO, accessed August 1, 2019, https://www.cooleygo.com/negotiating-term-sheets/.
76. Ancer, "Relationships and Power in Startup Ecosystems."
77. Bartus, "Negotiating Term Sheets."
78. Ancer, "Relationships and Power in Startup Ecosystems."

CHAPTER

Choosing an Accelerator Program

With the top programs, everybody in the VC community will be looking at you. But with some of these newer accelerators, especially regional ones or those in nontraditional verticals, you need to be sure that serious VC shops from outside your area take the program seriously and see its alumni as serious possibilities for funding.

Yael Hochberg, Rice University Professor of
Entrepreneurship; Managing Director,
Seed Accelerator Rankings Project

Significance of the Decision to Participate in or Forgo Accelerator Programs

Before considering which accelerator to do, founders have to first decide if they should do an accelerator at all. For instance, they have to consider the benefits accelerators offer (e.g., idea validation, accelerated learning, accelerated evolution, investment readiness, seed funding, advice/support network, investor/customer/ strategic partner access, help with legal structure, help with getting strategy right, help with executing the strategy, etc.), whether they need these benefits, whether accelerators are the best vehicle for accessing these benefits, and whether the right accelerators for them are actually accessible.[1] Notwithstanding that they may not know what they don't know, if founders believe the response to any of these questions is "no," then forgoing accelerator programs may make sense. Doing so means they don't unnecessarily dilute their equity, don't expose themselves to restrictive equity investment terms, and don't waste valuable time participating in a three- to nine–month accelerator program—which may come with steep opportunity costs. Not knowing what they don't know, founders can get the accelerator participation decision wrong. This can have grave consequences (e.g., if they decide not to enter an accelerator when they should, this may result in them not receiving validation about the viability of their idea, not understanding what is required to be investment ready, missing out on critical seed funding, missing out on access to transformational investors/customers/strategic partners, missing out on having incentivized/experienced/hands-on supporters, missing out on getting strategy right, missing the opportunity to get the legal structure right, and much more. The latter may lead to building a successful startup, only to end up losing it to others through early legal mistakes. Thus, this is not a decision that should be taken without careful consideration, without adequate understanding of the true value of accelerators, or without careful consideration of the real challenges of replicating the accelerator value proposition.

Significance of the Accelerator Choice Decision

Not all accelerators are the same. And although all accelerators deliver on the accelerator value proposition to some degree, not all accelerators can do so to a sufficient degree to make a meaningful difference to a startup's evolution. In Chapter 3 we noted that almost any startup can march into a bottom-tier accelerator or an accelerator on the lower end of the mid-tier accelerators. But not many make it to the top-tier accelerators. Yet there are stark differences in the benefits derived from top-tier vs. mid-tier vs. bottom-tier accelerators (e.g., a top-tier accelerator or good mid-tier accelerator may propel a startup to a billion-dollar exit; while a bottom-tier and low-end mid-tier accelerator may actually erode a startup's valuation, make the startup uninvestable, or ruin the startup altogether.) So, once a startup decides that it is worth doing an accelerator program, the choice of accelerator becomes one of the most important decisions in the startup's life. That decision can make or break a startup. Sometimes the choice of a wrong accelerator and its impact is clear and visible early. For example, after incurring significant costs relocating to New York for an accelerator program he thought would get his startup to the next level, YouGift founder Efrem Weiss was shocked to discover the reality of the program was very far from what the accelerator organizers made it out to be.[2] Rather than the mentoring sessions being one-on-one, the sessions were done as group chats over Skype in a crowded room. The accelerator space looked more like cheap student accommodations that had been through one too many binge parties—nothing like what was in the flashy brochures. And the accelerator program activities lacked in so many critical areas that they were a blatant waste of time. Further, the program had only provided founders $18,000 for 6% equity. Deflated, Efrem decided to go through the difficult process of pulling his startup out of the program after only two weeks. But this came at a cost. He returned home having lost valuable time and the little money he had left. Rather than being a launching platform, the accelerator had actually set him backwards, and made it less likely for his startup to survive. In less than a year, he was forced to shut up shop.

Efrem's story is a moderate case, relative to other poor accelerator choice horror stories. Typically, these horror stories touch on any number of surprises that confront founders once a startup program is underway. For example, such surprises can include startups discovering they have to pay back the accelerator investment if their startup does not succeed. Or startups being presented partway through the program with highly restrictive and unacceptable clauses in shareholder agreements that were not apparent in term sheets. Alternatively, startups may discover hurdles that make it virtually impossible for them to actually get their seed money. Other surprises include the structure of accelerator seed investments drastically bringing down a startup's valuation or putting off investors who otherwise would have been interested, accelerators with curriculums and activities that are of no actual value, accelerators with inept mentors and advisors, accelerators with investors/investment networks that have no intention of actually investing, and accelerators with advisors that provide advice that discredits founder judgments—only to end up doing more damage than if founders had just followed their own judgement. Sometimes the impact of a bad accelerator choice is more subtle. For instance, we spoke to an Oceania founder who explained that he was in fundraising conversations with three different investors, with one of them being more serious and in the term sheet negotiation stage. During this time, he received a referral/recommendation to apply for an accelerator program that was about to launch in his city. The serious investor wanted 30% of the company and the founder had asked for $250,000. The investor didn't want to put up all the $250,000 and was pitching his network for a co-investor. Advised strongly by the referrers to submit an accelerator application since he would get all the benefits the investor could provide and more without having to give up so much equity, the founder prepared an application and submitted it. Before he knew it, he was accepted and received a term sheet from the accelerator. He was talked into signing the standard term sheet in which the accelerator took 7% equity for a $10,000 investment. He signed it because he was not giving up much equity and was going to get the funds almost immediately. He desperately needed money to finalize worldwide patent fees for a law firm. When he told the investor the good news, the investor became irate, saying it was unbelievable that after all their combined hard work building up and pitching the startup's value at $1 million, the founder had gone ahead and drawn a $140,000 line in the sand regarding the startup's valuation. The investor sarcastically offered to purchase 70% of the company for $100,000 and, when the founder started to protest, was never heard from again. Only with the benefit of hindsight did the owner realize that the accelerator did him a huge disservice by talking him into signing the accelerator term sheet in the hopes of building up the valuation and raising much more money on demo day through the accelerator's "vast" investment network. The founder and his co-founders did not raise funding from the accelerator investor network on demo day nor, as of the time of our discussions with him, had he raised more than $50,000 from the accelerator network almost five years after the program.

Choosing the wrong accelerator is easy. It often involves snap judgments and limited understanding of the accelerator value proposition and of the aptitudes of different accelerators to deliver on this value proposition. It relies on heuristic-based advice, superficial analysis, and little depth of thought. It is often dominated by a desperate need for quick access to money, or is a satisficed last resort activity to keep the startup moving forward. Choosing the right accelerator is exactly the opposite.

What Makes Choosing an Accelerator So Challenging

The number of accelerators around the world has grown at dramatic rates.[3,4] Today, the number of accelerators globally has been estimated at somewhere between 3,000[5,6] and more than 10,000[7] (although we weren't able to verify the original source of the latter number, and, if true, we suspect it incorporates incubators). Nevertheless, the numbers continue to grow rapidly.[8,9] This is despite more and more accelerators adopting a franchise-type model, and having operations in many countries (which can obscure visible growth in the number of accelerator programs). For example, as well as having a presence in many U.S. states, Techstars is now a global accelerator with offices in Europe, Africa, the Middle East, and Oceania. Yet Techstars may be counted as a single accelerator when the number of accelerators is counted. As well as the vast number of accelerators, and the increasing diversity of accelerator locations, more and more accelerators are focusing on particular types of startups (e.g., early-stage, late-stage, software, hardware, services, IoT, Telco, NGO, corporate, etc.). The sheer number of accelerators, the increasingly global catchment area of the accelerators, differences in accelerator designs and focus, and differences in the benefits and costs of different startup ecosystems around the world make choosing an accelerator a challenge. For example, should founders go through each of the more than 10,000 accelerators globally to find the best one for them? How much time can they seriously devote to this task, and to what depth can they really analyze these? Should they just choose from top-tier accelerators? Or will this be a waste of time for their startup given the low acceptance rates for such accelerators? If an accelerator is not ranked, does this mean it isn't good? How can founders know how good the accelerator is? Should they choose a local accelerator or relocate interstate or even overseas?

For many founders, the accelerator choice decision can't just be a matter of going to accelerator rankings sites and choosing the highest-ranked accelerator. For starters, these rankings usually only have data available on top-tier accelerators, and the acceptance rates to such accelerators become lower and lower by the year (e.g., due to top-tier accelerators having more and more startups to choose from and more later-stage applicants). It may be easier to get accepted into Harvard Business School than into a top-tier accelerator. Further, making the right choice requires founders to know themselves, know their startup, and to carefully consider what may be the best fit for them. The best accelerator for a founding team may not necessarily be the top-ranked accelerator. The accelerator choice decision is made more all the more difficult given its high stakes, buyer-beware nature. That is, get it right, and the rewards can be enormous. Get it wrong, and the costs can range from merely treading water for three months, to startup purgatory,[10] and even accelerated failure.

What Makes a Good Accelerator

A good accelerator is one that can sufficiently deliver on the accelerator value proposition. That is, it can make a significant enough difference to a startup's evolution to warrant the opportunity costs of participation. The opportunity costs include what the startup could have otherwise achieved with the time spent in the accelerator, the benefit of not having to give up equity to the accelerator, the benefit of not having term sheet restrictions imposed by the accelerator to protect its equity (see Chapter 7), the benefit of flexibility with regard to the startup's valuation (e.g., the accelerator investment does not draw a line in the sand regarding the startup's valuation), the benefit of not having to incur particular costs to participate in the accelerator (e.g., relocation costs). This is not an exhaustive list. But, essentially, a good accelerator will create unique value for the startup that significantly exceeds the probable value that startup could have created through other means. We unpack some of the key elements of a good accelerator below (i.e., key elements of the accelerator value proposition that good accelerators sufficiently deliver on).

First, Do No Harm

Startups put a lot of trust into the accelerators they participate in. Implicit in this trust is the belief that accelerator organizers and advisors are more akin to a parental figure guiding startups onto the right path or to a medical doctor guiding a patient toward good health. So, one of the last things a startup would expect is for an accelerator to harm their startup in some way. Whether through poor advice, predatory investment terms, lying about the accelerator's capabilities, unfilled commitments, wasting founders' time, or any other multitude of issues common in accelerator horror stories—the harm is usually significant opportunity cost or, worse, startup fatality. Thus, a critical element of a good accelerator is the measures it takes to guard against harming the very startups it sets out to help. Such measures can range from selecting the right startups at the right stage to participate in the program,[11] being fully transparent about the actual accelerator experience, having founder-friendly investment terms, ensuring high-quality and impactful curricula, ensuring high-quality and accessible advisors, having high-quality/effective professional and support services, having equity-back guarantees if founders don't feel the program has been worth it,[12] etc. If some of these measures seem extreme, consider the measures taken to ensure that medical doctors first do no harm[13] (e.g., Hippocratic Oath, accreditation, medical negligence laws, and coroner's investigations). Table 7.1 shows the results of a study investigating the negative aspects of accelerator and incubation programs and their prevalence. Although generalizations cannot be drawn from the limited sample of eight start-ups, the prevalence distribution is nevertheless insightful. The study was undertaken by Kristina Lukosiute (research student at the University of Southern Denmark), Søren Jensen (associate professor at the University of Southern Denmark), and Stoyan Tanev (associate professor of technology entrepreneurship at the University of Carleton in Canada).

TABLE 7.1 Examples of Negative Aspects of Accelerator/Incubator Programs and Their Prevalence within a Cohort of Eight Startups

Element of Accelerator or Incubation Program	Negative Aspects of Program	Prevalence
Admission criteria	The program did not perform due diligence and assessment to ensure a quality startup cohort.	50%
	General workshops, courses, and lectures about entrepreneurship were not found to be suitable.	13%
	Startups received low commitment from program mentors and advisors.	50%
	The program did not meet the company's initial expectations.	25%
Network	The program's network was not aligned to the startup's product.	38%
	Startups were unaware of the program's ecosystem.	25%
	Startups did not use the office space provided for the program.	38%
Investment	The program did not provide direct or indirect access to investment.	25%
Equity	Equity investment terms made startups unattractive to potential investors.	13%
IP Protection	Participation in the program put intellectual property at risk.	13%
After the program	After the program, startups needed to join another program or to seek out business angels for support.	38%

Source: Adapted from Lukosiute, Jensen, and Tanev (2014).[14]

Seed Investment

A good accelerator will make a meaningful seed investment at a fair price for the equity it receives. It won't, for example, invest $10,000 for 10% when a startup's real valuation is $500,000. That would likely harm a startup by drastically lowering its valuation. Accelerators may get applicants who don't understand the implications of the accelerator's fixed investment amount and equity requirement. Good accelerators also typically have transparent, founder-friendly terms. This enables prospective applicants to review the terms and get legal advice on the terms—avoiding the exploding term sheet situation[15] (i.e., where startups are presented a never before seen term sheet with unacceptable terms, but a short window of time to accept it prior to the program start date, otherwise they forfeit participation in the accelerator altogether). Some accelerators present these exploding term sheets part way through the accelerator program, putting founders in a very uncomfortable situation.

Accelerated Learning and Skills Development

A critical element of the accelerator value proposition is that accelerators drastically speed up startup evolution by compressing years' worth of learning-by-doing into just a few months.[16] That's the promise and a main attraction to accelerators. But delivering on that promise is no easy feat, and not something every accelerator is capable of.[17] In great accelerators, founding teams leave the accelerator program transformed as entrepreneurs, strategic leaders, product builders, sales people, marketers, and operations managers. They also leave accelerator programs having applied this learning and skill base to transform their startups and significantly advance them in the startup evolution process. For example, a startup might enter an accelerator while in the early stages of customer discovery and leave the program having completed customer validation and even be part way through strategy/operational/financial validation. The founders will also have honed their pitching and fundraising skills—preparing them well for raising the funds necessary for the scaling stage. Delivering such impactful accelerated learning and skills development requires a committed network of great accelerator program designers and facilitators, advisors, mentors, alumni, and professional service providers. It also requires selecting the right startups to participate in the accelerator. Not all accelerators can make the type of investment required and attract the type of people and types of startups required to effectively deliver all this.

Accelerated Investment Readiness

Access to investment funding is the lifeblood of many startups, particularly startups with negative cash flow, and startups planning to scale significantly and or rapidly.[18] Sooner or later (usually sooner), these startups will find themselves needing to raise funding from experienced or professional investors with access to large amounts of money. For the unprepared and unlucky, fundraising is likely to be an opaque, difficult, time-consuming, chaotic, and demoralizing process that yields no results. Even for seasoned founders, fundraising can be a daunting and chaotic process that distracts them from running their business, costs money (e.g., loss of time that could have been used to grow sales), and results in no actual funding. Given the opaqueness and uncertainty of the fundraising process, it's critical for startups to be ready for it. That is, for startups to be investment ready. Startups are investment ready when founders are able to compel experienced or professional investors to fund them.[19] This readiness is partly driven by the nature of the startup (e.g., what its product is, market, team, traction), its stage of evolution (e.g., is it at the insight/opportunity recognition stage or at the scaling stage), and founders' fundraising skills[20,21] (e.g., can founders get in front of the right investors, pitch effectively, having the right fundraising tools to back up their pitches, effectively negotiate term sheets, and get through due diligence?).[22] Going through the fundraising process without being investment ready usually only results in wasted time, money, and energy—which can hurt a startup in apparent and non-apparent ways.[23,24] It can also send the wrong signal about founders' maturity.[25] Good accelerators understand how important investment readiness is for startups and their founders. As a result, a fundamental focus of their programs is accelerating each startup's investment readiness.[26] For example, this might involve pushing startups to rapidly advance through the startup evolution stages so as to be at a stage that enables them to get a look in from investors.[27] It might also involve pushing startups to build a track record of progress over the three-month accelerator timeframe that will excite investors, teaching startups how to get in front of the right investors, preparing founders to be able to deliver effective investor pitches, preparing startups to effectively address investor questions, preparing and being able to properly use pitch decks/ investor memorandums/business plans, and preparing startups to navigate the fundraising process once they get genuine interest from an investor. Startups often graduate from good accelerators being investment ready or, where their startup just couldn't get to a stage at which experienced or professional investors will invest, knowing how to navigate the fundraising process effectively once the startup gets to that stage.

In assessing an accelerator's capacity to get startups investment ready, founders can look for proxy indicators such as the number of that accelerator's alumni who have gone on to raise funding, how much they have raised, from which investors, at what valuations, how long after the program, etc. They can also seek out alumni reflections on how effectively an accelerator prepared their startup for navigating the fundraising process. Additionally, they can ask accelerator program organizers what they do to get startups investment ready—and then contrast different accelerator organizers' answers. Some accelerators can overinflate, exaggerate, or make up their alumni valuations and milestones to seem more successful. So, founders should take the cited success stories and valuations with a grain of salt (even when these are in the press). It may be wise to start by getting in contact directly with the alumni and asking their opinion of the accelerator prior to talking to the accelerator organizers. To get a true indication of alumni progress, founders can look on platforms like CrunchBase—which list fundraising rounds and milestones of startups (but subject to validated evidence of these milestones being achieved). Figure 7.1 suggests a possible relationship between the quality of an accelerator and the ability of that startup to raise funding.

	Follow-on %	Median Total Funding ($M)	Parameters:
Y Combinator	40%	3.50	- Follow-on defined as $750K raised post-accelerator - Accelerator date is April 2015 or before
Techstars	48%	3.01	
500 Accelerator	30%	2.30	
DreamIT Ventures	14%	2.04	
Mass Challenge	13%	2.89	
Alchemist Accelerator	39%	6.65	
Entrepreneurs Roundtable Accelerator	24%	3.08	
AngelPad	25%	2.70	
Capital Innovators	32%	3.72	
Portland Seed Fund	32%	2.60	
Most Active Accelerators Average	35%	3.01	

FIGURE 7.1 Proportion of Startups Participating in the 10 Most Active U.S. Accelerators in 2016 That Raised at Least $750,000 Funding within 12 Months of Graduating from the Accelerator (i.e., Raised Funding = "Follow-On" Funding)
Source: Adapted from Kaji (2016).[28]

Accelerated Product Development

A startup's product and its stage of development are critical to the startup's evolution. For example, it determines whether a startup can get customers and how many, whether a startup can generate revenue, what type of traction a startup can demonstrate, how far a startup is from finding product market fit, etc.[29] So, depending on the stage of development a startup's product is at, accelerating the startup's product development may need to be a high priority. Where this is the case, a good accelerator will prioritize that startup's product development, as opposed to preoccupying that startup with other activities that take time away from product development.

A good accelerator can draw on its network of technical and non-technical mentors, advisors, professional service providers, alumni, and potential customers for the startup's product to help founders to rapidly validate market acceptance (or rejection), and accelerate product development.[30] In contrast, a lesser accelerator may attempt to get all cohort startups to follow a fixed curriculum and set of activities, irrespective of product development being the priority for some startups. To gauge an accelerator's capabilities in this area, founders can draw on accelerator alumni reflections, as well as ask accelerator program organizers about the support provided to speed up product development.[31]

Getting Legal Right from the Start

It's not uncommon for founders to build a great business, only to exit with meager rations or, worse, to lose it all. Losing it all to whom? Losing it to a protracted and expensive legal battle, to a predatory investor, to a machiavellian cofounder, to an opportunistic business partner/former employer/past employee—or sometimes to an individual or entity genuinely wronged by the startup. It is common for founders to not think through, or to put off, potential legal issues until "later," when they may have the money to pay a lawyer, or when they may have "more" time.[32] After all, they have a product to build, sales to make, employees to hire, and a business to run. And they are under incredible time pressure requiring sink or swim prioritization. In such a context, legal issues can fall in the "important not urgent" category, and get put off until it is too late.[33] Harvard Business School professor Constance Bagley identifies some of the common legal mistakes founders make[34] in such a context, including failing to incorporate early enough, issuing founder shares without vesting, hiring lawyers not experienced with entrepreneurs and venture capitalists, only considering valuation during investment negotiations, waiting to consider international intellectual property protection, disclosing inventions without an effective non-disclosure agreement or prior to patent filing, starting a business while employed by a potential competitor or hiring employees without checking their agreements with current competitors (this may result in them actually owning IP those employees have worked on), overpromising and underdelivering (e.g., Theranos), and thinking legal problems can be solved later. Good accelerators will usually move quickly to identify legal issues and push startups to iron them out. For example, they may encourage startups to work with the accelerator's legal specialists to sort out incorporation, shareholder/ advisor/employee/business partner agreements, intellectual property protection, and other legal issues[35]—as it is not uncommon for such legal issues to get in the way of fundraising. Founders can gauge accelerators' offering in this regard through Alumni conversations, questions to accelerator alumni, and investigations of what types of legal advisors the accelerator has.

Getting Strategy Right

Increasing integration is blurring the boundaries between industries, markets, geographies, technologies, and platforms. And increasing complexity and volatility is making predicting the future more and more difficult.[36] As a result, strategy is becoming more and more important, yet more and more challenging to get right. For startups, getting strategy right means knowing the right things to do now, and in the future (strategic objectives). Startups also need to know how to do those things and actually get themselves to do those things (tactics and execution capability). Getting strategy right usually requires well thought out and compelling answers to critical long-term, medium-term, and short-term questions. For example, should the startup adopt an intellectual property strategy, an architectural strategy, a value chain strategy, or a disruption strategy?[37] (Joshua Gans, professor of technical innovation and entrepreneurship at the Rotman School of Management, delineates between "Intellectual Property" strategy, which focuses on maintaining control of IP and licensing it within the existing market place; "Disruption" strategy, which focuses on taking incumbents by surprise with rapid execution; "Value Chain" strategy, which focuses on creating value for partners in the existing value chain; and "Architectural" strategy, which focuses on creating and controlling a new value chain—often using a platform).[38] How should a startup effect the chosen strategy? How does all this relate to how the startup goes through the stages in the startup evolution process? When is the startup ready to move from customer discovery to customer validation stages? How does a startup find product/ market fit? What business model should be used? What does the sales and marketing roadmap need to be? How does the startup undertake strategy/operational/financial validation? These are all very important questions, and how they are answered and acted on can either propel a startup or suffocate it. Good accelerators can help startups find the right answers to these questions. They can also help startups develop the right strategic objectives and corresponding tactics. They can then help lead entrepreneurs to get themselves to do what needs to be done to execute strategy. Lesser accelerators lack the network of great accelerator program designers and facilitators, advisors, mentors, alumni, and professional service providers that can help startups get strategy right.[39] Or, they may have such a network but lack the ability to manage it effectively so that it provides optimal value for startups.

Exclusive Access to Investors, Customers, Strategic Partners, Cofounders

Although all accelerators aim to have a network of great accelerator program designers and facilitators, advisors, mentors, alumni, professional service providers, and cohort companies, not all these networks are the same. Some networks will be superior by virtue of the accelerator location, by virtue of the accelerator founders, by virtue of the accelerator funding accessible, by virtue of the accelerator track record, by virtue of the age of the accelerator, and many other factors. Also, due to a combination of two or more of these factors, some accelerators will be able to provide exclusive access to unique investors, customers, strategic partners, alumni, professional service providers, mentors/advisors, and cohort companies. Founders ought to consider what exclusive network access an accelerator can provide and what difference such exclusive access could make to their startup.

An Effective Support Network

Whether exclusive or not, a good accelerator's support network will effectively deliver on the accelerator promise. An effective support network has high-quality program designers and facilitators, advisors, mentors, alumni, professional service providers, and cohort companies (i.e., network team members who have the knowledge, skills, experiences, and capacity to impart know-how to founders). Plus, network members will be available and be easily accessible by founders. A lesser accelerator may have a low-quality network, or it may have a high-quality network but with members who are inaccessible (e.g., too busy, too far geographically, too aloof, too unapproachable, unable to prioritize founders' issues, lacking the motivation to get their hands dirty, etc.). Founders can discover the quality and accessibility of an accelerator's support network by looking into network members' profiles (these are usually listed on accelerator websites and further details can be found via LinkedIn). But founders should keep in mind that being listed and actually being accessible are not the same thing. By speaking with the accelerator's alumni, founders can assess how accessible and supportive alumni found different people in the accelerator network both during and after the program.

Professionalism, Confidence, and Other Ancillary Benefits

A good accelerator will transform a startup's professionalism and enhance its credibility with prospective customers, investors, strategic partners, prospective employees, and the community in which the startup operates. Acceptance into a good accelerator is also likely to enhance the founding team's confidence, by validating their ideas and validating that their startup is on the right path (once it gets onto that path). The accelerator may expand the founding team's expectations about what is possible for their startup. For example, Dropbox founder Drew Houston probably never expected his idea could be as big as it is today, had Y Combinator not expanded his expectations of what was possible. Getting into a good accelerator can also bring positive media attention, growth in web traffic, and additional traction enhancing sales. Finally, during the application process, a good accelerator will usually be respectful of founders' time, anxieties, and the business demands on them. The ability of accelerators to deliver on these latter benefits can be discovered through conversations with accelerator alumni.

What Makes an Accelerator Right for a Startup

The right accelerator for a startup is both a good accelerator (i.e., one that can sufficiently deliver on the accelerator value proposition to make a difference to a startup's evolution), and also a good fit for the startup. An accelerator that is a good fit for a startup is one that the startup has good odds of being accepted into (e.g., so that the startup is not wasting valuable time going through the application process). An accelerator that is a good fit for a startup can also work practically for the startup (e.g., it is in a location that founders can relocate to if needed, it occurs at a time of year when the whole team can be available to fully participate in the program, it has a curriculum that can align with the startup's critical priorities, etc.).[40] An accelerator that is a good fit for a startup will have a support network made up of the types of program designers and facilitators, advisors, mentors, alumni, and professional service providers who have the specific skills and know-how relevant to that startup. For example, if a startup has a business-to-business software as a service product (B2B SaaS), then it is likely to fit better with an accelerator that has a support network with deep technical and strategic knowledge of what is required to accelerate such a company's evolution. This would enable founders to draw on cohort company CTOs, mentors and advisors, alumni company CTOs/CEOs, advisors, and specialist B2B SaaS professional services providers. An accelerator that is a good fit for a startup may also have access to the startup's target customers, investors, and strategic partners. For example, when LEAPIN Digital Keys, a startup with Australian founders that we featured in the Case study in Chapter 3, went through a European accelerator, it was able to form partnerships with telecommunications companies based in England, and distributors and potential customers in Spain and Italy. While far from the founders' home location, the accelerator was ideal—since the access to such strategic partners and customers may not have been possible elsewhere. Finally, some accelerators specialize in accelerating startups' evolution from one particular stage to another (e.g., from customer discovery to customer validation, or from customer validation to strategy/operational/financial validation).[41] If a startup is accepted into an accelerator that specializes in getting the startup from the stage that it is at to the stage that it wants to get to, and that accelerator also happens to have the domain expertise and market focus relevant to the startup, then the startup is on a winner—even if the accelerator may not be the highest-ranked accelerator.[42] Good fit between an accelerator and a startup has been found to optimize founding team and support network engagement and chemistry.[43] Startup Yard Seed Accelerator staff suggest that founders ask accelerator program managers these eleven questions in order to assess the suitability or fit of the accelerator for their startup (see Table 7.2).

TABLE 7.2 Example of Questions Founders Can Ask to Assess Accelerator Fit for Their Startup

No.	Accelerator Fit Questions (to ask the accelerator or find out through other means)
1	Why is your accelerator interested in us?
2	Are you convinced by our pitch?
3	What do your investors want? Where is the money coming from?
4	Does the accelerator management team have a stake?
5	Why are your terms the way they are?
6	Have you ever fired a startup during the program?
7	What do you expect from us?
8	What is special about your ecosystem? Why should we go there?
9	Does the accelerator pay the mentors?
10	What entrepreneurial experience does the management team have?
11	Do you have partnerships with potential customers?

Source: Adapted from Startup Yard (2018).[44]

Yael Hochberg, Rice University entrepreneurship professor and managing director of the Seed Accelerator Rankings Project, had this to say about fit:[45]

> *If you're a healthcare startup, it doesn't matter if they're the best consumer internet VCs on the planet and the mentors are all consumer internet gurus; if you're doing healthcare, that's not the right fit for you.*

How to Choose the Right Accelerator

In the sections that follow, we discuss four important things that are critical to choosing the right accelerator. These include understanding what makes a good accelerator, knowing yourself and your co-founding team, doing the investigative work to access the right information about target accelerators, and considering alternative sources of accelerator benefits. Needless to say, this list is not exhaustive. It is only a starting point and we encourage entrepreneurs to expand it.

Understand What Makes a Good Accelerator

The adage "buyer beware" applies to accelerators.[46] We noted earlier that not only are some accelerators not worth the time at all, they can actually be outright dangerous for particular startups (e.g., providing dangerous advice, undoing the great work founders have already done). To guard against this, founders must do their research and due diligence (not so different to the way investors do their due diligence on prospective startup investments). This begins with founders having a clear understanding of what makes a good accelerator. That is, what does it take for an accelerator to deliver on the accelerator value proposition to a sufficient degree that it actually accelerates a startup's evolution—as opposed to setting it backwards. Once founders are clear that they are choosing only from a list of good or "good enough" accelerators, then they can proceed to considering issues of fit and acceptability of accelerator investment terms. Yael Hochberg had this to say about the importance of choosing a good accelerator:

> *Equity is an extremely precious thing to be handing away. You need to make sure that you're handing it away to an organization that will truly be able to help you.*

Know Thyself

Since good fit between an accelerator and a startup can have an outsized impact on what a startup gets out of an accelerator,[47] it is important for startups to pay a lot of attention to it when choosing an accelerator. Good accelerators do their best to select only startups that are a good fit with them and that they can genuinely have a significant transformative impact on. For example, a good hardware-focused accelerator will rarely accept non-hardware startups or hardware startups that it can't have a positive transformative impact on. But, ultimately, accelerator application reviewers may not understand a startup as well as its founders will, at least not merely based on the limited information gathered in the application process. For example, based solely on accelerator application information, application reviewers may not understand the startup's team dynamics and history, its customers and customer relationships, its customer acquisition process, its opportunity costs of participating in the accelerator program, or the technical details relating to the start-up's product development. As a result, startups themselves can play an important role in getting the right fit. For example, after getting a good understanding of an accelerator's strengths and weaknesses and shortlisting good accelerators, founders can think through the following questions: Which accelerator is the startup most likely to get accepted into (so as not to waste valuable time in the application process with no outcome)? Which accelerator support network is the best fit for the founding team (e.g., most relevant experience, easiest to access, most likely to have chemistry with the founding team, etc.)? Which accelerator will provide access to the most appropriate customers/investors/strategic partners for the startup? Is the founding team capable of relocating for an accelerator and still function effectively? What will the monetary costs of accelerator participation be (e.g., visa costs, flight costs, accommodation costs, day-to-day travel costs, etc.)? And what are the most likely opportunity costs of participating in the accelerator (e.g., we noted examples of startups' damaging their valuations and burning existing investor relationships to participate in an accelerator or forgoing substantial government grants because they reincorporated overseas).

Do the Investigative Work to Separate Reality from Spin

If investors took everything in a startup's investment pitch at face value, they would soon lose all their money. For this reason, they take due diligence, the investigative work to confirm/validate the truth of any assertions made, very seriously. Although the specific due diligence activities differ from investor to investor, examples of such due diligence work can include reviewing all key legal agreements such as existing shareholder/customer/strategic partner agreements, auditing financial reports and bank statements, reviewing source code, speaking with customers and strategic partners, reviewing patent filings, undertaking reference checks, etc.[48] The cost of these activities can be exorbitant.[49] But investors undertake extensive due diligence activities to separate reality from spin—because basing their investment decision on spin will most likely result in their losing millions of dollars. Similarly, startups need to do their due diligence on accelerator assertions to separate reality from spin. Because basing the accelerator participation on marketing spin (e.g., assertions made on the accelerator website, on accelerator-friendly press stories and blogs, or on accelerator-friendly networks) will most likely result in startups ending up in the wrong accelerator—and therefore losing valuable time, incurring significant opportunity costs, or even startup failure. The cost of this impact is probably as significant as the costs to VCs. Due diligence on an accelerator can include speaking with enough accelerator alumni to get a true picture of the accelerator experience and impact, finding data on alumni outcomes (e.g., how many are still really alive, how many have raised funding and how much, what milestones have these startups achieved before/during/after the program), finding data on accelerator performance relative to competitors (e.g., average funding, number of exits, size of exits relative to competing accelerators), asking good questions of accelerator program managers, investigating the accelerator's reputation with investors, getting advice from trustworthy sources with insider information, and much more. Essentially, founders want to find objective enough proof of the extent to which the elements of a good accelerator actually exist for the accelerator, and the extent to which the accelerator is actually a good fit for them. And they want to collect and triangulate primary and secondary information from a variety of sources to support their decisions. Ryan Shuken, expert in residence at Chinaaccelerator, put it this way:[50]

> *A VC will vet your idea, your team, your numbers and your potential, but most of all your people. Why shouldn't you do the same? Look at the people who run the program. Who are they? What are their experiences? How incentivized are they to give you everything they can to help you? Are you a data point or are you a partner?*

Consider Alternate Sources of Benefits

Accelerators are not the only source of rapid learning and all the other benefits of accelerator programs. Other sources of some of the accelerator benefits include incubators, angel investors, advisory boards, seed stage venture capital firms, and government support programs. Many government grants also increasingly come with ongoing coaching and mentoring. For example, the European Commission's Horizon 2020 Program grants include stipend money as well as a set number of hours with specialist coaches, advisors, and mentors. However, as identified in the introduction and in Chapter 1, in general these alternate sources have obvious limitations delivering on the full accelerator value proposition.[51,52] For example, regarding learning, angel investors may lack the formal structure, extensive support network, planned activities, cohort/alumni community, and compressed timeframe characteristic of accelerators. And venture capital firms may assign a single representative to advise/guide/monitor founders, whereas accelerators typically have an extensive and diverse network.[53,54] Irrespective of all this, founders can think through the benefits they are seeking and consider what they are only able to get out of accelerators vs. what they can replicate through potential alternate sources of such benefits. Where the benefits can be replicated at a lesser cost, then an alternative source may have lower opportunity cost. Where the benefits are unique to accelerators, then an accelerator may be the only way of accessing those benefits.

Case Study 6: An Unexpected Accelerator Experience[*55]

Accelerator Choice and Application

Our startup had been through our first accelerator nearly eight months ago, and we felt we had made some important progress as a result of accelerator participation. But now we were having some trouble with our vertical, and we needed deep domain expertise. We reasoned that since an accelerator helped us resolve our issues the first time, maybe it was the answer again. Maybe we could resolve our vertical-specific issues by going through an accelerator focused on our vertical. We stumbled upon an accelerator specific to our vertical, and we discovered it was really only accepting vertical-specific cohort companies. It wasn't in our city, but the managing director of the accelerator worked for a highly regarded startup in our vertical. It was going to be the inaugural program for the accelerator, so we expected there might be some teething issues, but other than that it was a good fit, so we decided to apply.

Acceptance, Accelerator Terms, and Relocation

Having been through an accelerator already, we got through the application process easily and were offered a spot in the program. When we received the

*Names, locations, and other identifiers changed for anonymity.

(Continued)

accelerator term sheet, we found it to be very similar to the first accelerator we went through. As we had worked hard to build the value of our startup since completing our first accelerator, it was disappointing for the valuation to be still the same as our first accelerator. But our thinking at the time was that all that mattered was that we resolve our issues and continue to make rapid progress. So, we began organizing for the relocation to the new city. Although flights weren't so expensive, accommodation in the new city was. Fortunately, we had some of the accelerator investment money to go towards it, when it would finally come in. We were fortunate to finally find a one-bedroom apartment within our budget and within walking distance to the accelerator campus. We ran into another founder participating in the accelerator who agreed to share the room in our apartment, in order to keep costs down. We set about finding two second-hand IKEA bunk beds to go into our one room. We also got some extra chairs and set up the kitchen table as a common working space.

Accelerator Space, Curriculum, and Stipend Payment

After sorting out our living arrangements, we decided to go familiarize ourselves with the accelerator campus. We decided to bring along the equipment and materials we would need on a day-to-day basis while at the accelerator. But when we arrived, we were surprised to find that the "campus" was actually just a busy co-working space with nowhere to store equipment and materials. This was quite different to our first accelerator, but we reasoned that the space is not where the accelerator's actual value would be coming from. Anyway, we had set up our apartment kitchen well—so we could just keep things there. We had spent most of the cash we could squeeze on flights, rental bond, and shopping to set up our living space. So, we were getting quite desperate for the accelerator stipend/investment money to come in. As the first day of the accelerator got underway, we debated whether we should ask about the investment money. We decided it might paint us in a bad light, and put it off until later in the week. When we finally asked one of the program facilitators, she advised that the accelerator wasn't actually making the investment—instead, a seed-stage venture capital firm (VC) was making the investment. This didn't seem bad on the face of it. Maybe it could be beneficial to have VC investor on our Cap table. We asked when the VC fund would transfer the $50,000 investment. She advised us that the investment depended on the VC, and that it wasn't necessarily going to be $50k, but a range up to $50,000 for some startups depending on valuation. She also notified us that before we could receive the funds, we needed to set up a C corp. We were angry and frustrated. If we received anything less than $50,000 we couldn't actually make it to the end of the accelerator program. And, although forming a C corp wasn't that complicated, it was going to delay payment, which might mean defaulting on our rental agreement.

Good Attorney/Bad Attorney

We put aside our frustration and set about registering a C corp ASAP. We were advised by the accelerator managing director (MD) to use the accelerator's "amazing" attorney who would be best for our situation. Thinking it might speed things up and keep costs down, we made contact with the attorney who promised to get back to us ASAP. But after a week, I had still not heard back from her. I called again a full week later and she finally fitted us in. She proposed a plan of action, but then proceeded to ask for an astronomical retainer. When we contacted the MD, she expressed shock and referred to the attorney as a "shark," saying she promised to offer the service for free. The MD referred us to another attorney, who finally did the work at no cost. We were relieved, but the whole process took three weeks. And by then we were defaulting on our rent and starting to wonder whether we would end up getting kicked out of our apartment before seeing any money from the accelerator.

House of Cards

Although it was still early, the whole accelerator seemed like a disorganized house of cards. We hardly saw the other teams because the accelerator space was simply a co-working space. We couldn't blame them for not being there. But we persisted, partly because we had already come so far and because we still hoped to make the most of meeting the founders the MD worked for. To make the most of the situation, we started to book meeting rooms and invite the other startups to work together. We also set up a Yammer group so everyone could chat together and share resources on the fly. The MD also hired two more accelerator staff. We started to feel optimistic that this could work out. The MD kept promising to link us with a great mentor, until it was announced via an online press release that the mentor had been hired by a competing accelerator. The MD then proceeded to message us at 3 a.m. trashing the mentor. She seemed irate. We received another message later suddenly turning on us and attacking us, saying that we weren't committed to the accelerator, we weren't participating, and that we needed to decide if we were "in or out." She accused us of not consulting with her and then threatened to kick us out if we didn't consult with her on every aspect of our company's strategy. We pushed back on her accusations and ultimatum, pointing out that there was nothing to participate in or commit to, outside of the get-togethers our team was organizing with the other teams. That we were actually helping her, so the attack and ultimatum made no sense. We got direct and expressed our disappointment that everything had been nothing but empty promises, backtracking, and disorganization.

A Hostile Learning Environment

We were later surprised to find that our roommate had received the same messages and threats at very early hours of the morning. But unlike us, he said

(Continued)

he had been kicked out of the program because apparently the mentors had negative feedback about him. Then, later, he was invited back in the program but only if he met some obscure demands. He was back in the program only to be kicked out again later. We were shocked to then receive a message from the MD about his being kicked out, on recommendation of the accelerator board and negative feedback from the mentors. She was probably not aware we lived with him. We told her that what she was doing was unacceptable; that even if what she accused him of was true, she was not creating a learning friendly environment. The next day he told us that he was back in the program again. We thought things would end there, but the drama continued with him being kicked out and readmitted repeatedly.

The Shifting Demo Day and Graduation Threats

We were relieved as demo day approached. But then we were suddenly informed that demo day was being moved almost a month out from the original planned date. The MD threatened that anyone not coming to demo day would not graduate from the accelerator, and that it was her decision who would graduate and not graduate. Our lease was due to run out a couple of weeks after the originally planned demo day. We had set it up this way to allow a few weeks for meetings and so forth after the accelerator. When we advised her that there was no way we would be able to stay until then, the MD suggested doing a private demo day for our company. We declined the suggestion, saying we didn't want special treatment. We didn't hear back from her for a while. But then, we had members of the accelerator staff telling us they were concerned about her mental health and well-being, since they had not seen her for a few days. Then randomly on a Sunday night, our roommate showed us an email he had received from her saying she had cancelled all the meetings he had organized with potential investors and advisors until he took a call from her. He was furious that she would do that, as she had not set up those meetings and was not a part of them. He refused to take the call with her. She blew up at him with very personal insults, saying he was the reason his co-founder had quit. But really, his co-founder had quit because she had promised to raise their startup at least $100,000 and advised that the co-founder could, therefore, quit his job and be in the accelerator program full-time. Of course, when he realized she could not deliver on that promise, he quit both the program and the startup. So, really, it was her fault, as we saw it.

Failure to Launch

We were surprised when accelerator staff later confided in us that there was no board making the decisions as the MD had made out. And that there weren't really advisors giving negative feedback. They also confided that the new accelerator staff the MD had hired were quitting because they had not been paid for months, and were uncomfortable with all the lying that went on. This was the last straw; we worked from the apartment until our lease ended then returned home. We almost couldn't believe what had happened to us. We later heard that ten investors and some startups turned up to demo day. We heard that when investors asked about our startup, the MD advised them that we were overseas chasing a deal. Strangely, we continued to hear from people she was referring our way, who said she spoke glowingly of us. To this day, we are still dumbfounded by our accelerator experience. It's like a jumbled dream we just can't make sense of. We feel some shame retelling this story. There must have been obvious signs. We don't consider ourselves fools, how did we miss them so badly? This story would almost be humorous, except that we lost a lot of valuable time and money—with nothing in return but humbling memories. And a painful reminder about habitual assumptions of professionalism. We are telling our story not out of blame or vindictiveness, but that it serves as a cautionary tale to other founders.

Notes

1. M. Bliemel, R. Flores, S. De Klerk, M. Miles, B. Costas, and P. Monteiro, "The Role and Performance of Accelerators in the AustralianStartup Ecosystem" (final report for the Department of Industry, Innovation & Science). Sydney, Australia: UNSW Business School, https://archive.industry.gov.au/industry/OtherReportsandStudies/Documents/The-role-and-performance-of-accelerators-in-the-Australian-startup-ecosystem.pdf.

2. R. Schatz, "How to Pick the Right Accelerator," *Inc.*, July–August 2014, accessed August 1, 2019, https://www.inc.com/magazine/201407/robin-schatz/how-to-choose-and-get-accepted-to-an-accelrator.html.

3. I. Hathaway, "Accelerating Growth: Startup Accelerator Programs in the United States," Brookings, February 17, 2016, accessed August 1, 2019, https://www.brookings.edu/research/accelerating-growth-startup-accelerator-programs-in-the-united-states/.

4. C. Clifford, "Within 10 Years, the Number of Accelerator Programs in the U.S. Has Increased Tenfold," *Entrepreneur*, February 18, 2016, accessed August 1, 2019, https://www.entrepreneur.com/article/271000.

5. R. Brown, S. Mawson, N. Lee, and L. Peterson, "Startup Factories, Transnational Entrepreneurs and Entrepreneurial Ecosystems: Unpacking the Lure of Startup Accelerator Programs," *European Planning Studies* 27, no. 5 (2019): 885–904.

6. Ibid.

7. Startup Yard, "This Will Make You Think about Accelerators," accessed October 14, 2019, https://startupyard.com/accelerator-in-the-21st-century/.

8. Gust, "Global Accelerator Report 2016," accessed October 14, 2019, http://gust.com/accelerator_reports/2016/global/.

9. "2016 Startup Activity," Kauffman Index, https://www.kauffman.org/~/media/kauffman_org/microsites/kauffman_index/startup_activity_2016/kauffman_index_startup_activity_national_trends_2016.pdf.

10. E. Griffith, "Why Startups Die Slow Deaths," *Fortune*, September 7, 2016, accessed August 1, 2019, https://fortune.com/2016/09/07/why-startups-die-slow-deaths/.

11. K. Lukosiute, S. Jensen, and S. Tanev, "Is Joining a Business Incubator or Accelerator Always a Good Thing?" *Technology Innovation Management Review* 9, no. 7 (2019): 5–15.

12. D. Cohen, "Improving Startup Success: The Equity Back Guarantee," Techstars Blog, September 4, 2014, accessed August 1, 2019, https://www.TechStars.com/content/accelerators/announcements/equity-back-guarantee/.

13. G. Hughes. "First Do No Harm; Then Try to Prevent It," *Emergency Medicine Journal* 24, no. 5 (2007): 314. doi:10.1136/emj.2007.047803.

14. Adapted from K. Lukosiute, S. Jensen, and S. Tanev, "Is Joining a Business Incubator or Accelerator Always a Good Thing?" *Technology Innovation Management Review* 9, no. 7 (2019): 5–15.

15. M. Arrington, "The Nasty Exploding Term Sheet," *TechCrunch*, March 23, 2009, accessed August 1, 2019, https://techcrunch.com/2009/03/22/the-nasty-exploding-term-sheet/.

16. I. Hathaway, "What Startup Accelerators Really Do," *Harvard Business Review*, March 2016, accessed August 1, 2019, https://hbr.org/2016/03/what-startup-accelerators-really-do.

17. Lukosiute, Jensen, and Tanev, "Is Joining a Business Incubator?"

18. L. Balachandra, T. Briggs, K. Eddleston, and C. Brush, "Don't Pitch Like a Girl! How Gender Stereotypes Influence Investor Decisions," *Entrepreneurship Theory and Practice* 43, no. 1 (2019): 116–137.

19. S. Blank, "Is This Startup Ready For Investment?" *Forbes*, February 24, 2014, accessed August 1, 2019, https://www.forbes.com/sites/steveblank/2014/02/24/is-this-startup-ready-for-investment/#b3f980f1d8fa.

20. A. Cremades, "The 10 Biggest Mistakes Entrepreneurs Make When Fundraising," *Forbes*, August 21, 2018, accessed August 1, 2019, https://www.forbes.com/sites/alejandrocremades/2018/08/21/the-10-biggest-mistakes-entrepreneurs-make-when-fundraising/#20827f044abe.

21. S. Palmer-Derrien, "Five Tips for Getting Your Startup Investment Ready," *SmartCompany*, accessed August 1, 2019, https://www.smartcompany.com.au/startupsmart/advice/five-tips-for-getting-your-startup-investment-ready/.

22. Blank, "Is This Startup Ready For Investment?"

23. D. Brown, "5 Things to Avoid When Raising Startup Funding," *Inc.*, September 7, 2018, accessed August 1, 2019, https://www.inc.com/david-brown/5-things-to-avoid-when-raising-startup-funding.html.

24. Cremades, "The 10 Biggest Mistakes."

25. C. Clifford, "Top Silicon Valley Venture Capitalist: These Are the 2 Biggest Mistakes New Entrepreneurs Make When Asking for Money," CNBC, May 8, 2017, accessed August 1, 2019, https://www.cnbc.com/2017/05/08/biggest-fundraising-mistakes-entrepreneurs-make.html.

26. A. Kang, "Accelerators: A Critical Component in Scaling Up Environmental Entrepreneurship," accessed August 1, 2019, https://www.wri.org/blog/2012/12/accelerators-critical-component-scaling-environmental-entrepreneurship.

27. Blank, "Is This Startup Ready For Investment?"

28. Adapted from S. Kaji, "How Helpful Are Accelerators to Getting Funded?" accessed August 1, 2019, https://www.cbinsights.com/research/top-accelerators-follow-on-funding-rates/.

29. M. Andreessen, "EE204 Business Management for Engineers and Computer Scientists," accessed August 1, 2019, http://web.stanford.edu/class/ee204/ProductMarketFit.html.

30. S. Cohen, D. C., Fehder, Y. V. Hochberg, and F. Murray, "The Design of Startup Accelerators," *Research Policy* 48 (2019): 1781–1797.

31. Ibid.

32. C. Bagley, "Top Ten Legal Mistakes Made by Entrepreneurs," accessed August 1, 2019, https://hbswk.hbs.edu/item/top-ten-legal-mistakes-made-by-entrepreneurs.
33. A. Kwapisz, "Do Government and Legal Barriers Impede Entrepreneurship in the U.S.? An Exploratory Study of Perceived vs. Actual Barriers," *Journal of Business Venturing* 11 (June 2019), e00114, https://doi.org/10.1016/j.jbvi.2019.e00114.
34. Bagley, "Top Ten Legal Mistakes Made by Entrepreneurs."
35. B. Mollen, "How Do Startup Founders Manage Legal Issues and Compliance?" Gust Launch, accessed August 1, 2019, https://gust.com/launch/blog/startups-manage-legal-compliance.
36. R. Busulwa, M. Tice, and B. Gurd, *Strategy Execution and Complexity: Thriving in the Era of Disruption* (Routledge, 2018).
37. J. Gans, E. Scottand, and S. Stern, "Do Entrepreneurs Need a Strategy?" *Harvard Business Review*, May 2018, accessed August 1, 2019, https://hbr.org/2018/05/do-entrepreneurs-need-a-strategy?referral=03759&cm_vc=rr_item_page.bottom.
38. Ibid.
39. Lukosiute, Jensen, and Tanev, "Is Joining a Business Incubator?"
40. S. Cohen, D. C., Fehder, Y. V. Hochberg, and F. Murray, "The Design of Startup Accelerators," *Research Policy* 48 (2019): 1781–1797.
41. "Choosing an Accelerator: 11 Questions to Ask," StartupYard, accessed August 1, 2019, https://startupyard.com/choosing-accelerator-11-questions/.
42. Ibid.
43. Ibid.
44. Adapted from "Choosing an Accelerator: 11 Questions to Ask," StartupYard, accessed August 1, 2019, https://startupyard.com/choosing-accelerator-11-questions/.
45. P. Andruss, "What to Look for in an Accelerator Program," accessed August 1, 2019, https://www.entrepreneur.com/article/225242.
46. Ibid.
47. "Choosing an Accelerator: 11 Questions to Ask."
48. R. Ragozzino, "The Effects of Venture Capital Firms on Entrepreneurial Firms' Strategic Alliances and Liquidity Events," in *The Oxford Handbook of Entrepreneurship and Collaboration*, ed. J. Reuer, S. F. Matusik, and J. Jones (New York: Oxford University Press, 2019).

49. Ibid.
50. R. Shuken, "Choosing an Accelerator in China: Then Running It," accessed August 1, 2019, https://medium.com/@ Chinaccelerator/choosing-an-accelerator-in-china-then-running-it-70c9f3b79a11.
51. S. L. Cohen, "How to Accelerate Learning: Entrepreneurial Ventures Participating in Accelerator Programs" (PhD diss., University of North Carolina at Chapel Hill, 2013).
52. S. Cohen and Y. V. Hochberg, "Accelerating Startups: The Seed Accelerator Phenomenon (2014)," accessed August 1, 2019, http://seedrankings.com/pdf/seed-accelerator-phenomenon .pdf.
53. Cohen, "How to Accelerate Learning."
54. Cohen and Hochberg, *Accelerating Startups.*
55. D. Cohen, "A Horrifying Accelerator Story That You'll Need to Read Twice," *Hi, I'm David G. Cohen,* August 29, 2013, accessed August 1, 2019, http://davidgcohen.com/2013/08/29/a–shocking-accelerator-story-that-youll-need-to-read-twice/.

How to Get the Most out of an Accelerator

If you don't plan ahead, accelerators will dominate your time with mandatory meetings, workshops, and events. You will surrender your life to the accelerator schedule for three months.

Lyle Stevens, co-founder Mavrck;
alumnus, Techstars

Plan Ahead

In order to compress years' worth of learning-by-doing into months, and still significantly transform founders and their startup, accelerators will have a lot going on during the accelerator program. Founders may find the experience akin to drinking from a fire hose. From the very first day of the accelerator, startups will face a flurry of activity that includes events, workshops, meetings, mentoring sessions, urgent deadlines, and dynamically changing schedules. While a lot is on offer, not everything will be mandatory or a priority for each startup, and founders need to avoid being pulled into many different directions, and thus wasting valuable time. If they don't, accelerators may dominate their time with activities that aren't crucial. Alex Iskold, managing director of Techstars' New York accelerator, strongly advises startups to be clear on their company goals—and then to work backwards from those goals when setting goals to achieve during the accelerator.[1] After doing this, founders should then set and pursue the monthly, weekly, and daily goals that will drive achievement of the overall accelerator goals. He warns that unless founders are clear on overall company goals and work backwards from these goals, they may surrender to the often noisy, chaotic, serendipitous, competitive, and distracting nature of accelerator programs.[2] While surrendering does not necessarily mean they won't get value from the accelerator, it typically limits how much value founders get out of the accelerator and how much progress their startup makes.

Clarify Priorities and Plan Your Time

Once founders are clear on what they want out of the accelerator, they need to think carefully about what they will prioritize in the accelerator, and how they will allocate their time to make sure priority activities and outcomes are delivered. Jessica Stacey, Venture Partner at the London-based BGV accelerator, recommends that founders focus on the top three priorities, or things they want out of the accelerator, and make sure that work and progress towards achieving these does not slip.[3] If it does, founders may find themselves spending time and effort on the wrong things. Doing the right things to achieve the priorities is as important as having the right priorities. For example, Lyle Stevens, Mavrck co-founder and Techstars alumnus, observed that while raising money typically dominates most cohort startups' priority lists, startups don't always spend their time on the activities most likely to accelerate fundraising. That is, rather than prioritizing their time around events and activities that directly maximize their traction, they prioritize investor exposure and introduction activities[4]—which, without enough traction, may be of low priority.

Founders need to be strategic about how they, as a team, allocate their time to get maximum value from the accelerator. Both Jessica Stacey and Lyle Stevens recommend that founders divide and conquer in order to participate in more activities, learn more, and do more follow-up.[5,6] For example, Lyle Stevens noted that startups can have the first team member taking charge of investment readiness/ fundraising activities, the second team member taking charge of product development activities, another taking charge of sales-related activities, and the third team member taking care of legal and professional service–related activities and any other remaining activities. But he warns that if they do this, founders should establish a way to know how the team is progressing, where each team member is at with their goals, how to support them, how to share information/learning, and how to approach decisions that require input from other team members. This is another reason why accelerators are usually turned off by solo founders—what they get out of the accelerator program can be restricted significantly by their inability to divide and conquer.[7,8]

Show That You Are Committed

John Harthorne, a board member at the MassChallenge accelerator (which has offices in Boston, Israel, Mexico, Rhode Island, Switzerland, and Texas), contends that accelerators and their investor network are on the lookout for smart, driven, and dedicated teams that are passionate about execution.[9] Teams that have these qualities in abundance are likely to better engage the accelerator's network, receive greater support, and thus get more out of accelerators. So, it's important for founding teams to demonstrate these qualities with both their actions and results. Just how do startups do this? For starters, they can show up to more events and activities.[10,11] Ash Rust, Sendhub co-founder and Sterling Road managing partner, points out that the aim of accelerator events and activities is to help startups learn to avoid the most common pitfalls—it's hard to do this if founders don't attend[12] Each missed event or activity is also a missed chance to meet and build valuable relationships with speakers who could be future investors, who could provide valuable time-saving insights, and who could provide access to customers or strategic partners that could change a startup's fate. For example, Steve Dunn, LEAPIN Digital Keys co-founder and H-Farm accelerators alumnus, considers himself lucky that he pushed himself to attend a networking event in the first week of an accelerator, where he struck up a conversation with a mentor who was friends with the CEO of the world's largest architectural hardware company. The mentor did an introduction to this CEO, who then later joined LEAPIN Digital Keys' team as an advisor. The CEO advised Steve on many aspects of business development, especially relevant to the industry, including offering a piece of advice that became a critical part of the startup's strategy. That advice was for the startup to steer clear of attempting to manufacture its own smartlocks, especially deadbolt attachment smartlocks. The CEO explained that his company had spent many years and many millions of dollars trying to do that with a different technology. Steve would later find out just how invaluable this advice was, as he watched competing startup after competing startup attempt to manufacture their own smartlocks—only to lose vast sums of money and end up going into bankruptcy.

Ash Rust suggests that founders start strong with full attendance at orientation and early social events.[13] And then have the right team members in attendance at all core sessions (e.g., team members who are engaged, actively listening, and are capable of picking up and acting on ideas that may change the business); but perhaps teams can seek the advice of accelerator program managers about the relevance of specific optional sessions to their startup. Young Entrepreneur Council (YEC) founding member and White House Top 100 Entrepreneur award recipient, Ash Kumra, suggests that entrepreneurs go all in. That is, that they dedicate their time to the accelerator program as it is an endeavor that requires their full focus.[14] In addition to your actions, your results should demonstrate your commitment. If you are really showing up and going all in, your results should show it. Stephanie Kaplan, founder of Her Campus Media, advises founders to keep in mind that they want to show that their startup is truly going places—that it is going to be even more successful if advisors get behind it.[15] Nothing says this stronger than how a startup behaves and the milestones it achieves during the accelerator.[16]

Go Fast

A big appeal of accelerators is the opportunity for startups to compress years' worth of learning and progress into the typical three-month accelerator duration. Most accelerators' designs are focused on enabling startups to do more, faster.[17] Going fast requires founders to first be strategic about what activities, if performed, will result in the greatest progress (e.g., growing revenue, building key partnerships, getting investment ready), what the optimal sequencing of these activities is, and how to ensure that they are done in the least amount of time possible (i.e., with the least amount of time wasted). Techstars' New York managing director Alex Iskold advises that this begins with founders realizing that they are on the clock.[18] And not, for example, writing extra code if it is not absolutely essential or chasing customers who will take too long to close. He also advises founders to constantly be looking for shortcuts as a way to be able to do more, faster. He suggests that founders can do this by, for example, always asking how something can be done faster[19] and always being on the lookout for actions that will make the greatest contribution to progress. Earlier, we noted that Jessica Stacey and Lyle Stevens recommend that founders divide and conquer in order to participate in more activities, learn more, and do more, faster.[20,21] Steve Dunn recommends that founders pay particular attention to how they spend their accelerator stipend or investment money to maximize how long it lasts and its impact. Once it runs out, a startup's speed may be seriously constrained (e.g., if it is unable to pay for critical things).

Get Customer Discovery and Customer Validation Right

We noted earlier Marc Andreessen's strong view that getting into a great market with a product that can satisfy that market is the only thing that matters for startups that are not there yet.[22,23] However, it is one of the greatest challenges startups face. And, according to Andreesen, it is the number one killer of startups. It goes without saying, then, that founders who have not found product/market fit need to prioritize finding it while in the accelerator; or at least making significant progress towards finding it. Finding product/market fit requires getting customer discovery right (i.e., problem/solution fit, MVP, sales funnels), and getting customer validation right (i.e., product/market fit, business model, sales and marketing roadmap). For startups that have not completed these two stages of startup evolution (most startups joining accelerators), the accelerator is an invaluable resource for knowing what to do, how to do it, when to do it, and when it has been sufficiently done to be able to move onto the next stage. Jumping the gun on customer discovery or customer validation activities, or believing you have got them right when you really haven't, can result in wasted time/ effort or, worse, can kill an otherwise promising startup. Theranos Inc. is a good case in point of a startup that jumped the gun on product/ market fit and started to scale a product that wasn't ready—only to come crashing down, with the founder finding herself facing a federal trial and possible prison time for misleading investors, doctors, and patients.[24] Accelerators can help startups get customer discovery and customer validation right, enabling them to test and iterate the right way, to test and iterate faster, to learn the right things from each iteration, to know when to pivot, and to know what to pivot to (e.g., what has the most promise). Within a good accelerator network, all types of strategies, tactics, and tools to get customer discovery and customer validation right will be on offer (e.g., via accelerator program managers, accelerator mentors/advisors, accelerator alumni, cohort startups, prospective customers, etc.)

Get Strategy Right

Strategy for startups is difficult to get right, especially with the conflicting prescriptions of strategy tools and frameworks more suited to large organizations than startups. But founders can't just turn a blind eye to it. Getting strategy right enables founders to do the right things, at the right time, and in the right way.[25] It also enables founders to know what not to do, thus avoiding fatal missteps (e.g., wasted time, money, and energy). Startups can draw on the accelerator's network to identify the best approach to setting strategic objectives, to identify tactics for achieving those strategic objectives, to identify the best approach to execution and identifying approaches to validate both strategic objectives/tactics and execution approach. Coming out of the accelerator, having gotten strategy right, is invaluable, as it will continue to pay dividends long after the accelerator ends. On the other hand, not getting it right while in the accelerator may result in a startup getting it wrong afterwards and undoing any gains made while in the accelerator. We noted earlier that LEAPIN Digital Keys received advice from an industry stalwart to not manufacture their own deadbolt smartlock. The startup was able to use the rest of the accelerator program to work with mentors to help devise realistic tactics and actions for developing its smartlock product without actually manufacturing it itself. Without the accelerator mentors' help to get the strategy right, the startup would have spent its scarce time and money on the wrong things and probably long been out of business—as has happened with many of its competitors.

Get Legal Right

In Chapter 7, we noted that if they don't get legal structures right from the start, startups can succeed—only for the founders to lose it all. Getting legal structures right is typically difficult for founders due to challenges in knowing/finding the right legal experts for a startup, and due to challenges affording such expertise. For this reason, the accelerator is a great opportunity to both have access to the right legal experts and, typically, at no cost (or at very accept-able rates, depending on the nature of a startup's legal needs). Once founders get the legal foundation right (e.g., right legal structures, right agreement templates/tools, resolution of any legacy legal issues etc.), they can build the startup with confidence, knowing that what they are building is truly theirs.

Get Investment Ready or Raise Investment

In Chapter 7 we noted that investment readiness is partly driven by the nature of the startup (e.g., what its product is, market, team, trac-tion), its stage of evolution (e.g., is it at the insight/opportunity rec-ognition, customer discovery, customer validation, or scaling stage), and the founders' skill at fundraising (e.g., can founders get in front of the right investors, pitch effectively, having the right fundraising tools to back up their pitch, effectively negotiate term sheets, and get through due diligence?). Notwithstanding that getting customer discovery and customer validation right is one of the biggest con-tributors to investment readiness, the accelerator provides one of the best opportunities for startups to understand what investment readiness actually looks like, to achieve investment readiness, and to raise investment (e.g., from a primed investor network).[26] While most founders may be aware of what it may take to get genuine inter-est from an investor, Figure 8.1 outlines some additional fundrais-ing stages that startups may need to be ready to navigate effectively before they can raise investment.

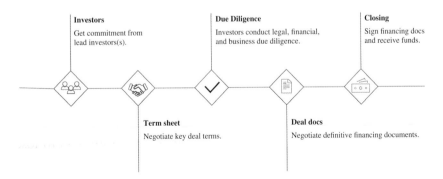

FIGURE 8.1 Key Stages of a Typical Financing Process for a Startup Funding Round
Source: Adapted from Scannavino (2018).[27]

Perfect Your Pitching, Storytelling, and Business Communication

Lyle Stevens points out that raising money, securing strategic partners, closing customers, and making star hires is exponentially difficult without a solid company story and pitch.[28] Steve Dunn adds that general business communication and relational skills are equally important (e.g., for networking and attracting supporters, explaining your idea clearly in different settings, etc). With specialist pitching, storytelling, and business communication experts, as well as a curriculum configured to hone startups' pitching, storytelling, and business communication skills, the accelerator is one of the best environments to develop these skills.[29] Founders who are not particularly strong in this area can maximize the value they get out of accelerators by getting out of their comfort zone and embracing all that the accelerator has to offer in this area.

Building Your Network within the Network

Good accelerators have a vast network of people who can provide two important types of value to startups. First, they can provide access to the right potential investors, strategic partners, advisors, board members, and customers. Second, they can act as a support network (e.g., providing strategic/technical advice, coaching/mentoring founders, providing hands-on help, being a source peer support/empathy, etc.). Since a good accelerator network is usually vast, and some of the best network members can be drawn on by lots of startups (e.g., cohort companies, alumni companies), founders can maximize the value they get out of the accelerator program by curating their own network within the network.[30] For example, this can involve founders identifying the people best placed to help their startup and engaging and building rapport with these people. Steve Dunn suggests that carving out enough face-to-face time to build and maintain relationships is extremely valuable. And Alex Iskold has this advice for founders:[31]

> Obsessively collect people and connections. The network will help accelerate your company after the program. It will help you with this business and all your next businesses. It is your resource and your set of shortcuts around the business world. If you don't obsessively connect, you are missing out. You will literally be at a disadvantage compared to other founders who are doing this correctly.

Jake Newfield, former VP of Business Development at Alumnify (a 500 Startups Alumni company), adds that good accelerators have a first or second connection to thousands of successful entrepreneurs and investors. With the right approach, founders can access all the resources they need to grow their company.[32] For example, they can ask for introductions and referrals, they can ask for hands-on support with particular customer engagements, they can sign up star entrepreneurs and investors to their boards, and much more. But founders shouldn't forget about other founders also participating in the program—they could turn out to be some of the most valuable connections if leveraged in the right way. Essentially going through the same experience, they can be a valuable source of camaraderie, hands-on support, and sharing of practices/tools. For example, a cohort company CTO may know how to simply solve a technical problem that may have cost a lot of valuable time and money. Alternatively, peer founding teams may link a startup to great employees, co-founders, investors, and customers. Not all startups work out, if your startup is unfortunate enough to be one that doesn't, it may just be that another startup embraces you as co-founder. Or perhaps as a contractor while you get back on your feet. Irrespective, the network that founders assemble can continue to accelerate a startup and to support the startup's cofounders long after the accelerator program ends.[33]

Resolve Any Difficult Issues

Startups may enter an accelerator with a range of legacy issues that have simply been too difficult to resolve (e.g., legal issues, shareholder issues, co-founder equity split issues, co-founder disputes, etc.). Left unresolved, these issues can sap morale and hamper a startup's progress. The accelerator is an opportunity to get help from people who have more than likely encountered and resolved these issues before. But this requires founders to be open and honest about these issues. This can be challenging, especially since founders may have glossed over these issues during the accelerator application process or presented themselves as a well-oiled machine during the accelerator interview. But BGV accelerator venture partner, Jessica Stacey, warns founders that secrecy is their enemy.[34] Without being honest about such issues, and getting help with what might be fatal problems, founders may be building on shaky foundations.

Maximize Learning

An important aim of accelerator designs is enabling accelerated learning to occur. But while accelerators can lead a horse to water, it is up to entrepreneurs how much they drink, if at all. Entrepreneurs who think they know it all, who are unwilling to trust accelerator advisors/mentors (after having selected the right accelerator), and who are unwilling to get out of their comfort zone, may simply be unteachable—except maybe by failure. For those who want to learn, maximizing learning is one of the biggest ways to ramp up what they get out of an accelerator. How can founders maximize learning? First, they can show up to more events and activities, as each of these may contain the critical insight that transforms a startup. But as well as showing up, founders must be engaged, actively listen, ask clarifying questions, and take notes. To get to more events, we noted earlier that founders can specialize and then divide and conquer. For example, one founder may focus on legal/accounting and attend every activity related to that. Another founder may take the lead on networking and strive to make as many relevant connections as possible and to engage these connections as much as possible. Second, founders can proactively seek out advice/coaching/mentoring at every opportunity, often at any time and nearly instantly. Since almost everything they need to learn potentially resides within the accelerator network, it may just be a matter of asking the right people the right questions. Third, Alex Iskold advises founders to take all the feedback that comes their way (the good, the bad, and the ugly), and that they shouldn't ignore recurring themes in this feedback.[35] Fourth, Jessica Stacey advises that startups can gain great learning from chats with cohort companies and should, therefore, show up at the office even when there are no sessions on and build relationships with the other founders.[36] But Lyle Stevens warns founders that there can be unnecessary competition between cohort companies, and founders need to find a way to get over it quickly so they can benefit from having those peers as a sounding board and to hearing their perspectives and experiences. Finally, Alex Iskold and Mavrck co-founder Lyle Stevens recommend that founders take time to process, synthesize, combine, distill, and share all the information/intelligence/learning gathered so the team can act on it.[37,38]

Case Study 7: One Co-Founder's Approach to Making the Most of the Techstars Accelerator Experience[*39]

Knowing how incredibly competitive the best accelerators are, our team realized how lucky we were when we got accepted into Techstars (2014 Boston class). We wanted to do everything possible to make the most of the program. Right from the start, our mentality was "how do we take advantage of every opportunity this presents us?" We started by thinking through what our company goals were and which of them Techstars was best suited to help us achieve. We finally agreed on the smart goals to achieve during the accelerator. That is, goals that were specific, measurable, achievable, realistic, and time bound. We framed each goal as below:

> ... reach X customers by Y date; raise $X by Y date; launch X product by Y date; recruit X roles by Y date; validate business model X by Y date; validate target market X by Y date.

We knew the goals were really going to stretch us, but with smart and disciplined focus we could deliver on them. We figured that using our time intelligently and getting prioritization right was going to be critical. So we discussed what would be the best time management strategy. We agreed that we should divide and conquer in order to get to more events and activities, as well as to be more actively engaged at these events and activities. Then, we strategized who would attend what events, what their role and goals would be, and what the team's expectations of them would be. As CEO, I would spend 90% of my time on meetings that resulted from the accelerator. Other co-founders would spend 50% of their time on accelerator activities relevant to them, and non-founder employees would spend 20% of their time on accelerator activities relevant to them. We wanted to keep our schedules flexible to adapt to last-minute accelerator schedule changes, drive-by meetings, or unexpected opportunities.

As the CEO, I knew it was my responsibility to keep everyone accountable, aligned, and on track, as well as to make sure that we shared information and learning for the divide and conquer strategy to work. I established one daily meeting, three weekly meetings, and one meeting that was regular but not at a fixed time. The meetings drew on agile scrum practices that everyone was familiar with. The daily meeting was a standup event (a meeting in which everybody took two to three minutes to explain what they had achieved the previous day, what they aimed to achieve today, and anything they were waiting on others for). The first weekly meeting was a 60- to 90-minute prioritization

[*As told by the startup's lead founder, adapted from the reference provided.]

(Continued)

or reprioritization meeting (identifying what was a priority to achieve that week in order to stay on track with our smart goals). The second weekly meeting (or meetings to be more precise) was a 15- to 20-minute one-on-one that I would have with each member of the team so they could voice any concerns and challenges. Since we were still coding our product, the third weekly meeting was one that already existed outside of the accelerator. It was our established weekly demo/sprint retrospective/sprint planning meeting. In this meeting, the dev team would do a demo to show the rest of the team where the product was at, reflect on what had gone well/not gone well in the previous week, and share the plan for the upcoming week. The dev team also had its own daily SCRUM meeting for day-to-day coding issues. The last weekly meeting reviewed progress toward each team member's objectives, key results, metrics, and corrective actions to be taken.

I knew it was going to take a lot for me to keep up, as all these regular meetings were in addition to accelerator-related meetings and appointments. Even conceptually, this seemed exhausting. But I needed to make sure that I didn't set a bad example or become the bottleneck for other team members. I needed to really change the way I approached things by default. I knew my biggest challenges/opportunities were going to be spending time on low-priority things, getting distracted by email, and not saying "no" to enough unexpected commitment requests. My plan to solve the email challenge was a decision I made to step away from my email inbox and only check/respond to emails three times a day (in the morning, at lunch, and in the evening). To better prioritize, I decided that I would not accept meetings more than two weeks in advance. I had lots of situations in the past where something really high priority came up, but I had already committed to something less important several weeks ago. Finally, I knew I needed to be more disciplined to stick to my planned schedule.

With all the effort we had put into planning for the accelerator, we were finally ready for the rubber to hit the road. As the accelerator program start date approached, Helmuth von Moltke's insight "*no plan survives first contact with the enemy*" and Dwight Eisenhower's insight ". . . *plans are useless, but planning is invaluable*" kept crossing my mind. If we needed to modify our plan once the accelerator started, we were ready to do so. But we were confident any modifications wouldn't be major and would still be focused on achieving the same aims.

Notes

1. A. Iskold, "7 Ways to Get the Most Out of an Accelerator Program," TechStars, March 10, 2016, accessed August 1, 2019, https://www.TechStars.com/content/accelerators/nyc/7-things-to-do-to-get-the-most-out-of-an-accelerator-program/.
2. Ibid.
3. "21 Tips for Getting the Most out of a Startup Accelerator Programme," Bethnal Green Ventures, July 14, 2015, accessed August 1, 2019, https://bethnalgreenventures.com/blog/21-tips-for-getting-the-most-out-of-a-startup-accelerator-programme/.
4. L. Stevens, "How to Make the Most of Your Startup Accelerator Program Experience," *TechCrunch*, May 7, 2015, accessed August 1, 2019, https://techcrunch.com/2015/05/07/how-to-make-the-most-of-your-startup-accelerator-program-experience/.
5. Bethnal Green Ventures, "21 Tips for Getting the Most."
6. Stevens, "How to Make the Most."
7. T. Cooney, "Editorial: 'What Is an Entrepreneurial Team?,'" *International Small Business Journal* 23, no. 3 (2005): 226–235.
8. W. B. Gartner, K. G. Shaver, E. Gatewood, and J. A. Katz, "Finding the Entrepreneur in Entrepreneurship," *Entrepreneurship Theory and Practice* 18, no. 3 (1994): 5–10.
9. "15 Entrepreneurs Give Tips on Getting the Most out of an Incubator or Accelerator," Young Entrepreneur Council, accessed August 1, 2019, https://venturebeat.com/2012/04/29/15-tips-to-get-the-most-out-of-an-incubator-or-accelerator/.
10. M. Moensted, "Networking and Entrepreneurship in Small High-Tech European Firms: An Empirical Study," *International Journal of Management* 27, no. 1 (2010): 16–30.
11. E. Chell and S. Baines, "Networking, Entrepreneurship and Microbusiness Behaviour," *Entrepreneurship & Regional Development, An International Journal* 12, no. 3 (2010): 195–215.

12. A. Rust, "How to Make the Most of a Startup Accelerator," accessed August 1, 2019, https://hackernoon.com/how-to-make-the-most-of-a-startup-accelerator-222c02b7b5e2.

13. Ibid.

14. "15 Entrepreneurs Give Tips."

15. Ibid.

16. Ibid.

17. Iskold, "7 Ways to Get the Most."

18. Ibid.

19. Ibid.

20. "21 Tips for Getting the Most."

21. Stevens, "How to Make the Most."

22. M. Andreessen, Product/Market Fit: "The Only Thing That Matters Is Getting to Product Market Fit," Stanford University, accessed October 23, 2018, http://web.stanford.edu/class/ee204/ProductMarketFit.html.

23. M. Andreessen, "12 Things about Product-Market Fit," Andreessen Horowitz, accessed March 6, 2019, https://a16z.com/2017/02/18/12-things-about-product-market-fit/.

24. K. Clark, "Theranos Founder Elizabeth Holmes to Stand Trial in 2020," *TechCrunch*, June 28, 2019, accessed October 15, 2019, https://techcrunch.com/2019/06/28/theranos-founder-elizabeth-holmes-to-stand-trial-in-2020/.

25. J. S. Gans, S. Stern, and J. Wu, "Foundations of Entrepreneurial Strategy," *Strategic Management Journal* 40 (2016): 736–756.

26. Rust, "How to Make the Most of a Startup Accelerator."

27. Adapted from N. Scannavino, "Startup Fundraising: Financing Process," accessed August 1, 2019, https://medium.com/law-decrypted/startup-fundraising-financing-process-2afa6d9e6bc3.

28. Stevens, "How to Make the Most."

29. F. Liu, J. Ma, and R. Li, "Which Role Model Is More Effective in Entrepreneurship Education? An Investigation of Storytelling on Individual's Entrepreneurial Intentions," *Frontiers in Psychology* 10 (2019): 836, doi: 10.3389/fpsyg.2019.00837.

30. D. L. Hoffman and N. Radojevich-Kelley, "Analysis Of Accelerator Companies: An Exploratory Case Study of Their Programs, Processes and Early Results," *Small Business Institute* 8, no. 2 (2012): 54–70.

31. Iskold, "7 Ways to Get the Most."

32. J. Newfield, "5 Ways to Get the Most out of an Accelerator Program," accessed August 1, 2019, https://www.inc.com/jake-newfield/5-ways-to-get-the-most-out-of-an-accelerator-program.html.
33. Iskold, "7 Ways to Get the Most."
34. "21 Tips for Getting the Most."
35. Iskold, "7 Ways to Get the Most."
36. "21 Tips for Getting the Most."
37. Iskold, "7 Ways to Get the Most."
38. Stevens, "How to Make the Most."
39. Adapted from L. Stevens, "How to Make the Most of Your Startup Accelerator Program Experience," *TechCrunch*, May 7, 2015, accessed August 1, 2019, https://techcrunch.com/2015/05/07/how-to-make-the-most-of-your-startup-accelerator-program-experience/.

What to Expect after the Accelerator Ends

The moment following demo day, you're a has-been. It's hard to imagine when you're in it and the center of attention of the startup community, but soon there will be a next batch.[1]

Tal Raviv, growth product manager, Patreon;
co-founder, Ecquire; alumnus, DreamIT
Ventures and Growlab

What Happens after the Accelerator Ends

During the accelerator, founders are under intense pressure to learn quickly, achieve critical milestones, and beat the ticking clock of demo day. In the frantic pressure and activity leading up to demo day, the spotlight is on them, as program managers and mentors constantly look over their shoulder to confirm the latest progress, and demo day facilitators start to set up for the big day. But then, suddenly, demo day is done, and the accelerator is over. All the pressure and attention are gone. The sudden switch in pace can be bewildering. Describing it as the "post accelerator cliff," Chloe Daniel, from the German Tech Entrepreneurship Center (GTEC), compares the experience to a post-exam blur, where founders may start to suddenly feel the effects of the exhaustion, fatigue, and burnout resulting from the accelerator's pressurized environment.[2] As accelerator program managers start to prepare for the new batch of startups, founders may find that they are on their own, and that all the support, advice, and resources that were readily available during the accelerator are suddenly not so easy to access. Experts who provided their services for free during the accelerator may suddenly want to charge full fees. And advisors who were readily available and responsive during the accelerator may suddenly prioritize their clients and be too busy.

The Need to Maintain Momentum

With the ticking clock of demo day and the watchful eyes of accelerator program managers and mentors suddenly gone, it can be easy for founders to slide back into the same routines and ways of running their company before the accelerator. Keenan Koizumi, from The Refiners seed fund, warns founders that this is the last thing they want to do.[3] Although it might be a relief not to be operating at hyperspeed for three months straight, founders need to find a way to maintain the pressure and the rate of progress. There are several benefits to doing this. For starters, maintaining that rate of progress engages co-founders and the rest of the team to both stay and commit more effort to the startup. Second, it is a great opportunity for founders to institutionalize that approach to rapid progress as the company's way of working. And a startup that maintains that way of working and rate of progress is almost unstoppable. Third, although a startup may not succeed in raising funding, signing heavyweight strategic partners or premium clients during the accelerator, it still has the opportunity to do so after the accelerator. For example, Chloe Daniel points out that European investors typically like to take their time to understand startups and their product—this can take many months of conversation.[4] So, founders should be aware that everyone will be watching the startup's progress closely after the accelerator and that, depending on its progress, investors, strategic partners, and prospective clients may suddenly go on the offensive and start courting the startup—instead of the startup always being the one courting them.

What to Do after the Accelerator

Once founders accept how critical it is to maintain the momentum and rate of progress achieved during the accelerator, the challenge becomes: how do they do it? Dror Pearl, head of IBM's Global Technology Unit that oversees the IBM Alpha Zone accelerator based in Israel, advises startups to think about "the day after" before the accelerator even begins, or at least at the start of the accelerator.[5] That way, they can plan ahead for life after the accelerator. For example, based on that plan, founders may prioritize activities during the accelerator that capitalize on the types of support they will not have access to or be able to replicate once the accelerator is over. Or founders may undertake activities that maximize the support they can receive after the accelerator ends.

Plan Ahead How You Will Maintain the Sense of Urgency

Drawing on Dror Pearl's advice that "the day after" should be thought through and planned for at the early stages of the accelerator, founders can do several things to ensure a seamless transition to post-accelerator life. For example, one startup we spoke to staggered out meetings with key mentors and advisors several months out after the accelerator. Prior to each meeting, the startup had to meet agreed-upon progress milestones. So for this startup, the accountability and sense of urgency did not just die off after demo day, and continued to galvanize the team. Another startup we spoke to had taken a similar approach and established an advisory board to replace the watchful eyes of program managers and mentors holding the startup accountable during the accelerator. The advisory board was assembled during the accelerator and drew on the advice of accelerator program managers and mentors. The startup had already had one monthly meeting and pre-booked advisory board meetings for the next twelve months after the accelerator. Chloe Daniel points out that, following the accelerator, most startups need the right office space and tech infrastructure to replace what they had at the accelerator space.[6] Planning for this in advance can prevent startups from getting distracted by such issues, so they can focus on maintaining or exceeding the accelerator progress rate. Many accelerators are held in shared labs, shared offices, and incubation spaces where office space is sometimes offered at discount rates to accelerator alumni. Founders seizing on such an opportunity can maintain continuity of the accelerator routines and pace. This can be invaluable for some startups. For example, INTACT Healthcare founder, Nicholas Caporusso, had the following to say about the space issue:[7]

> Removing this sort of hassle helped us keep our momentum going. We could focus on product and reaching out to the right people without getting distracted.

Establish Ongoing Mentoring

Chloe Daniel notes that a key benefit of accelerators is that founders are continuously talking with people who have been there, done that, and who have an active interest in founders and their startup. Founders need to keep this going after the accelerator. Thus during the accelerator, they should be on the lookout for accelerator mentors who are motivated and have the capacity to do this after the accelerator. This may, at least in part, depend on the rapport founders have managed to build with the desired mentors during the accelerator. After all, there may be competition for access to the best mentors' time and attention. As we noted earlier, pre-setting regular catch-ups with mentors can also enable them to plan ahead to accommodate the mentoring sessions in their schedules. Startups can have a range of mentors for the whole team or for particular founders. And these mentors can support them with a range of issues. For example, a lead entrepreneur may have an accelerator startup alumnus CEO as a one-on-one mentor for support with lead entrepreneur issues. A founding team CTO may have both a corporate CTO and an accelerator startup alumnus as mentors. And the whole founding team may have a couple of mentors who act as a board for the startup without being formal board members. The challenge for founders is finding the right combination of mentors and establishing sufficient meeting regularity and ad hoc mentor access to derive full value from the mentoring relationships. Startups leaving accelerators without such mentors can ask the accelerator for introductions to people who may be a good fit for them.

Keep Investors Engaged

We discussed earlier that many startups may not raise funding during the accelerator or that they may not be investment ready for some time after the accelerator has ended. But sooner or later they may be investment ready (e.g., when they achieve compelling traction milestones). At this point, existing investor relationships can be invaluable—especially for cash-poor startups. If they have kept accelerator investor contacts engaged and maintained those relationships, they may be able to avoid the opaque, time-consuming, chaotic, and distracting aspects of the fundraising process—particularly where brand-new investors need to be engaged. Plus, investors within the accelerator network may have more founder-friendly terms. Nurturing the relationship and communicating compelling progress are likely to be the main things that keep investors interested. The former may build trust, but the latter is what ultimately matters to investors.

Keep Accelerator Organizers Engaged and Leverage Them Fully

Although they may be quite occupied while a program is underway or about to be underway, most accelerator program managers aim to provide post-program support.[8] But typically, how much post-program support they provide depends on the founders. Founders have to ensure that organizers are kept informed of the startup's progress, challenges, and action plans. This helps to ensure that their startups are kept in the minds of organizers instead of being slowly forgotten after the program.[9] Startups kept in the minds of organizers are likely to receive more advice, referrals, and even hands-on support. Chloe Daniel recommends that founders provide regular monthly status updates to accelerator program directors.[10] For example, these can include a monthly phone call or email discussing what the startup set out to achieve, what it achieved, the challenges it is facing, and plans for the upcoming month. As well as keeping accelerator organizers informed, startups can ask for their input into critical decisions (perhaps they know an alumnus startup that faced and solved that issue or someone else in the accelerator network who is the best in the world for input into that decision). Startups can ask program managers for introductions to particular companies and for hands-on support with particular issues. For example, Steve Dunn asked accelerator program managers for hands-on support to manage complex strategic partnerships and fundraising projects. Steve found that program managers, many of whom have had ten to twenty years of experience negotiating deals, contracts, and partnerships, had an innate ability to read between the lines of email correspondence and meeting minutes, to offer "live" negotiation tips and advice. Without this hands-on support from an experienced, trusted, and incentivized advisor, closing the deals would have been much more challenging.

Nurture Existing Relationships/Make New Connections

Dror Pearl recommends that founders never stop nurturing the relationships established during the accelerator, and that this should be a top priority.[11] With business becoming more dynamic, you never know which contact's circumstances may change for them to suddenly open the door that makes all the difference to your startup. The contacts to nurture are not only advisors and mentors but also the professional service providers (e.g., lawyers, accountants, and fundraising/business model/technical advisors), accelerator startup alumni, and cohort companies that went through the accelerator at the same time as the startup. Regarding the latter, Bart Clarysse, Mike Wright, and Jonas Van Hove investigated acccelerator networks and found that the alumni network can be an important source of mentors and investors, since alumni may be motivated to give back to the community that supported them.[12] The challenge for founders is how to prioritize their networking/relationship nurturing time, and how to get the most out of it.

Look Forward, Not Sideways

Cohort companies may see themselves jockeying for finite accelerator resources (e.g., access to top mentors' time, funding, etc.), or to make the most progress during the accelerator. Some founders may deliberately seek or try to induce such competition to drive themselves and their teams. As a result, a strange competitive dynamic can develop that makes relationships between cohort companies complex. This dynamic can continue even after the accelerator, as startups stalk their peers online to constantly check their progress. Dror Pearl advises that startups avoid such competition as it can create unnecessary distraction and stress.[13] Both during and after the program, they should concentrate on their goals, the schedules set for themselves, and how they are doing against these goals and schedules. Rather than look sideways and compare themselves to other companies, they should instead focus on their goals and on building supportive relationships with cohort startups so they can learn from them.[14]

Notes

1. T. Raviv, "After Two Startup Accelerators, What I Wish Someone Had Told Me," *Ecquire*, April 20, 2012, accessed August 1, 2019, http://ecquire.com/blog/lessons-from-two-startup-accelerators/.
2. C. Daniel, "Surviving the Post-Acceleration Cliff: What Startups Really Need to Succeed, *Medium*, November 27, 2015, accessed August 1, 2019, https://medium.com/silicon-allee/surviving-the-post-acceleration-cliff-what-startups-really-need-to-succeed-fb26abdfa1fe.
3. K. Koizumi, "What to Do after Your Accelerator Program," *The Refiners*, July 5, 2017, accessed August 1, 2019, https://www.therefiners.co/blog/what-you-do-after-your-accelerator-program.
4. Daniel, "Surviving the Post-Acceleration Cliff."
5. D. Pearl, "What Happens the Day after the Accelerator Program Ends?" *GeekTime*, November 4, 2014, accessed August 1, 2019, https://www.geektime.com/2014/11/04/what-happens-the-day-after-the-accelerator-program-ends/.
6. Daniel, C. (2015). "Surviving the Post-Acceleration Cliff."
7. Ibid.
8. Ibid.
9. Ibid.
10. Ibid.
11. Pearl, "What Happens the Day after the Accelerator Program Ends?"
12. L. Wadid (ed.), *Technology Entrepreneurship and Business Incubation: Theory, Practice, Lessons Learned* (World Scientific, 2016).
13. Pearl, "What Happens the Day after the Accelerator Program Ends?"
14. Ibid.

Appendix: Founder Resource Directory

A hack that takes a tenth of the time may be more useful than an elegantly engineered solution, even if it has to be thrown away later.
Reid Hoffman, founder, LinkedIn

Resource Directory Overview

This resource directory is divided into three parts. Part 1 contains the reflections of founders going through different accelerator programs around the world. Part 2 contains the reflections of program managers operating different accelerators around the world as well as tertiary entrepreneurship educators teaching entrepreneurship and researching entrepreneurship education. In Part 3 we have curated key resources founders can draw on for different aspects of the accelerator experience. For example, they can find curated information for evaluating accelerators, for navigating different aspects of the accelerator process (e.g., preparing accelerator applications, preparing for interviews, starting the accelerator, networking, preparing for demo day, etc.). In this part, we also curate tips and advice from a range of founders who have gone through accelerators on how to approach almost all aspects of the accelerator experience. Finally, for each region of the world (Asia, North America, Europe, Africa/Middle East, South America, Oceania), we list some of the most popular accelerators, their focus, and their notable alumni startups.

Part 1: Founder Reflections

Founder Reflections Overview

This part contains reflections from three anonymous founders who have been through more than one accelerator each (see Table A.1 to A.3). One took their startup through three accelerators in three different continents. Another took their startup through two accelerators in two different countries on the same continent. And another took their startup through seven accelerators in two different continents. The benefit of these anonymous reflections is that entrepreneurs can be frank, since no startup is identified, no accelerator is identified, and no country is identified. Following these reflections, we direct you to another five reflections, which are not anonymous (see Table A.4). These five reflections are from entrepreneurs who have raised funding and exited their startups. We identify their startups, when they were founded, the founders' names, the accelerators they went through, the funding raised, and the exits that have occurred. We follow these up by directing you to another 35 reflections from founders who went through diverse accelerators around the world. In these 35 reflections, the startup names and accelerators are also identified. Our aim in the different types of reflection is to provide examples of the diversity in founders' challenges, thinking, and intentions that drive the decision to enter accelerator programs. And then their approach to applying, their accelerator experiences, and their accelerator outcomes. Through the mixture of anonymous but highly detailed founder reflections, well-known founder reflections, as well as less detailed and perhaps less commonly known founder reflections, we hope you can triangulate different responses and glean additional insights to help you choose the right accelerator, get the most out of it, and accelerate your startup.

Founder Reflection #1

Startup and Accelerator Overview

TABLE A.1 Key Startup and Accelerator Details Relating to Founder 1 Reflection

Industry	IoT
Startup's stage of evolution	Customer validation
Accelerator type	General, industry-specific, technology-specific
Local or overseas accelerator	Overseas

Finding the Accelerator

Our startup had some good successes locally. But progress had stalled. It felt like our investor discussions would always reach a certain point, and then just go totally cold. Investors would just ghost us. We tried everything from completing MBA programs, to participating in government startup programs, to going on televised shark tank competitions. We felt like investors locally were afraid of our tech or afraid to part with the amount of money we were looking for. When they did offer money, they wanted a lot of equity (30%) for only a few hundred thousand dollars. That was never going to do anything meaningful for us. And although government programs sometimes offered millions of dollars for no equity, they seemed to focus on particular types of technologies (mainly life sciences, healthcare, agriculture, etc.). At the same time, we were starting to see overseas competitors emerge and form big partnerships, raise large sums of money, and sign big customers, even though we believed their technology was inferior to ours. We were in a double bind in the sense that it helped to give our idea credibility locally, but then people turned around and said we now had competitors. We started to wonder whether we should go overseas. But it was a big decision. And we didn't know how to do it. We saw some press for a local accelerator that was breaking new ground and bringing in heavyweight overseas investors and advisors, the type we had always admired. We quickly looked into the accelerator and decided to put in an application.

Accelerator Application and Accelerator Experience

The accelerator website directed us to F6s.com for filling out and submitting the online application. The application questions were different from what we had been used to, but we filled them out the best way we knew how and submitted it. We were thankful the application didn't ask for business plans and financial projections, which were always painful to do. We didn't hear anything for a few weeks and assumed we hadn't been accepted. Then we got a call from an overseas heavyweight we had always admired, congratulating us on getting into the program. We felt like things were finally going to change for us. We were generally looking to establish a presence in the regions where the accelerators were held. I probably don't need to explain to you what happened in the accelerator. But in general, we made some very valuable contacts who gave us great advice. And we learned a lot. Basically, we realized what being investment ready was, and we were steered off a course we were about to take, that would definitely have resulted in failure. But we still didn't raise funding and found ourselves having made a lot of progress but still essentially being in the same situation. That is, needing to raise large sums of money for our type of product, and not having the types of investors willing to put up those amounts.

Now, we actually went through three different accelerators, so I'll tell you about the second one. Around a year after graduating from our first accelerator, we began applying to U.S. accelerators. At this stage, we had just released the next iteration of our product, completed in our home country, this time around with customer trials. As we had a paying customer, we were under more pressure to deliver. We worked hard to deliver a more advanced product. But at the same time, we also learned from these customer trials that we were still a long way off from having our product commercially ready. The only way we could develop more features and get the product commercially ready, we concluded, was to raise significant funding. As we were unsuccessful in raising funding after completing the first accelerator in our home country, like many of the other alumni from that accelerator, we started looking at accelerators in the United States. We had concluded that the startup ecosystem in our home country was not going to cough up that type of money, so we set our sights on the United States. We got accepted into a U.S. accelerator and started packing our bags.

The U.S. accelerator program went well, and we were very close to raising the type of funding we needed from an investor. But then we had visa complications, and getting the money was essentially contingent on resolving those complications. We couldn't resolve them in the end. Although fundraising was much easier in the United States (minus the visa issues), we found getting traction in the U.S. market difficult (perhaps due to coming from overseas). In contrast, we found we were getting more traction in Europe. We had recently signed some large strategic partners in Europe. So, after the U.S. accelerator, we set our sights on Europe. We wanted to establish a presence in Europe and decided that doing an accelerator there may be the way to go. By this stage we had given up on the U.S. market. Getting traction there was difficult, whereas we found we were getting more and more traction in Europe, without too much effort.

We had recently signed some large strategic partners in Europe. We had also been attending many trade shows with our partners and getting some local sales in Europe. Further, our strategic partners there offered us everything we needed to continue developing our product (it would have cost millions to access those types of resources). So, it made sense for us to move to Europe as, at the time, we would be closer to existing EU customers. We could only travel around Europe on holiday visas for short periods, so we knew we had to find an accelerator that could support us with the visa application process, and offer support in finding local accommodation, as well as settling into the EU culture. Within two months of sending off the first round of applications on f6s.com, we were in Europe participating in a leading accelerator.

After the Accelerator

After each accelerator, we had many meetings with potential investors. At times we had six or more meetings with potential investors. But in each case, we did not raise capital from the accelerator network. However, we have had lots of serendipitous/unexpected opportunities from people we met during accelerators (e.g., connections of connections). These have been invaluable to our progress. We found accelerator managers generally accessible and ready to help whenever we needed them.

Tips for Founders Considering Applying for an Accelerator

Choosing an Accelerator

I would say, make sure you choose an accelerator that is well established and has a reputation for successful alumni. We found success both overseas and locally, so you don't necessarily have to go overseas. It depends on things such as where you are based physically, and what stage your startup is at, and where you intend to take your startup. Also, the startup should consider doing an accelerator in a strong startup ecosystem. I've read reports and statistics that say Silicon Valley is the best startup ecosystem on the planet, and that it is the best place in the world to get a startup off the ground; so if you believe the science, and you are interested in making your company a success in the shortest time possible, I would advise founders to apply for Silicon Valley accelerators. Building your startup in some locations can be like building a curry shop in the middle of the desert; people may encourage you to do it (e.g., for national pride reasons like trying to create local employment etc.), but if you do it, you're going to get minimal support and it's going to be that much harder to sell your curry. Also, you will be at significant risk of getting beaten by a competitor that emerges and goes to the best location for that type of startup.

The Accelerator Application

When applying, make sure you keep it short, sharp, succinct. Give exact numbers. Be honest. Be yourself. If you are using videos or doing a demo, make sure everything works okay. On one occasion during an accelerator interview, the video software tried to load on two windows, so there was an echo, and it was very difficult to hear (I couldn't work out the problem until towards the end of the inter-view). In another the webcam was upside down—for some reason there were compatibility problems with the conferencing software. Also, be careful with questions about the market size. It's hard to gauge if interviewers want a lot of detail or just a 10-second answer. We had a short 10-second answer prepared, and also a long stats-rich answer, just in case.

The Accelerator Term Sheet

Think carefully about the implications of the equity terms. Some accelerators have equity options. We thought this was great but found investors who had concerns about it. Saying it creates uncertainty, and they didn't like uncertainty in the cap table. That is, they don't know when the accelerator will exercise their options and effect the shareholding arrangements. Also, look out for non-dilution clauses. Accelerators, like all investors, should dilute every time a new inves-tor comes on board.

During the Accelerator

Be professional at all times, be punctual, attend everything, and be prepared to go out of your comfort zone. Take full advantage of networking opportunities, be prepared to learn and be coachable. Look out for consultants/coaches/lawyers/advisors etc. promising the world to you (e.g., promising raising capital, introductions to potential investors, etc.) and then wanting to charge hourly rates, retainers, and high fees. And finally, be prepared to work hard. And actually do it.

Raising Investment

You can raise investment, but it depends on the accelerator and the investment network, and whether the accelerator is in an investment hotspot. If all of that is right, then you need a neat and clean cap table, with not many shareholders, and the shareholders should be active contributors (e.g., not good having a co-founder who has a lot of equity, but no longer has anything to do with the startup). Don't try to raise capital too early. If you can't tick the investment-ready boxes, then you are just wasting your time. For example, if you don't have a strong team with startup experience/qualifications from good universities or if you don't have revenue, returning customers, an accepted MVP, a clean cap table, and clean ownership, then you should consider other options such as bootstrapping, grant applications, and so on. And make sure you work hard to get everything ready for due diligence when talking to investors; and be prepared that this can take time.

Final Thoughts

Our startup would not have made it without each of the accelerators we went through. Going through three accelerators means we gave up a lot of equity. But the alternative was we wouldn't have survived, like several of our competitors who raised large sums of money, went with the wrong technologies, and then went bust.

Founder Reflection #2

Startup and Accelerator Overview

TABLE A.2 Key Startup and Accelerator Details Relating to Founder 2 Reflection

Industry/vertical	FoodTech
Startup's stage of evolution	Customer validation
Accelerator type	Industry-specific accelerator
Local or overseas accelerator	Local

Finding the Accelerator

I received an email from the accelerator organizers wanting to catch up with me to discuss the accelerator opportunity. I was quite surprised, as it was a great accelerator. We were at the MVP/Prototype stage, so we had built our MVP or prototype already, and even tested it. What we really needed was backing and people with experience to support us to continue. We had already been through an accelerator, which was good for the first half of the program. But in the second half of the program, the accelerator had dropped the ball, and that half was basically a waste of time. We didn't even get the full funding we were promised. So, although this next accelerator was high profile, we decided to do a lot of due diligence. Eventually, we confirmed they were fantastic.

The Accelerator Application and Accelerator Experience

We put in an application but basically, we were very confident, as we were recruited to the accelerator and had previously been through an accelerator already. We had a good MVP and most of the information required in the application we had on hand from our previous accelerator. So, the application took no longer than 15 to 20 minutes. For the interview, we already had our pitches, pitch decks, and financial forecasts memorized and on automatic. There were some questions about business models, things outside of our control, and the vision/mission thing. We found these surprising and difficult. Especially the vision/mission. It was a difficult sell. It is essentially a sell. I think people either buy it or they don't. I don't know what these guys thought.

When the program kicked off, we were surprised by how much we learned in a very short period of time about how to create and build a sustainable business. We met so many new and interesting people from all over the world. And we got to learn from some of the best in the industry. We realized we did not really understand business models at all, and yet our business was dependent on having a good business model. So, we're really glad the accelerator helped us understand that, and also helped us to develop and validate the business model.

We were also surprised by how professionally run the program was; and how many investors, advisors, and mentors were domain experts in our industry and readily understood our product. There were lots of prospective corporate clients, and they were actually the ones seeking us out, trying to understand our business and setting up meetings with us and other parts of their organization. We ended up signing three corporate clients from the accelerator's network. We were shocked when, several weeks before demo day, a serious investor approached us. In less than four weeks after meeting him, we finalized a deal and raised $500,000. I am still in disbelief about how simple it seemed—since our previous efforts with other investors always started out cordially, only for us to hit a stone wall of silence. We weren't actually expecting to raise funding from the accelerator. We just thought it would help get us investment ready.

After the Accelerator

When the accelerator ended, we had a whole bunch of meetings with customers and strategic partners. We eventually closed some of the strategic partnerships after we returned home. Raising money changed the game for us. Rather than making a minimalist existence on the accelerator investment, we suddenly could afford an appropriate working space. We could hire a business development person, and we could actually pay for important professional services. This made a big difference, as suddenly our revenue started to take off in leaps and bounds. We made a lot of great friends from different parts of the world. When the accelerator ended, they became good resources for moral support and input into decisions. Most of the time they were either going through the same issues or had just been through them.

Tips for Founders Considering Applying for an Accelerator

First, when selecting an accelerator, make sure you get the industry and personality fit right. When we compare the first and the second accelerator, we were a much better fit with the second one, which made everything a lot easier. Plus, we weren't pretending to be what we weren't. Second, make sure the accelerator is reputable and will follow through on their word. Any fluffiness regarding funding is not going to cut it. If they don't give all the funding, the shortfall may be the make-or-break amount for your startup. Especially if you make plans assuming you will receive all the funding. The accelerator should also show commitment and pay up front. Make sure there is a hard agreement in place specifying what the accelerator will deliver, and what happens if they don't. I am disappointed to give this advice, but it happened to us. Halfway through the program, they bailed out of giving us our funding. Don't expect that it will not happen to you.

If you are not careful, you can definitely choose the wrong accelerator. You will end up losing valuable time and wasting money on travel. Take your due diligence on the accelerator seriously. We didn't the first time; it never really occurred to us. And talk to people who have gone through the accelerator before—you'd be surprised what you can learn about the accelerator from them. Talk to friends and family about what is right for you, people you trust, and who are talented in this area. For instance, someone spoke against the **** accelerator, but I could see it was his own expectations that were a mismatch, rather than the actual program delivery. Hence, I decided to move forward in spite of it; and it was the best choice ever. Also, for terms, talk to a lawyer or someone who is not just good, but great with contracts, and works in a very important position within the firm for that area.

Lastly, read *Lean Startup* by Eric Ries, get an MVP (can be wireframe drawings), test it if possible, get it produced, create a presentation, follow Airbnb online slides—that is what I did, get an accountant who can help you stress-test and build the financial forecasts, know your numbers, and practice presenting. And relax—don't be too rehearsed. The right opportunity will come your way, just jump—you've got this.

Founder Reflection #3

Startup and Accelerator Overview

TABLE A.3 Key Startup and Accelerator Details Relating to Founder 3 Reflection

Industry/vertical	Robotic process automation software
Startup's Stage of Evolution	Insight or opportunity recognition
	Customer discovery
	Customer validation
Accelerator type	Various
Local or overseas accelerator	Local and overseas

Finding the Accelerator

We've been through all sorts of accelerators, about seven in total—and mostly in Korea and Europe. What I can say for sure is that although they have many common elements, the actual experience and impact are not the same. The actual experience and impact can vary drastically. It can be like the difference between having a professional surgeon operate on you and having a person off the street read a random surgery book and then operate on you. The experience and impact can differ drastically. We mostly heard about these accelerators through news media, social media, emails, and direct or indirect invitations. For some, we saw a Facebook post in a startup group; for others there was a story in the news media. Sometimes we directly received an email about an upcoming accelerator program. When it came to choosing an accelerator, we generally tried to imagine what kind of value the accelerator could deliver to us and the cost of that value to us.

The Accelerator Application and Accelerator Experience

In our first accelerator, we were very early stage. We saw the accelerator as a first step to prove our business model. The questions were challenging the first time around. Mostly because we didn't understand them. And also, because we were still very early stage, and the questions asked about issues we had not considered yet. Issues that weren't yet relevant to us. From our experience in the first accelerator, we found that the questions that went beyond the particular stage we were at were usually difficult for us. We also found the revenue questions difficult, because we had no revenue. No one was buying our product yet. If you don't have proper traction, revenue questions are just hard. Questions about product/market fit are also difficult if you don't have traction or a good understanding of what product/market fit means—and how to know if a startup has found product/market fit. For subsequent applications, we developed and tested answers to all these types of questions so they ticked all the right boxes.

Our first interview sucked. We stammered through the questions, which were far more difficult in the interview due to time pressure. Looking back, I am not sure how we got in. Over time, our approach to the interview has been refined through trial and error. For the latter accelerator applications, the approach was to prepare and rehearse our story, create a good pitch, and rehearse it so it becomes automatic. Also, creating a good pitch deck really helped. Throughout the application process and after, you never know when you will need either the story, the pitch, or the pitch deck. After the first two accelerators, we had basically honed the best responses in both the application questionnaire and the interview. But that doesn't mean we got into every accelerator. Basically, I think the better the accelerator, the less it is about the quality of the responses and the more it is about how much of a sure bet the startup is. By that I mean, it's difficult to get the quality of the application and interview responses beyond the quality of the actual startup. On the other hand, your application responses could be terrible, but if the actual startup is great, then that's what matters. The issue is, that for many startups, it isn't so clear how good the idea is. So well-prepared responses can make it clearer and get you across the line.

The terms for most accelerators we went through were standard, more or less a version of the Y Combinator ones, which you can find online. We did give up equity in some accelerators and not others. But with the benefit of hindsight, we would never give up equity again. Except perhaps to a later-stage VC accelerator or an accelerator that takes very small batches and can give each cohort company a lot of hands-on support. Then, the equity may be worth what a startup receives. But basically, there should be a very good reason for giving up equity. We've learned that the hard way.

After our first accelerator, we were more focused on using accelerators to access the right corporate clients in different regions. At this stage, it was mostly each accelerator's network that we were interested in and, specifically, the types of prospective clients it could give us access to.

After the Accelerator

We found most accelerators to essentially still be willing to help us after the accelerator. But in limited ways. We made a lot of effort to try and leverage the accelerators' ecosystem after each accelerator. We thought that was the way to maximize the value from the accelerator. Sometimes we had great serendipitous opportunities come from someone who knew someone, who then knew someone else.

Tips for Founders Considering Applying for an Accelerator

Most accelerators we went through were focused on early-stage start-ups. I think that is true for most accelerators in general. So, as far as being ready goes, I think once it is close to its MVP, every startup is accelerator ready.

It is critical that you pick the right accelerator. And you should always consider the stage you are at. It does not make sense to apply to accelerators that do not fit you or your stage. You should also check the accelerator's industry specialization, its market specializations, the appropriateness of its location, the quality of the mentor and advisor expertise, whether it takes equity, and, most important, what its business model is (does it make money from corporate sponsors or from government, or does it make money from cohort company exits, or does it make money some other way). By understanding the accelerator's business model, you can understand its interests and how those interests might shape what the accelerator does and the value it is able to really offer. Remember, as your startup presents an ideal picture of itself, so does the accelerator.

Once you have chosen an accelerator, you should have clear goals before starting it. Be clear about why you are doing the accelerator, exactly what value you intend to get out of it, and how you will get that value out of it. Also, most accelerators are hands off but can complicate your startup's processes and decision making. The final bit of advice is to follow the accelerator process, but still critically evaluate what you are being asked to do and remain flexible to change.

Final Thoughts

Does a startup need an accelerator to make it? I'm not really sure. I know that in the early stages we probably would not have made it without an accelerator. But could we have gotten by without accelerator 3 onwards? Possibly. We haven't made it yet. So, I can't really say. We've definitely realized that accelerator acceptance and participation can give the illusion that the idea is good, and the business model works. But ultimately, only traction and actual product/market fit can give such assurances.

Additional Founder Reflections

The following additional founder reflections can be accessed by getting a copy of Luke Deering, Matt Cartagena, and Chris Dowdeswell's book *Accelerate: Founder Insights into Accelerator Programs*. It is difficult to get a soft copy, but you can order a hard copy via Amazon.com. We have identified the specific page numbers where you can find each case. Each is approximately two pages in length. Within the same book, and in the same chapter titled "The Accelerator Program Experience," you can find another 35 additional but short (approximately a quarter of a page) reflections from different entrepreneurs who did different accelerators around the world. These short reflections are useful because the founders usually focus on one or two issues that were significant for them. As you read through the 35 short cases, some clear themes will start to emerge.

TABLE A.4 Key Startup and Accelerator Details Relating to the Additional Six Founder Reflections

Startup Name	Founders	Founding Year	Accelerators	Funding Raised	Notes	Page #
Digital Ocean	Ben Uretsky Jeff Carr Moisey Uretsky Mitch Wainer Alec Hartman	2011	Techstars Boulder (2012)	$305.4 million		128
SendGrid	Tim Jenkins Jose Lopez	2009	Techstars Boulder	$80.4 million	Acquired by Twilio for $3 billion on Oct. 15, 2018.	111
Localytics	Raj Aggarwall Henry Cipolla Andrew Rollins	2008	Techstars Boston (2009)	$69.8 million		118

Startup Name	Founders	Founding Year	Accelerators	Funding Raised	Notes	Page #
Cloudability	Mat Elllis	2011	Techstars Cloud 500 Startups Portland Seed Fund Portland Incubator Experiment	$39.8 million	Acquired by Apptio on May 16, 2019	112
Uboogly	Carly Gloge Isaac Squires Gavin Lee	2012	Techstars Boulder (2012)	$2.7 million	Acquired by Cartwheel Kids on Oct. 15, 2014	124
Overlay Studio	Kevin Heap Spencer Smith Joe Wilson	2013	Boom Startup	$1.7 million		119

Part 2: Accelerator Program Manager and Entrepreneurship Educator Reflections

Accelerator Program Manager and Entrepreneurship Educator Reflections Overview

In this part, we provide accelerator program manager and entrepreneurship educator reflections on accelerators and on the challenges of teaching entrepreneurship see Table A.5 to A.8. We focus on the reflections of two different stakeholders who have similar goals. The first stakeholder is accelerator program managers, who design and facilitate the delivery of accelerator curriculums and related activities to realize the accelerator value proposition—in particular, accelerated learning. The second stakeholder is university entrepreneurship educators, who usually also undertake entrepreneurship education research or, at least, engage with the latest entrepreneurship education research. The entrepreneurship educators providing the anonymous reflections each had accelerator programs at their university, although their teaching was somewhat disconnected from the accelerator programs. The purpose of these reflections is to provide two contrasting views of entrepreneurship education. In doing so, we hope founders can triangulate the information, spot unique insights, and understand some of the strengths and shortcomings of different entrepreneurial learning vehicles. The reflections from accelerator program managers are a good guide for people looking to prepare accelerator applications. In subsequent editions of this book, we hope to expand the number of reflections from both program managers and entrepreneurship educators. We also hope to include the reflections of more investors who, this time around, we had not anticipated would be so difficult to pin down for a few hours of interview time.

Accelerator Program Manager Reflection #1

Accelerator Overview

TABLE A.5 Key Accelerator Details Relating to Program Manager #1 Reflection

Accelerator type	General accelerator but with each program having a specific focus
Industry/vertical/focus	Agnostic
Startup evolution-stage focus	Customer discovery and customer validation

Value of Accelerators

An accelerator is a program for startups to quickly understand if there is a market for their product/service or not. It's a process that startups go through to test their ideas and commercialize them rapidly. It is also a process for them to cooperate with each other and with corporate partners. It's essentially a program for accelerating everything a startup needs to do. Government programs don't have the right support, and people running those programs don't understand the market and startups so well. Incubators are based on renting a space/real estate. The accelerator creates a process and a place to bring corporates together. Sometimes incubators, government support programs, and accelerators can mix and work together.

Accelerators have taken off because of a real need in the market. The market need is not only for the startups, but for corporates too. We have found that corporates are struggling to understand innovation, to hire innovators, and to develop new products/services.

Corporates need to understand that cooperating with startups is a good exercise for them. A good accelerator creates a smooth process for the startup to test their solution directly with customers, whether consumer, SME, or Corporate. We've had some great alumni success stories with big exits and return on investment. We have sold our stakes in a few companies at various rounds of fundraising. Dealing with lots of big corporates and partnering with them is also a big outcome of our accelerator. Another great outcome is when corporates work with startups, and the corporates become clients of the startup.

Choosing an Accelerator

Startups can choose the wrong accelerator. It all depends on the offer from the accelerator, and the stage and the need of the startup. Getting it wrong means insufficient or wrong support for the startup to get the outcomes described above. Founders should find out if an accelerator is the right fit for them and the stage of development their startup is at.

The Accelerator Application

We look for a combination of things in the accelerator applications we receive: product, technology, how advanced they are, and whether the team is strong? We advertise throughout networks and through the startup online platforms a couple of months before the program starts. Then we receive a bunch of applications, go through the applications, and invite startups to pitch at our lab, or we do Skype interviews with overseas teams. We ask all sorts of questions in our application; you can see our previous applications online. We look for revenue, strong teams, and strong technology.

A startup can be too early to make it through the application if revenue, the team, and the technology are still very underdeveloped. Sometimes startups make it into the accelerator too early. We usually find they are not 100% committed to the program. They can't or don't take advantage of the business contacts and connections. We scout startups based on business needs. They don't necessarily have to stay for the duration of the program; but if they don't stay for most of the program, they miss out on many important opportunities.

The Accelerator Interview

The accelerator interview is important to understand the human side of the startup. In the interview, we want to check if the founders really believe in what they are saying; we want to see how they tell it and how they speak. Founders who get the interview right clearly communicate their passion, their product, and their opportunity. We don't like it when a startup is hiding things. We also don't like it when they think they know everything.

Accelerator Costs

Typically, equity-taking accelerators ask for an equity option of between 5 and 10%. The equity investment process usually involves signing term sheets after the program begins. The purpose of the term sheet is to outline all the terms and conditions of the investment. Besides the cash investments, startups get other tangible benefits like accommodation, food, and an accelerator working space.

The Accelerator Curriculum

Our curriculum varies from program to program. Around one and a half years ago we stopped running the usual three-month accelerator program. Our program structure is a mixture of mentoring sessions, with presentations, group sessions, ongoing coaching, and so on. We have specific mentors for specific startups, from all over the world, that we bring into each program. We have the equivalent of five full-time program managers. They work on proposals, contracts, budgeting, financial forecasting, general facilitation, scouting, designing deal flows, nurturing, and maintaining good relationships. Our program managers are salaried employees. Startups can make the most of our curriculum by attending everything. A lot of thinking and discussion are put into putting together the set of activities that combine to create the most value for the particular cohort of startups. As well as attending everything, they should work closely with our corporates. We partner with some of the biggest corporates. It is a great opportunity to have so much of the corporate managers' time, engagement, and proactive support. Typically, it can be a real fight for entrepreneurs to get that sort of access to senior managers.

Fundraising

Of course startups can raise money in an accelerator! They certainly do in ours. You can check on our website and blog posts. We always publish everything, and not just our successes. To raise funding, founders have to work hard, be active, present to as many people as possible, and, of course, meet certain touch points. An investment-ready startup basically looks like some of the successful companies listed on our website that I just referred to. No, cohort companies are not at risk of a lower valuation by participating in an accelerator.

Networks

We value our relationships with corporates from many different industries very highly. And we invest a lot in them. We work in different industries from automatic, to manufacturing, to banking. We have eyes on everything. A lot of times we have melting pots between different corporates and different sectors. And our network is continually growing both locally and globally. So of course, our network is very different from networks entrepreneurs might build themselves. Even a single high-profile entrepreneur would not have the type of network that we have.

Final Thoughts

A standout opportunity for startups in our accelerator is our extensive partnership with most of the leading corporates, and the engagement and motivation of these partners to collaborate with cohort startups.

Accelerator Program Manager Reflection #2

Accelerator Overview

TABLE A.6 Key Accelerator Details Relating to Program Manager 2 Reflection

Accelerator type	Vertically focused
Industry/vertical/focus	High-tech
Startup evolution-stage focus	Customer discovery and customer validation

Value of Accelerators

Accelerators are time-boxed programs for early-stage startups, designed to increase speed and efficiency for accomplishing milestones. Accelerators differ from incubators and government startup support programs in that there is more emphasis on achieving specific goals of the startup. And interactions with other teams are also a very important feature of accelerators for expanding personal networks and increasing implicit learning. Accelerators fill in a gap for early-stage funding and provide validation for later-stage investors. As far as their value to startups, accelerators provide early capital, access to customers, access to talent, access to networks, access to quality mentorship, and external accountability. They also fill skill gaps. The best outcomes startups have achieved through our accelerator have included closing series A, signing major enterprise clients, and finding the right technical talent.

Choosing an Accelerator

Yes, startups can choose the wrong accelerator. Founders should choose carefully to avoid wasting time and focus. When choosing, they should evaluate the accelerator's industry-specific connections (especially for B2B), the accelerator's deep network of "active" mentors, and how engaged and well-functioning the accelerator staff and team are.

The Accelerator Application

We use global accelerator application platforms (f6s, vator, gust, etc.) for our applications. We shortlist the applications we receive to select the top fifty (as chosen by the internal team/accelerator staff); we then distribute them to stakeholders for multiple criteria voting. The top 20 are moved to the interview stage (a 30-minute face-to-face or virtual interview). Based on the interview performance, we select the top 12 and make offers to them. We ask what we consider standard questions, common to most accelerators. When is a startup ready for our accelerator? It depends on the stage and focus of the startup (e.g., concept stage vs. defined product). At the very least, a startup needs a core team that is passionate about the problem they are trying to solve. If a startup gets into an accelerator too early, it can negatively impact the quality of the interactions with the other teams.

The Accelerator Interview

The point of the accelerator interview is to gauge the interpersonal and communication skills of the team and probe for more in-depth insights not covered in the application. Startups that successfully make it through the interview understand their problem statement, provide evidence of specialized knowledge, and are engaging. Startups that are eliminated typically argue with the interviewer, especially if we have a SME (subject matter expert) on the interview panel. Would we accept a company with a great application but a terrible interview? Yes, if we felt we could provide a positive impact, and if the company seemed to be coachable.

Accelerator Costs

We have two versions of the accelerator, one with funding that is considered an investment (3–6% equity) and another that is free (no equity), as it only includes a travel stipend (around $5–10k). We invest at the current round terms; and if there hasn't been a priced round, we use a SAFE (simple agreement for future equity) or convertible note. The purpose of our term sheet is to be transparent with startups upfront. Besides the seed investment, we offer startups access to potential customers, mentors, and investors, with the main value being establishing pilot programs with our enterprise sponsors.

The Accelerator Curriculum

Our curriculum is delivered over three months. Month 1 is focused on understanding startups' specific gaps/needs and defining an action plan. Months 2 and 3 are similar—organizing interactions with sponsors, potential customers, mentors, and so on. We have industry-focused and skill base–focused mentors. We have daily mentor meetups, weekly standups, weekly network events, and weekly special topic workshops. We usually have three program managers, one focused on event management, one focused on mentors and partner engagement, and another focused on team interactions. But all overlap on roles. All our program managers are paid a salary, with no performance bonuses. Cohort companies can make the most of the program by engaging with the programming, attending events, and interacting/engaging with other companies.

Fundraising

Yes, startups can raise money in accelerators. But only if they develop the relationships during the program, and don't wait until demo day. Also, they have to start early, and not just rely on the program to provide all the introductions. As well as that, they have to get their solution MVP ready and have positive feedback from potential customers. We keep in close communication with regional investors from the beginning of the program. That is what our investor network is looking for. Are cohort companies at risk of a lower valuation by participating in an accelerator? No.

Networks

Networking involves creating connections during the accelerator that can lead to potential customers, strategic partners, star employees, advice, and so forth. Compared to networks entrepreneurs might build themselves, accelerator networks are like networking on steroids.

Final Thoughts

Our accelerator is unique due to it being very vertical/industry focused. Another standout opportunity of our program is that we have pilot programs with enterprise companies. Getting these would otherwise take startups months, if they ever get them.

Entrepreneurship Educator Reflection #1

Entrepreneurship Educator Overview

TABLE A.7 Key Accelerator Details Relating to Entrepreneurship Educator 1 Reflection

Position	Senior Lecturer, Entrepreneurship and innovation
Teaching level	Undergraduate
Highest level of education	PhD
Startup experience	Extensive/active

Entrepreneurship Education Approach

The approach to entrepreneurship that I have developed over the last 20 years is based on systematic research into the learning motivations and expectations of the students in each class. Overall, there may be 1 to 3 students out of a class of 80 to 100 who state at the beginning of course delivery that they are interested in starting their own enterprise. As a result, I focus on education "about" entrepreneurship, and give my courses an "enterprise" flavor so that students can understand how to apply the principles of entrepreneurship to themselves, to their families, to their community, as well as in their business context. Another aspect that I focus on is to develop students' understanding of basic models, theories, and frameworks. This sometimes poses a challenge because students have a perception that entrepreneurship is purely an applied activity, so I remind them that theory is the most practical thing that you can learn, because theory gives you the tools to best estimate what might happen in the future.

Entrepreneurship Education Challenges

The major challenge is that, in my opinion, entrepreneurship is one of the most difficult/challenging subjects to teach. Entrepreneurship is a complex field of practice, as it requires decision making across all aspects of business activity, in situations where there are high levels of uncertainty, in a global and dynamic socio-technical context. In practice, that means that undergraduate students in particular just do not have the life experience or business understanding to fully grasp the complexities and intricacies of this field. For that reason, I have gone to a fair degree of effort and thought to distil the key aspects of entrepreneurship and "package" them in a way that students can come to grips with those aspects; in other words, I aim to teach just the essentials and to keep these as simple as possible. This requires a great deal of experimentation with different activities and an assessment of the engagement value of these activities in a continuous improvement process. This continuous improvement process was recognized with a National Award for Teaching Excellence.

"Teaching about," "Teaching for," and "Teaching in" Entrepreneurship

Another challenge is to make entrepreneurship relevant to the particular audience, so that they are able to engage with the particular approach. In practice this means distinguishing between "teaching about," "teaching for," and "teaching in" entrepreneurship.

Myth of the Genius Entrepreneur

A further challenge is the public perception of entrepreneurship that is projected by successful entrepreneurs. My observation is that when entrepreneurs talk about their experiences, or their business, they tend to talk in a very prescriptive manner (such as "you need to do this," "you need to do that"). In other words, they construct empirical generalizations, drawing on their own very limited experience. This causes problems because their operating context may be quite different from the one faced by their audience. In addition, there are topics that entrepreneurs very rarely talk about—like the importance of timing, as well as the real importance of plain luck. They seem to feel a need to have an audience believe that the success of their venture was entirely due to their own genius/brilliance.

Negative Perceptions of Entrepreneurship

Yet another challenge I have experienced is the negative view of business and entrepreneurship that is held by a significant number of undergraduate students entering university. I have experience in dealing with the public schooling system, and I have identified very strong anti-business views among teachers. So, I am not surprised when, from time to time, I receive caustic or abusive emails, typically from social sciences/law students, who object to my promotion of entrepreneurship, as they associate it with rapacious, unethical, and greed-driven behaviors.

I suggest that the "Universities are for Losers" attitude captures public perceptions quite well. This reflects the common view that what is important in entrepreneurship is just to get out and do it. People reading such an article do not realize that the successful entrepreneurs who hold these views are probably the 1 or 2 in 10,000 who have been successful, and that their success may be more due to luck, timing, and connections than they are willing to admit.

Entrepreneurship Education at Universities

A strength of university entrepreneurship programs is that entrepreneurship is being exposed to more and more students in universities. I would like to think that the general idea of enterprise is one that stays with students, so that when they have business experience and more maturity, they may feel more confident about starting their own enterprise and be more prepared to ask for help in doing this.

But the university programs that I have looked at try to do too much. They include too many complex models for typical (and even good) students to be able to grasp and to understand. A good indicator of the problem is to look at the content of a typical textbook for an entrepreneurship foundation course; 600 pages of small print for a 10-week or 13-week course is simply unrealistic. There is no way that even a highly motivated student can work their way through such a tome. At the same time, the way that the content is presented is often complex and makes the topic a real challenge. Another major shortcoming is that there seems to be a fixation with measuring the number of startups that result from an entrepreneurship education program. (Those who teach mathematics do not fixate on how many of their graduates become mathematicians.) This attitude is particularly perplexing, given the average age of entrepreneurs, and the evidence that entrepreneurs need a sound background (e.g., 10 years of learning) in a technology, or market, in order to be able to recognize and evaluate viable opportunities. For this reason, when I set up the entrepreneurship discipline at my university, I proposed that it be developed along the lines of the Cornell University model, where enterprise is a core course in each faculty, but it is tailored to the context and needs of the particular field of study. In this way, the aim is to instill a culture of enterprise, as distinct from entrepreneurship. The intention was to develop an "enterprise university" that would aim to give every student exposure to the principles of "enterprise" in a manner that was aligned with their discipline.

Future of Entrepreneurship Education at Universities

This is a difficult one. The current trend (at least in our country) is that teaching is being increasingly done by "teaching academics," who deliver seven to eight different classes a year. This means that these instructors increasingly use course materials associated with a textbook. With this level of workload, it is not possible for educators to be content experts in each area in which they teach. In effect this means that students are not learning from a person who is immersed in the field but are being instructed by someone who happens to know how to use textbook materials. This is what I see happening in other areas of instruction, and I see no reason why entrepreneurship should be different. This trend is exacerbated by senior academics (professors) being appointed primarily to deliver research output (published papers in the right journals and research funding), and this tends to lead them to reduce or avoid teaching. This is an international trend.

Entrepreneurship Education in Universities versus in Accelerators

As stated earlier, in my opinion tertiary entrepreneurship activities should focus on "enterprise," and on giving students an understanding of the frameworks/models/principles of entrepreneurship. In other words, to give people an understanding of the process, without requiring them to actually do the process. Nonetheless, I recognize that it is possible to "do entrepreneurship" as a tertiary course, but the numbers would need to be very limited in order to provide appropriate/adequate support. In my opinion, educating "for entrepreneurship" is the only viable approach when dealing with large numbers of students.

In my view, accelerators and incubators focus on "teaching in" entrepreneurship, where mentors work with a small number of would-be entrepreneurs and help them tailor/pivot their activities as they work their way through the entrepreneurship process. The key thing is that the performance/outcome/output measures are connected with the number of (successful) startups, which is quite different from the large-scale university entrepreneurship/enterprise program. Accelerators and incubators can effectively use (successful) entrepreneurs who give the activity a measure of industry credibility.

Entrepreneurship Education in Government Programs

I am not sure exactly what these programs consist of, but my guess is that they are designed for people who have decided to start an enterprise. In other words, the approach would be along the lines of educating "for entrepreneurship" and "in entrepreneurship."

Entrepreneurship Educator Reflection #2

Entrepreneurship Educator Overview

TABLE A.8 Key Accelerator Details Relating to Entrepreneurship Educator 2 Reflection

Position	Sessional lecturer, entrepreneurship
Teaching level	Undergraduate and postgraduate
Highest level of education	Masters x 2
Startup experience	Extensive/active

Entrepreneurship Education Approach

For me, entrepreneurship education is all about helping the student learn how to think differently, apply various tools, and develop insights based on the input from the market around them. As a sessional lecturer who is basically brought in to fill a capacity gap, I don't profess to be able to fairly represent the university in describing their approach. But my impression is that it is a typical academic approach, where it is more about focusing on the content than it is about helping the students (with whatever background they might have) to integrate the entrepreneurial wisdom gathered by trial and error to create their own, new reality.

Entrepreneurship Education at Universities

The relative strength of tertiary programs is that they at least are generally not perpetuating the Hollywood myth of entrepreneurship and its superficiality, and provide real frameworks and knowledge. But, like any university program, my observation is that academic rigor has a higher priority than actual learning outcomes for the students. I have the sense that tertiary entrepreneurship education programs are generally seen as academic exercises, and not necessarily of great practical use.

Entrepreneurship Education Challenges

The biggest challenge is going against the hype around entrepreneurship, ideas of unicorns, that shine of shows like "Shark Tank," and the used car salesman dubiousness that all this attracts. It is difficult to develop the understanding that while there are specific mindsets and tools that can be applied, it all requires quite a bit of time and effort, and thus is not a get-rich-quick scheme. There is no way around trial-and-error, iteration, and market-focus.

Future of Entrepreneurship Education at Universities

The future of all tertiary education is uncertain, as the area is being disrupted. Assuming universities are willing to adapt, tertiary entrepreneurship education will be less monolithic, module/theme-based, and highly flexible to match the needs of the students, while ensuring a basic standard of knowledge and understanding.

Entrepreneurship Education in Universities versus in Accelerators

Based on my assumption that most people do not distinguish between accelerators, incubators, co-working spaces, and government entrepreneurship programs, I will treat them as one group. I realize that there are certainly exceptions and do not want to criticize them. While tertiary entrepreneurship focuses on academic content versus mental heuristics and tools, accelerators/incubators/ government programs/co-working spaces attempt to help through physical spaces and the provision of mentorship/guidance from so-called seasoned experts.

    While these approaches are very popular lately, I question if they are necessarily such a great thing. Technology now makes it really easy (and relatively inexpensive) to conduct business from just about anywhere, and access just about any information—so I don't see anything special about them. My sense is that they are a simplistic, easy, and physical solution to a complex problem, which involves new mindsets and perspectives. For public officials and community leaders, ribbon-cutting ceremonies are more public and easy to grasp than other, more difficult solutions (and make for better pictures in the media).

    Regarding the function of these spaces to bring people together, there are plenty of other options for that, and they do not incur the cost of creating and maintaining physical spaces. I would also surmise that the inhabitants in such spaces will be focused on their own venture. And I don't mean this in a mean or arrogant way, but there is a real risk of the blind leading the blind in such spaces where everyone is trying to make a go of their venture.

An impressionable wannabe-entrepreneur might observe somebody doing something that is not necessarily the right thing for their venture and unknowingly waste time and resources trying to make it work for them.

There is also a real question around mentorship/guidance resources. My personal observation is that they are usually well-meaning, but often misguided in their recommendations. This is partly due to their own demographics, often being (in a terrible generalization) frustrated accountants in their fifties having expertise in taxes, but not the world of Lean Startup Methodology, the Business Model Canvas, or effectuation—or even the less numerate functions of marketing, sales, human resources, and leadership.

Then there are the "sharky" service providers preying on unsuspecting wannabe-entrepreneurs; these sharks use entrepreneurship spaces as hunting grounds. Hopefully that isn't all too negative.

Part 3: Curated Accelerator Resources

Resources to Help Founders Choose the Right Accelerator

In Table A.9, we have curated key resources you can use to search for accelerators by a range of criteria (e.g., location, average alumnus fundraising, average alumnus exit value, accelerator rankings, sector/focus, etc.). You will also find resources to help you look deeper into particular accelerator regions and particular accelerator alumnus startups (when did they start, when did they enter an accelerator, which accelerator did they enter, how much funding did they raise, where are they now, etc.) We hope founders can use this table to find different accelerators and to assess the quality of the accelerator.

Resources to Help Founders Prepare Accelerator Applications and Plan for the Start of an Accelerator

Curated resources in Table A.10 include: how to find entrance criteria for particular accelerators, how to prepare the accelerator application (e.g., how to prepare your video, how to prepare your team, how to present your startup online, how to make your accelerator application stand out, a primer of accelerator curriculum requirements, a primer of demo day requirements, etc.).

TABLE A.9 Resources to Help Founders Choose the Right Accelerator

Resource Type	Resource Name	Resource Description	Resource Location	How to Use This Resource
Accelerators by location and exit totals, and funding raised for startup participants	List of accelerator programs and their locations	A comprehensive and up-to-date table of accelerator programs, their locations, links to the programs, exits, and funding amounts	https://www.seed-db.com/accelerators	Check the table of location and click on the link to the program, when on the accelerator website, follow the instructions on how to apply
	Top 10 startup accelerators based on successful exits	A list of the most successful accelerators including the number of exits, and some examples of successful exit startups	https://www.forbes.com/sites/alejandrocremades/2018/08/07/top-10-startup-accelerators-based-on-successful-exits/#72df8fb94b3b	Check this article if you want to choose an accelerator based on successful exits
Accelerator rankings	Top-ranked accelerators in the USA (updated yearly)	The top accelerators in the USA ranked	http://www.seedrankings.com/#rankings	Go here to see a list of the best accelerators in the USA, including links to their websites
Accelerators by sector	List of accelerators grouped in categories, A-Z starting with AI and finishing with Woman	List of accelerators organized in different categories such as locations, type, sector, etc.	https://thembaisdead.com/list-of-startup-accelerators-and-incubators/	Go here to see the list of the most successful startups by investment amounts, and the accelerators organized into different categories such as sector

Resource Type	Resource Name	Resource Description	Resource Location	How to Use This Resource
Accelerator data	Global accelerator report by Gust	A comprehensive report on accelerators with a good analysis of corporate involvement	http://gust.com/ accelerator_ reports/2016/ global/	Go here to see a trend of what's happening in accelerators across the globe (unfortunately Gust did not publish any more of these reports after 2016)
Accelerator alumni network and startup data	Discover information about Innovative companies	An extensive list of hundreds of thousands of companies, and details about their funding rounds, and who the funders are, and what the names of the accelerators that the company has graduated from are	https://www .crunchbase.com/	Go here to see when a startup alumnus was funded, by whom, and for how much

Resources to Help Founders Navigate Key Stages of the Accelerator Experience

Curated resources in Tables A.11 and A.12 are organized by key accelerator-experience stage to help founders navigate different stages of the accelerator experience. There are resources to use before applying for an accelerator, resources to use while navigating the process of applying, resources to use while navigating the accelerator curriculum, resources to use while navigating demo day/the lead up to demo day, and resources to use while navigating the post accelerator stage etc.

TABLE A.10 Resources Help Founders Prepare Accelerator Applications and Plan for the Start of an Accelerator

Resource Type	Resource Name	Resource Description	Resource Location	How to Use This Resource
Accelerator entrance criteria	f6s.com #1 for startup deals, accelerators, and funding	Main site for accelerators listing their programs. Register a profile and submit accelerator applications here.	https://www.f6s.com/	Set up a new account, then set up your profile, search currently available for submissions accelerators. Submit your application by filling in the online forms, and attaching supporting evidence. e.g., PowerPoint presentations.
Accelerator application resources	How to shoot great video for your accelerator application	A short article from *Forbes* and video to describe how you should set up a video shoot of your team talking about your startup.	https://www.forbes.com/ sites/mikalbelicove/2013/01 /04/how-to-shoot-great-videos- for-your-business/?utm_content =buffer6ecad&utm_medium= social&utm_source=inkedin. com&utm_campaigr= buffer#442c75f65f21	Watch the video to get tips on how to quickly, easily, and cheaply set up a professional video of your team talking about your startup.
	How to register a U.S. company online (and a bank account)	A legal website showing how to register a company anywhere in the USA in minutes.	https://www.legalzoom.com/ business/business-formation/ inc-pricing.html https://www. globesamerica.com/ https:// freshdesk.com/general/how-to- incorporate-a-us-corporation- from-outs-blog/	Sign up and pay for the all-inclusive company registration services including all documentation.
	How to prepare a team	An article from *Entrepreneur* journal that describes how to go about assembling a top-class startup team.	https://www.entrepreneur.com/ article/335126	Get tips on how to go about building a strong team.

How to name your startup	A short mashable article giving lots of tips on how to name your startup.	https://mashable.com/2013/07/20/startup-name/	Get tips on how to go about getting a great name for your startup.
How to prepare marketing messages and design for websites	An article in a leading startup blog that analyses 20 of the most successful startups websites, explaining what they have in common and giving many great examples.	https://www.hotjar.com/blog/2014/08/07/we-analyzed-the-homepages-of-30-successful-startups-and-here-is-what-we-learned/	Get tips on website design for successful startups. The site is a little dated in terms of design, but the fundamentals are generally the same as now.
How to make your accelerator application stand out	An article in *Entrepreneur* journal of seven ways to make your accelerator application stand out from the rest.	https://www.entrepreneur.com/article/246303	The managing director of Techstars tells the things they are looking for in applications for the next Techstars NYC class that most likely apply to any accelerator.
DropBox's 2007 Y Combinator application (in full)	See the full and original successful application to Y Combinator in 2007 by DropBox co-founder and CEO Drew Houston, and an analysis of the application in this *Business Insider* journal article.	https://www.businessinsider.com.au/dropbox-y-Combinator-application-from-2007-by-drew-houston-2013-9?r=US&IR=T	An example of a successful accelerator application form.

(Continued)

TABLE A.10 (continued)

Resource Type	Resource Name	Resource Description	Resource Location	How to Use This Resource
Accelerator program curriculum resources	A guide to seed fundraising	An investor gives a guide to how to go about raising a seed round for your startup including how much to raise, valuing your company, negotiating and closing deals, rules to follow, etc.	http://www.imaginek12.com/manualseed.html	Use this guide for an overview and explanation of how to prepare your startup for a seed round.
	How to write an Investor information memorandum with an example template	A *Medium* online journal article that provides a template of a typical Investor memorandum document for raising a round of investment, plus analysis and links to videos and other useful resources.	https://medium.com/@alitamaseb/a-template-for-startup-executive-summary-or-investment-memo-for-vcs-cb434f47e502	Go here if you are looking for a successful template for an investor memorandum.
	How to build your MVP	A *Medium* online journal article that provides a good how-to guide for building MVP's	https://medium.com/swlh/how-to-build-an-mvp-in-the-right-way-in-2018-f538df0f2bba	Go here to learn about the steps involved in building a MVP, and what to watch out for as you go along.
	How to do a competitive analysis—a step-by-step guide	A digital marketing agency provides a detailed guide into how to carry out an extensive competitor analysis for your business plan / Investor IM.	https://conversionxl.com/blog/competitive-analysis/	Use this guide if you're struggling with what to write in the competitive analysis section of your business plan/investor IM.
	The top seven legal documents for startups	An article from *Entrepreneur* journal that explains seven of the most common legal documents for startups with links to example template legal documents.	https://www.entrepreneur.com/article/253997	Go to this guide for full example agreements for your startup.
	Tech startups	A ten-part special report on accelerators and tech startups in *Economist* journal	https://www.econorrist.com/special-report/2014/01/16/a-cambrian-moment	Go here for a special report into everything about accelerators and tech startups.

Accelerator demo day resources	How to design a pitch deck that makes investors say "yes"	A leading digital design agency provides an in-depth design guide for an investor pitch deck.	https://www.canva.com/learn/design-a-pitch-deck-that-makes-investors-say-yes/	Go here for lots of design tips with many examples of well-designed slides.
	Airbnb's Y Combinator pitch deck	See the full and original successful Airbnb pitch deck from when they went through Y Combinator and an analysis in *Business Insider* online journal.	https://www.businessinsider.com.au/airbnb-original-startup-pitch-deck-2019-6?r=US&IR=T	Read this article for a good analysis of Airbnb's Y Combinator pitch deck, and to see how far they have come since they graduated from Y Combinator.
	5 body language tips for pitching to investors	A *Forbes* article that gives body language tips for pitching to investors.	https://www.forbes.com/sites/carolkinseygoman/2013/10/23/5-body-language-tips-for-pitching-to-investors/#50524 9b85767	Go to this article if you are worried about your body language for pitches, and if you are looking for suggestions on how to improve your stage presence.
	An introduction to public speaking fear	A public speaking training agency full of well-known / famous speakers provides a five-part series to how to become a better public speaker with links to free e-books.	https://www.throughlinegroup.com/2018/04/22/an-introduction-to-public-speaking-fear/	Go to this article if you have nerves or anxiety to learn how to deal with them, including lots of physical exercises you can do.

TABLE A.11 Resources to Help Founders Navigate Key Stages of the Accelerator Experience

Resource Type	Resource Name	Resource Description	Resource Location	How to Use This Resource
Accelerator application	Before applying for an accelerator, here's what you need to know	Program managers from dozens of accelerators around the world tell you what you should prepare and have done before applying to their accelerator.	https://www.gan.co/blog/ever-applying-accelerator-heres-need-know/	Read this article to get an idea of exactly what a specific accelerator is looking for, straight from the mouth of the program managers, before applying to an accelerator.
	Four tips for getting accepted to an accelerator	Founder and co-CEO of Techstars David Brown gives four straightforward tips for getting into accelerators.	https://www.inc.com/david-brown/4-tips-for-getting-accepted-to-an-accelerator-program.html	Read this article to get an insight into the four main things a leading accelerator program manager is looking for when accessing startup applications.
	Five tips on how to make your accelerator application stand out	A program manager of a medical device accelerator in the United States tells us what he's looking for when he assesses accelerator applications.	https://medium.com/@TMCInnovation/5-tips-on-how-to-make-your-accelerator-application-stand-out-2a8b984b4a3f	Read this article to see how a program manager provides his take on all the main reasons for what you should do to get into an accelerator with simple understandable justifications.
	Seven ways to make your accelerator application stand out	The managing director of Techstars in NYC tells us what he is looking for in the NYC Techstars applications.	https://www.entrepreneur.com/article/246303	Read this article to learn what you need to do to get into a top-class accelerator, and see some examples of successful Techstars companies' application videos and elevator pitches.

Ten top accelerators share their advice for getting into their programs, including 500 Startups, Techstars, Y Combinator and more	A great article with quotes from managers of all the top accelerators with bits of advice, alumni statistics, and general info about the accelerator and why it's successful.	https://blog.conversionfanatics.com/top-accelerators-share-best-advice-getting/	Read this article for a good high-level overview about what the ten best accelerators in the world are looking for in their applications, and to get the names of successful alumni that you can look up too.
Seven Lessons from 500, YC, Angelpad alum—how to prepare for any accelerator interview	Good article on the 500 Startups website with program managers discussing the mistakes entrepreneurs make in interviews.	https://500.co/7-lessons-from-500-yc-angelpad-alum%E2%80%8A-%E2%80%8Ahow-to-prepare-for-any-accelerator-interview/	To learn what mistakes not me take after you have been offered an interview.
How to ace your interview with 500 Startups	A 500 Startups program manager tells how to ace an interview.	https://500.co/startup-accelerator-interview/	Get tips on what to say and what not to say in an interview.
Interviewing with an accelerator—the do's and don'ts	A leading startup accelerator program manager gives hints on what to say or not to say in an accelerator interview on their accelerator website.	https://startupyard.com/interviewing-with-an-accelerator-a-few-dos-and-donts/	Get tips on what to say and what not to say in an interview.
How to prepare for a first-stage interview with an accelerator	A leading startup accelerator program manager gives hints on what to say or not to say in an accelerator interview.	https://medium.com/katapult-accelerator/how-to-prepare-for-your-first-stage-interview-with-an-accelerator-e6a4a6ef2709	Get tips on what to say and what not to say in an interview.

(Continued)

TABLE A.11 (continued)

Resource Type	Resource Name	Resource Description	Resource Location	How to Use This Resource
Accelerator program structure/ curriculum	Anatomy of an accelerator; curriculum	A high-level argument about whether accelerators should or should not be following curriculums and why or why not.	https://medium.com/swlh/ anatomy-of-an-accelerator-1-curriculum-b121811f55ee	Go to this article for the links, rather than the article content. There are links to articles with endless links to articles that could form a curriculum in any accelerator, such as free guides and courses for entrepreneurs, free image editors, free SEO and website analyzers, etc.
	Designing an accelerator program	Although this article is set out as if you were trying to design your own accelerator program from the ground up, it's packed full of statistics.	https://howdo.com/innovation-tools/corporate-accelerator/ program-design/	Go to this article for examples of startup curricula, and many links to resources, quotes from leading accelerator program managers, bits of advice from everything on how to find co-founders, to selection criteria for acceptance.
	The accelerator curriculum guide	A 20-page pdf/PowerPoint presentation prepared by a nonprofit organization, which lists and analyzes typical content and provides week-by-week lesson plans.	https://youngfoundation.org/ wp-content/uploads/2013/02/ The-Accelerator-Curriculum-Guide-February-2013.pdf	Go to this presentation to get an idea of what types of activities, content suggestions, and learning outcomes you get from participating in accelerators. See lots of photos and diagrams of activities too.

	Designing the startup curriculum	Lessons a program learned through the years as I've worked on developing curriculum for entrepreneurship, which I think are unique to successful accelerator programs.	https://www.rockstart.com/blog/designing-startup-curriculum/	Get a good idea of the rationale and philosophies of a program manager when it comes to accelerator curriculum.
	CoPhilly accelerator program curriculum	An accelerator lists the week-to-week curriculum for their accelerator.	http://cophilly.com/curriculum/	Read this article to see a typical week-by-week breakdown of what happens in an accelerator.
Accelerator demo day	Pitch the future at your accelerator demo day	A program manager provides some advice about what your aims for demo day should be about, and what you should be pitching on demo day.	https://medium.com/m8-ventures/pitch-the-future-at-your-accelerator-demo-day-b01d34533424	Read this article to get some fresh program manager insights about what demo day is about, and how you can take full advantage of it.
	A guide to demo day presentations	A Y Combinator program manager gives a very detailed guide about how to structure your demo day presentation, techniques to use, how your slides should be, and more.	https://blog.yCombinator.com/guide-to-demo-day-pitches/	Read this article to get everything you need to know about making a killer pitch on demo day. Also packed with lots of further reading, examples of good pitch decks, stacks of advice, techniques for pitching, etc.

(Continued)

TABLE A.11 (continued)

Resource Type	Resource Name	Resource Description	Resource Location	How to Use This Resource
	Advice on pitching (for demo day)	An Y Combinator program manager gives straight, short bullet-point advice about how to deliver your pitch on demo day.	http://www.aaronkharris.com/advice-on-pitching	Read this article for straight-to-the-point, no-nonsense advice on how to deliver your demo day pitch. Also, at the bottom of this article is a discussion/chat thread where startups ask direct questions to the program manager to better understand his points.
	How to present to investors	Paul Graham, the godfather of accelerators, the man that started the accelerator concept, gives 14 do's and don'ts about demo day and pitching to investors.	http://www.paulgraham.com/investors.html	Read this article to hear all the do's and don'ts you should consider for your demo day pitch or for any pitch to an investor at any time. This comes from Paul Graham, the guy that started the accelerator phenomena so it packs even more weight for this reason.
	Pitch deck examples from successful startups	The original pitch decks of Facebook, Uber, and Airbnb are listed on this site.	https://slidebean.com/blog/startups-pitch-deck-examples	Read this example to see the pitch decks, like you should have for demo day, from the most successful startups on the planet.
	How to design a better pitch deck	A Y Combinator program manager gives an in-depth guide to how to design your slide deck for demo day—article features on the Y Combinator website	https://blog.yCombirator.com/how-to-design-a-better-pitch-deck/	Read this article to get advice and tips on the design of your slides for demo day.

	What we learned from Techstars demo day	Two program managers from a Prague-based accelerator called Startup Yard visit the London Techsters demo day and offer an honest appraisal of the day.	https://startupyard.com/what-we-learned-from-demo-day-techstars-london-2015/	Read this article to see the honest opinions of lesser-known startup program managers, observing the better-known startup demo day, and all the learnings from experience.
Accelerator post demo day support	What happens after Y Combinator	A few stories of some Y Combinator alumni and what they did after demo day.	https://www.fastcompany.com/3044333/what-happens-after-y-Combinator-the-marathon-after-the-sprint	Read this example for some stories about the hard work some Y Combinator accelerator alumni did after demo day.
	What happens after demo day	A U.S. accelerator program manager provides some good advice and tips about what to do and what to expect after demo day.	https://www.tennessean.com/story/money/2014/08/18/entrepreneurs-comes-demo-day/14202453/	Read this article if you're looking for some direction after demo day, or not sure what to expect after an accelerator finishes.
	Attention startup accelerators: Your job is not over after demo day	An interview with an accelerator program manager/angel investor giving examples of what they do after demo day to help startups succeed.	http://johngreathouse.com/attention-startup-accelerators-your-job-is-not-over-after-demo-day/	Read this article to get an idea of the types of things accelerators do for startups after demo day.
	Beyond demo day; Startups find success after the AUC Venture lab	A program manager discusses what happened to some of their alumni after demo day.	https://www.aucegypt.edu/news/beyond-demo-day-startups-find-success-after-auc-venture-lab	Read this article to find about how an accelerator supports alumni after demo day, and for getting inspiration from alumni success stories.

(Continued)

TABLE A.11 (continued)

Resource Type	Resource Name	Resource Description	Resource Location	How to Use This Resource
	Should your startup close a small seed round prior to demo day?	Useful advice from a lawyer specializing in advising start-ups about when it is best to close a seed investment round.	https://startuplawyer.com/accelerators/should-startup-close-seed-round-accelerator-demo-day	Read this article for legal advice if you're not sure if you should be raising capital during the accelerator or after demo day.
	Six ways Startup Yard helps alumni post program	A program manager of an EU accelerator describes six ways how they help alumni post accelerator.	https://startupyard.com/6-ways-startupyard-helps-alumni-post-program/	Read this article to learn more about what support you would expect to get from the program managers post accelerator.
	Surviving the post accelera-tion cliff	A journalist from *Medium* online journal interviews a number of accelerator program managers about how to survive after the accelerator is finished.	https://medium.com/silicon-allee/surviving-the-post-acceleration-cliff-what-startups-really-need-to-succeed-fb26abdfa1fe	Read this article to get ideas on what to do after the accelerator to find advice from many different program managers.

TABLE A.12 Resources to Help Founders Navigate Key Stages of the Accelerator Experience

Resource Type	Resource Name	Resource Description	Resource Location	How to Use This Resource
Accelerator application	Insights from a YC alum on how to prepare for the Y Combinator interview.	A Y Combinator alumnus gives tips and insights into how to prepare for an accelerator interview.	https://mattermark.com/insights-yc-alum-prepare-y-Combinator-interview/	Read this article to get an idea about what to expect during the accelerator interview and what to do and what not to do.
	YC accelerator reverse engineering.	An in-depth article full of what to say and what not to say in your accelerator application responses, from YC program managers and entrepreneurs, and alumni.	https://standuply.com/blog/yc-application-advice/	See examples of responses to questions, what to write, what not write.
	A copy of a 2017 successful Techstars application.	See the full application that got a startup into the 2017 Techstars cohort.	https://blog.coastlinemarket.com/the-application-that-got-us-into-techstars-2017-c63ecdfeac12	An example of a successful accelerator application form.
	How we got into Techstars, after we were rejected at the interview stage of Y Combinator.	A startup gives examples of how they got into Techstars.	https://blog.routific.com/which-startup-accelerator-is-right-for-you-729e87d424ef	Get tips for a startup that was accepted into Techstars, but rejected from Y Combinator.
	A copy of a 2017 successful Y Combinator application.	See the full Y Combinator application of Simple Habit—a startup that was accepted in 2017 Y Combinator program.	https://www.businessinsider.com/successful-y-combinator-application-yunha-kim-simple-habit-meditation-startup-2019-5/?r=AU&IR=T	An example of a successful accelerator application form.

(Continued)

TABLE A.12 (continued)

Resource Type	Resource Name	Resource Description	Resource Location	How to Use This Resource
	How to make a great pitch deck—including 50 pitch deck examples from 500 Startups and Y Combinator alumni.	An article from an Y Combinator alumnus that featured in their blog with 50 Best Pitch Deck Examples from 2018 That Got the Investors Talking (At 500 Startups & Y Combinator).	https://www.konsus.com/blog/35-best-pitch-deck-examples-2017	You will need to submit a pitch deck in your application to any accelerator. Here you can see 50 examples of great pitch decks and an analysis of what makes each deck great.
	We got accepted into Techstars and we turned them down.	An accelerator alumnus on their blog gives examples of what to say and not to say in a Techstars interview.	https://talkroute.com/got-accepted-into-techstars-turned-it-down/	Learn about interview techniques, what to expect in an interview.
Accelerator program structure/curriculum	Six lessons learned from tech accelerators according to CEOs.	*Forbes* interviews a number of startup founder accelerator alumni and summarizes six main lessons learned.	https://www.forbes.com/sites/laurencebradford/2017/12/26/6-lessons-learned-from-tech-accelerators-according-to-ceos/#391c115f52b7	Read this article if you're looking for some high-level things to expect during the accelerator program.
	What an accelerator taught me that I couldn't learn at Google.	An *Entrepreneur* journal article full of tips and a comparison of a accelerator alumnus founder who compares his previous work at Google to going through an accelerator.	https://www.entrepreneur.com/article/270269	Read this article if you not sure about the benefits of going through an accelerator, or perhaps getting a full-time job in a tech firm such as Google.

Startup accelerator comparison Y Combinator vs. Techstars.	A founder who graduated from both Y Combinator and Techstars compares curricula from both programs, and many other things such as demo day and fundraising.	https://www.freecodecamp.org/news/startup-accelerator-comparison-y-Combinator-vs.-techstars-b4080d0c93c8/	Read this article if you are not sure which of the top accelerators you want to apply to, Techstars or Y Combinator.
Five Things you'll learn in the 500 Startups accelerator program	A 500 Startups alumnus founder discusses the five main things he learned during an accelerator program.	https://500.co/5-things-you-learn-startup-accelerator-program/	Read this article if you're interested in knowing what you will learn in 500 Startups or generally what main take-aways you can get out of an accelerator told by an accelerator alumnus.
Ten things I learned by spending three months at Katapult accelerator.	An alumnus of an accelerator from Norway discusses the top ten things she learned during the Katapult accelerator in Oslo.	https://www.majaequity.com/media/2018/6/15/10-things-i-learned-by-spending-3-months-at-katapult-accelerator	Read this article if you're looking for a European spin on what key learnings you can expect in an EU accelerator.

(Continued)

TABLE A.12 (continued)

Resource Type	Resource Name	Resource Description	Resource Location	How to Use This Resource
Accelerator demo day	How I pitched my first startup.	A Techstars alumnus startup discusses all the things you can do right or wrong on demo day, and all the things their startup did right or wrong.	https://keen.io/blog/how-i-pitched-my-first-startup/	Read this article to get an in-depth idea of what a startup goes through at Techstars in preparing and pitching at demo day. Also includes their pitch video.
	Seven tips to make your investor pitch a no-brainer.	A co-founder gives seven great tips about what to do and what not to do on demo day	https://blog.close.com/demo-day-pitch	Read this blog to get ideas on how to crush your demo day pitch.
	Our startupbootcamp Cape Town Journey demo day blog.	A co-founder from South Africa describes the experience of demo day and publishes the video of her presentation.	https://blog.browniepoints.africa/sbccapetown-journey-demo-day/	Visit this article to see a start-upbootcamp alumnus.
	The road to demo day, a founder's perspective.	A 500 Startups alumnus founder discusses what it was like to pitch at demo day for 500 Startups. Some other founders are also interviewed to describe their demo day experience too.	https://500.co/road-cemo-day-founders-perspective/	Read this blog to get an idea of what to expect at a leading accelerator programs demo day.
	Demo day experience, entrepreneurs in their own words.	A NYC accelerator interviews some of their alumni to describe the experience of demo day, the highlights, and what they got out of it.	https://www.blackstone.com/media/press-releases/article/blackstone-launchpcd-demo-day-experience-entrepreneurs-in-their-own-words	Read this article to get quotes and honest reflections and to see the emotions of founders who pitch on demo day.

Accelerator post demo day support	What the Y Combinator experience actually looks like.	An article full of full-size photos capturing what to expect during and after Y Combinator accelerator.	https://www.snappr.co/startup-snapshot/what-the-y-Combinator-experience-actually-looks-like	Go to this article to see lots of professional photos capturing the experience of attending Y Combinator.
	Reflecting on my summer at 500 Startups.	A 500 Startups alumnus founder looks back on his experiences in 500 Startups, lessons learned, gives tip and advice on what happens after and during the accelerator.	https://www.tkkader.com/2011/09/reflecting-on-my-summer-at-500startups/	Go to this article to get insights into what it was like to attend 500 Startups and what to expect during and after the program, and the lessons the founder learned.
	When joining a startup accelerator program is a bad idea.	An article that analyzes why it might not be a good idea for some startups to enter accelerators, with lots of statistics about what happens to startups after the program finishes.	https://arkenea.com/blog/dont-join-startup-accelerator-program/	Read this article to get a negative view of startup accelerators, and how they might not be appropriate for some startups, especially considering the high rate of failure after an accelerator program finishes.
	You've finished your startup accelerator, so now what?	An accelerator alumnus founder gives lots of advice and tips about what to do after an accelerator finishes.	https://under30ceo.com/youve-finished-startup-accelerator-now/	Read this article to get more insights into the value of networking, and how you can use the networks you made during the accelerator to your startups advantage.
	Life post accelerator.	A Techstars alumnus founder writes in *Forbes* about what life is like in the six weeks after an accelerator.	https://www.forbes.com/sites/groupthink/2014/12/03/life-post-accelerator-maintaining-forward-momentum/#f76001b40e3b	Read this article for a professionally written analysis of what to expect in the six weeks after demo day, and what you should do to survive the emotional ride

(Continued)

Asia

TABLE A.13 Examples of leading accelerators in Asia

Accelerator Name	Location	Marketing Message from Accelerator Website	Vertical/ Sector	Notable Alumni	Link
Impac Tech	Singapore Thailand Japan	Empowering impact-driven technologies.	Technology-focused	Mindfi, Wellderly, Ark, Emo Health	https://impactech.com/accelerator-program/
VS. V	Vietnam	A leading accelerator that invests in world-class early-stage startups.	ICT, IoT	Lozi, Ship60, Base Enterprise, True Juice	http://www.siliconvalley.com.vn/
Chinaccelerator	China	First accelerator to launch in Asia. We are a landing pad for cross-border startups, from the world into China, and from China to the world.	Internet	Snapask, Shopal, 247 Tickets, Bitmex	https://chinaccelerator.com/
TLABS	India	We love founders who are building disruptive and amazing things. We call ourselves "Support Stage Investors" to support you in doing #epicshit.	Technology-focused (internet and mobile)	Niche Ai, Peersme, HopOn, GetMyUni	http://www.tlabs.in/

Name	Country	Description	Focus	Portfolio	URL
Sparklabs	Korea	Global startup accelerator founded by entrepreneurs for entrepreneurs	Internet, online gaming, mobile, e-commerce, digital media, healthcare, IoT, and hardware sectors.	UrbanBase, Memebox, TreePlanet, Wanted Lab	http://www.sparklabs.co.kr/lb/index.php
IdeaSpace Foundation	Philippines	Turning ideas into reality	IT, agriculture, food technology, infrastructure, energy.	Portfolio Launcher, Pinoy Travel, Stream Energy, JustGo	http://www.ideaspacefoundation.org/
Plug and Play Asia Pacific	Indonesia, Singapore	Our passion is to see startups succeed.	Startups with MVPs.	Soulscape, Bustikeet, Fixir, Surge	http://apac.plugandplaytechcenter.com/about/
Tribe Accelerator	Singapore	Accelerating smarter cities through blockchain.	Blockchain and Fintech & Insurtech, mobility & supply chain, data & telecommunications, energy & sustainability.	Acrue, Chorus Mobility, Digix, Halo,	https://tribeaccelerator.co/
Startup Bootcamp Singapore	Singapore	The leading global accelerator program focused on financial innovation.	Fintech, Insurtech	Aim, Banhji, Bankguard, CherryPay	http://www.startupbootcamp.org/accelerator/fintech-singapore.html

North America

TABLE A.14 Examples of Leading Accelerators in North America

Accelerator Name	Location	Marketing Message from Accelerator Website	Vertical/Sector	Notable Alumni	Link
Angelpad	NYC, San Francisco	We are ranked the top U.S. accelerator by MIT's seed accelerator benchmark—every year since 2015.	Technology including SaaS, marketplaces, advertising, API, Mobile, Healthcare, AI, Data, B2B, B2C.	Postmates, Buffer, AllTrail, Pipedrive, Mopub	https://angelpad.com/
StartX	Stanford University, California	We believe that as entrepreneurs we can achieve more as a group than we can as individuals.	Biotech, medical devices, ardware, fintech, cleantech, health IT & deep tech.	Nearoy, Boosted, Protcol labs, Limbike	https://startx.com/accelerator
Y Combinator	Mountain View, California	Y Combinator created a new model for funding early-stage startups.	Technology ventures.	Airbnb, Stripe, Dropbox, Coinbase, Instacart	https://www.yCombinator.com/
Amplify	Los Angeles	Amplify backs LA's strongest teams at the earliest stages.	Technology ventures.	FloQast, Clutter, Winc, AlphaDraft	http://amplify.la/
Chicago New Venture Challenge	Chicago	New Venture Challenge (NVC) is recognized as one of the top-ranked accelerator programs in the nation.	Technology ventures.	AgileMD, Appiness, Braintree, Grubhub	http://www.chicagonvc.com/

Name	Location	Description	Focus	Companies	URL
MuckerLab	Los Angeles	Not in Silicon Valley? Not a problem. Based in Los Angeles, Mucker provides capital and support for startups outside Silicon Valley.	Technology ventures.	AuditBoard, Emailage, Honey, UpKeep,	https://www.mucker.com/
Techstars	Seattle, Los Angeles, Boulder, Kansas City, NYC, others	Techstars is the worldwide network that helps entrepreneurs succeed.	We fund all types of startups.	Sendgrid, Digital-Ocean, Zipline, Outreach Pillpack	https://www.techstars.com/
500 Startups	Silicon Valley	We believe in great founders. We help them thrive.	500 invests in a diverse range of companies in the tech industry, from marketplaces to SaaS, from media to AI.	Twilio, Udemy, Talkdesk, Gitlab, Ipsy	https://500.co/
MassChallenge	Boston, Texas	More than an accelerator. We are a community of innovators working together to solve some of the world's most massive challenges.	Early-stage startups across all industries, from anywhere in the world. For our vertical accelerators.	Relayrides, Ksplice, Joytunes, Thinx, Drync	https://masschallenge.org/
DreamIt	NYC, Philadelphia	DreamIT ventures is a fund and accelerator focused on startups with revenue or pilots that are ready to scale.	Healthtech, Securetech, Urbantech	Level Up, Trendkite, SeatGeek, Houseparty, Adaptly	https://www.dreamit.com/
Creative Destruction Lab	Toronto	Creative Destruction Lab helps innovators transition from science projects to high-growth companies.	seed-stage, hi-tech, energy, healthcare, cities, general.	Audible Reality, Biome Renewables, Galaxy.AI, LabsCubed, Luminari, Nix Sensor, Squad	https://www.creativedestructionlab.com/companies/

Europe

TABLE A.15 Examples of leading accelerators in Europe

Accelerator Name	Location	Marketing Message from Accelerator Website	Vertical/Sector	Notable Alumni	Link
Barclays Techstars	London, UK	A unique program designed to take your business further. We're fintech-focused and overflowing with opportunities	Fintech	Pierce Matrix, Bear, Abe Ai, Alpha Exchange, Core.bi	https://www.barclays accelerator.com/
Startup Bootcamp	London, Berlin, Amsterdam, Italy, Spain, Germany	Accelerating Innovators, Gain access to the most relevant connections in your industry.	Technology ventures	Sunrise, Realyr, Bundle, Viewsy, Fuel up	https://www .startupbootcamp.org/
MassChallenge Switzerland	Switzerland	Founded in 2016, MassChallenge Switzerland has quickly become a leading driver of innovation and entrepreneurship in Europe by connecting startups with the experts and resources they need to grow.	We accept applications from early-stage start-ups across all industries, from anywhere in the world.	Ambrosus Technologie, TasteHit, Haya Therapeutics, Mixf t Inc	https://masschallenge. org/programs-switzerland/
NDRC	Ireland	Best Place to Start.	We invest in and support the most promising early stage technology based startups.	Logentries, Soundwave, iCabbies, Way2Pay	https://www.ndrc.ie/

Name	Location	Description	Companies	URL
Seedcamp	London	We invest early in world-class founders attacking large, global markets and solving real problems using technology.	Bloomsbury AI, Wefox, TansferWise, Ui Path	https://seedcamp.com/
Techstars London	London	Techstars London—Home to a thriving international community of tech, founders, innovators, and investors.	Coconut. Lifebit, Kencko, Pesky Fish	https://www.techstars.com/programs/london-program/
50 Partners	France	Successful entrepreneurs empowering promising startups	Monsieur Drive, Snap Event, Guarantors, Brigad	http://en.50partners.fr/
Impact	Spain	Impact is considered among the world's best emerging accelerators.	8 Fit, Glamping Hub, Situm, Healthia	https://www.impact-accelerator.com/
Rockstart	Netherlands	We support startups by providing access to capital, market, community, and expertise in four domains.	Codeplace, Wercker, Postcron,	https://www.rockstart.com/
Founder Institute	Poland, Netherlands	Get to Traction and Funding in Warsaw with the world's largest pre-seed accelerator.	Appota, Travelcar, Peerby, Itembase	https://fi.co/s/warsaw

Africa and the Middle East

TABLE A.16 Examples of Leading Accelerators in Africa and the Middle East

Accelerator Name	Location	Marketing Message from Accelerator Website	Vertical/Sector	Notable Alumni	Link
Techstars Israel	Israel	An accelerator program that offers entrepreneurs unprecedented access not only to a world-leading bank, but also to Techstars international mentor and investor relationship.	Financial technology, cyber security, insurance tech and enterprise software.	Salaryo, Uhura, Vala, Mada Analytics	https://www.techstars.com/barclays-tel-aviv-program/
Activs paces	Cameroon	#1 Technology Innovation Hub in Cameroon. Building world-class technology entrepreneurs.	Technology startups.	SkylaBase, Feem, Ense, Zinger Systems	https://www.activspaces.com/
Turn8	UAE	Investing in Innovation with Global Reach.	Startups with MVPs.	Kanari, PixelBug, Melltoo, Junbot	https://turn8.co/
XL Africa	South Africa	Connecting startups across Africa with mentorship and access to investors.	Technology startups.	Asoko Insight, Rasello, Sendy, Timbukto	https://www.xl-africa.com/

Name	Country	Description	Sector	Portfolio	URL
Startup90	South Africa	Ideate! Innovate! Accelerate! Launching high-growth, high-impact startups with our accelerator program.	Finance, healthcare, agriculture & energy sectors.	Medbook, Wanos, Tidy and Co, TechTuition	http://www.startup90.com
Savannah	Kenya	Africa's leading technologyseed fund & accelerator.	Technology startups.	Safi Analytics, Podozi, Aerobotics, Smile Identity	http://savannah.vc/
The Junction Israel	Israel	The Junction is the leading pre-seed program for startups in Israel.	Technology.	Simplee, HoneyBook, Houseparty, Mobilize	https://f2vc.com/the-junction/
Flat6labs	Egypt, Tunisia, Beirut, Bahrain, Abu Dhabi, Saudi Arabia	Accelerating entreprenuership in Mena.	Technology startups.	CollectionAir, Instabug, Integreght, Jumpsuite	https://www.flat6labs.com/
Avatech	Iran	Avatech is a startup accelerator that provides entrepreneurs with the necessary ingredients to succeed.	We are mainly looking for startups working in the digital space with a big enough potential market and the ambition to grow fast.	Taskulu, Easypaz, Reyhoon, 2nate,	http://avatech.ir/en/

Latin America

TABLE A.17 Examples of Leading Accelerators in Latin America

Accelerator Name	Location	Marketing Message from Accelerator Website	Vertical/Sector	Notable Alumni	Link
Startup Chile	Chile	Join the leading accelerator in Latin America.	Tech startups	Cabify, CargoX, Mercardo Transporte, Glamit	https://www.startupchile.org/
Wayra	Argentina, Brazil, Chile, Columbia, Mexico, Peru, Venezuela	We scale startups. We are the most global, connected, and technological open innovation hub in the world.	SaaS, big data, artificial intelligence, fintech, agtech, Smart Cities, IoT, among others	Brandtrack, Brightflag, Marfeel, Uplanner	https://ar.wayra.co/
Imagine Lab	Chile	At Imagine Lab, we accelerate our startups and open the doors for them to scale in various markets.	Tech startups	Hostify, Cappo, Swinesmart, Livin	https://imaginelab.cl/
500 Startups Mexico	Mexico	500 Startups—Investing in Spanish-speaking startups since 2011.	Fintech transportation tourism education ecommerce enterprise, consumer civic tech / health	Clip, Yaxi, MexicoDestinos, Cemeantoja	https://latam.500.co/latam/
NXTP Labs	Argentina	We invest in Latin American tech companies generating positive impact at scale.	We look for strong teams running an MVP.	Eartits, Wehostels, ComentaTV, Flipter	https://www.nxtplabs.com/

BlueBox Ventures	Mexico	We believe in a future that motivates creativity and boosts the talent of incredible startups and powerful corporations.	Agile startups revolutionizing industries	Briq.mx, Homie, Guschat, ChiaMia	https://www .blueboxmx.com/
Masschallenge Mexico	Mexico	MassChallenge strengthens the global innovation ecosystem by accelerating high-potential startups across all industries, from anywhere in the world.	We accept applications from early-stage startups across all industries, from anywhere in the world.	Totolines, Urbvan, Bitso, Bayonet,	https://masschallenge. org/programs-mexico
Artemisia	Brazil	A new business generation is transforming Brazil.	Education, health, housing, early childhood, financial services, food, energy, mobility.	Banco Perola, Clinica SIM, Geekie	https://artemisia.org.br/
Seed Accelerator	Brazil	Seed–startups and entrepreneurship ecosystem development, an innovation factory in Minas Gerais state!	Technology-based businesses from around the world that want to develop in the state of Minas Gerais can apply.	Beved, Tracksale,	http://seed.mg.gov.br/

Oceania

TABLE A.18 Examples of Leading Accelerators in Oceania

Accelerator Name	Location	Marketing Message from Accelerator Website	Vertical/Sector	Notable Alumni	Link
BlueChilli	Australia	We build startups. We help founders build products, gain pilots, secure investment, and establish their first team.	Global tech startups	Folktale, Benchon, SafetyCompass	https://www.bluechilli.com/
Muru-D	Australia	We're a startup accelerator running programs in Australia that helps tech founders scale their business smarter and faster. And we're backed by Telstra, a world-class technology company.	Technology startups	Caitre-d, Cuberider, Fluid Education, Funetics	https://muru-d.com/
Lightning Lab	New Zealand	Lightning Lab is Creative HQ's three-month, mentor-intensive, business acceleration program.	Technology startups	Jrny, Offcut, Choice, Sulufiti	https://www.lightninglab.co.nz/

Name	Country	Description	Portfolio	URL
Plug and Play	Indonesia	We are building this accelerator program together with Gan Konsulindo (a local investment firm in Indonesia), Astra International, Bank Negara Indonesia, Bank Tabungan Negara, and Sinar Mas.	ReadyPulse, Vudu, Retrovo, Addthis	https://www.plugand-playtechcenter.com/indonesia/
Flux accelerator	New Zealand	We back ambitious founders building global startups from New Zealand.	Genoapay, Narrative, Jasper, Chipi	https://www.fluxaccelerator.co.nz/
Startmate	Australia	At Startmate, we help exceptional people build iconic companies, and we're powered by the most successful entrepreneurs and venture capitalists in Australia.	Happy Inspector, Work180, Flirtey, Everproof	https://startmate.com.au
GnB accelerator	Indonesia	First global accelerator in Indonesia dedicated to progress and innovation that brings together the people, the funding, and the partners that drive business velocity	Xwork, Ahlijasa, Simplidots, Plomo	https://gnb.ac/
Slingshot	Australia	Slingshot is the most active corporate accelerator in Australia.	Autoguru, CarNext-Door, Episoft, Openagent	https://www.slingshotters.com/

Examples of Leading Accelerators Globally by Region

In these tables, we highlight some of the leading accelerators in the world by region (i.e., leading accelerators in Asia, North America, Europe, Africa/Middle East, South America and Oceania). These may be useful if you want a quick glimpse into the standards, acceptance criteria, program design, and other factors in relation to accelerators in different parts of the world.

Index